VALENTINO
THE FIRST SUPERSTAR

NOEL BOTHAM

metro

Published by Metro Publishing Ltd, 3 Bramber Court,
2 Bramber Road, London W14 9PB, England

First published in hardback in 2002

ISBN 1 84358 013 6

British Library Cataloguing-in-Publication Data: A catalogue record
for this book is available from the British Library.

Design by ENVY
Typeset by Mac Style Ltd, Scarborough, N. Yooskhire

Printed and bound in Great Britain by CPD (Wales)

1 3 5 7 9 10 8 6 4 2

Papers used by Metro Publishing Ltd are natural, recyclable products
made from wood grown in sustainable forests. The manufacturing processes
conform to the environmental regulations of the country of origin.

Pictures reproduced by kind permission of The Moviestore Collection, The Kobal
Collection and The Vintage Magazine Archive.

Every attempt has been made to contact the relevant copyright-holders but some
were untraceable. We would be grateful if the appropriate people could contact us.

'To generalise on women is dangerous.
To specialise in them is infinitely worse.'

Rudolph Valentino 1926

Prologue

IN THE STILL warm November sunshine, Rudolph Valentino and close friends Norman Kerry, the actor, and Paul Ivano, a technical adviser, strolled unhurriedly along Sunset Boulevard, occasionally pausing to window-shop in the stylish and expensive new boutiques which were springing up in the affluent movie capital.

Rudy's latest picture, *The Sheik*, was already breaking box-office records and Paramount, who were-receiving over 1,000 letters a week from besotted fans, had hailed him as their first superstar. The vain, Italian born actor adored the hero worship and the lavish praise of friends like Charles Chaplin, Dougie Fairbanks and Mary Pickford.

But the deification of Valentino as the god of love, and the acknowledgement of his unique status as the first male sex symbol, had already created an unprecedented behavioural transformation in the way fans needed to express their adulation and devotion. This deification was also about to manifest itself in a frightening and completely unanticipated way.

As the three friends paused outside the window of a fashionable new menswear shop, a woman recognised Valentino and screamed his name. In seconds it triggered a stampede, as every woman within hearing distance rushed towards them.

It was the first example of a unique and bizarre phenomenon, and Valentino and his friends were totally unprepared for the sheer hysterical ferocity of the fans' attentions.

He was, he admitted afterwards, 'scared witless', and believed they were trying to maim or kill him.

'Now we know why they're called fanatics,' laughed Kerry, trying to brighten the young Italian's spirits, and soon they were all able to smile about the incident. Valentino remained apprehensive, though, about the future. He was sure this would not prove to be an isolated incident and that other such mobbings would almost certainly follow. And he was to be proved right.

The world's first superstar was suddenly confronted by an unforseen drawback to his unique status. Being the first man to cause international mass hysteria among women, who had been exposed – via the silver screen – to his smouldering sex appeal, was highly flattering. But in becoming the heady release valve for millions of grey, romantically barren lives, he had also become a target. They craved more of what he offered on screen and believed he could deliver in person.

This was primal chemistry at work. This was love and lust and sex and savagery, served up just the way they loved it. At last, there had appeared a virile, dominant and demanding hero, who knew what he wanted and made sure he got it.

In *The Sheik*, he had released an animal magnetism which women found irresistible. The fan magazines coined a new word to describe him – 'heart-throb' – and eminent psychiatrists and psychologists tried to analyse and explain this curious social phenomenon with learned phrases like 'emotional vulnerability', 'sexual immaturity', 'public hysteria' and 'lack of inhibitory checks'.

But to the impressionable girls and women, the young and the mature, who sat in darkened cinemas transfixed by that flickering image on the big screen, the secret was much more obvious. It was the magic of that dark desert devil, the great lover, the movies' first he-man sex symbol.

English writer Elinor Glyn had at that time coined a new word to describe sex appeal: 'it'. Millions of women popularised the expression by declaring, unanimously, that Rudolph Valentino most certainly had 'it'.

Coping with the phenomenon was not easy for Valentino, for there was no one to whom he could turn for advice. He was the first of a new breed, a new genre of movie actor – the prototype model for future generations, the first Hollywood superstar male sex symbol.

Though it is highly doubtful if anyone who saw the penniless Italian immigrant – plying for trade among the society women who came to New York's sleazy cabaret dance halls seeking a male prostitute for a brief moment's imagined love – would have predicted his leap into immortality.

FROM THE moment he first began to crawl, the world's first superstar was in trouble, his mother remembered years later. 'Rodolpho seemed to have an exceptional nose for trouble, and it for him,' she told her neighbours. 'He had a rare, natural talent for mischief-making.'

Mademoiselle Beatrice Babin was a French peasant girl, a fun-loving, pretty and intelligent teenager who loved to dance, when she met Giovanni Guglielmi, a young, Italian veterinarian who was then working in a travelling circus. After their marriage, they returned to Castellaneta, a dusty and unattractive small town, untouched by the passage of time or progress, which lay, uninspiring and unexciting, in the instep of the boot of Italy. Its name, he told her, was derived from the many ancient citadels which still punctuated the sun-baked skyline.

But Beatrice was happy. Her husband's veterinary qualifications may have been of dubious origin but his work with the domestic animals in the region was competent enough for him to earn a regular living and the trust of his hard-up clientele. Their house, in a better part of town, had three rooms, an improvement on her own family's home in France and superior to those of most of their impecunious neighbours in Castellaneta.

The flat-roofed house, built of heavy white stone, had once had its front wall painted, a sure sign of comparative wealth in this rural outpost of nineteenth-century Italy. And the mere fact that Giovanni could afford new outfits for his family each year placed him among the upper echelons of the town's mainly illiterate, working-class inhabitants.

Neither Giovanni nor his beautiful wife had any ambition to leave the sleepy, uncomplicated community of little more than

6,000 souls. They were truly contented, both with each other and with their lot. Their third child Rodolpho's naughtiness did upset Beatrice, but she was convinced that he would improve as he became older.

But fate had much disappointment and tragedy in store for her in the years to come.

The Guglielmis' first child, a daughter, also named Beatrice, would die aged eight. Giovanni would then follow his daughter to the grave 12 years later. But before then, three other children – two sons and a second daughter – were to be born to Beatrice, and survive into adulthood. They were Alberto, Rodolpho and Maria.

Rodolpho was born in the early morning of 6 May 1895 and was baptised in the local church with an impressive army of names – Rodolpho Alfonzo Raffaelo Pierre Filibert Guglielmi di Valentina d'Antonguolla.

He was always different from the others, his mother claimed. 'He was a very stubborn child, right from being a toddler. He was a very naughty boy, disobedient and rowdy, but I could never stay mad at him, not when he was little. He had such a beautiful face. Like a cherub.'

Rodolpho's cherubic face brought the kisses and hugs he detested from relatives and his parents' friends and was more often set in a fixed scowl than a smile, and his dark, attractive eyes were frequently lost in some private, personal daydream.

Many years later, Rodolpho's childhood friends and neighbours, the sisters Rita and Ada Maldarizzi, would recollect, 'He was a daddy's boy. His poor mother could never control him. Even as a very small boy he would disobey her. He even refused to go to church and would shout and spit if his mother tried to force him.

'He was a real terror, even more so after his father took him to visit the capital city of Taranto as a special millennium treat when 1900 came. Once he had seen the bigger town with its motor cars and big buildings, it was as though Castellaneta had become a prison cell. He was desperate to leave our town from then on, even though he was only five years old when it happened.'

Taranto was a mere 23 miles from Castellaneta and was a developed and comparatively modern city. There, clinging to his father's hand, Rodolpho had marvelled at the height of the buildings, the multitude of horse-drawn carriages and the noisy motor vehicles which zig-zagged madly about the streets, their drivers hooting furiously on hand-worked horns, leaving clouds of smoke billowing in their wake.

From then on, it was there where Rodolpho wanted to be, where life was exciting and fast and fascinating. Yet it seemed that his whole future, his entire life, must be tied, irrevocably, to the tiny, suffocatingly quiet town of Castellaneta.

Despite this, as childhood friend Ada Maldarizzi recalled, he made little effort to improve himself academically in order to fulfil these boyish ambitions. 'There were no formal schools,' she said. 'We received our education from the parish priest and from local, married women and spinsters, who gave lessons in their front rooms in return for much needed cash. But Rodolpho hated studying. His father would regularly beat him and force him to go to classes with the priest but it never lasted for long.

'He preferred to be off playing truant with his head in the clouds, picturing himself as some great mythical hero or mighty warrior, playing in the olive groves. Sometimes his younger sister Maria, or my sister Rita, or I, would skip our classes to play with him – and then we would all get into trouble. But it was worth it. His make-believe adventures were far more fun than stuffy lessons in church. Even the certain knowledge that we would get a spanking and that a supperless evening lay ahead couldn't spoil our enjoyment. Our world of make-believe was so much nicer than the reality in our lives.'

At the age of five, an experiment with his father's cut-throat razor left Rodolpho with a horizontal slash across his right cheek, creating a life-long scar. Even though they knew the truth, he told his friends in Castellaneta it had been inflicted during a mighty duel – which he, of course, had won. And 25 years later, he was uniquely consistent in telling reporters of a wholly fictitious account of his childhood for the benefit of his fans, and that he had received the scar in a duel. But this time the duel was set in Paris and was over a lady's honour!

At the age of 11, cruel reality was to invade Rodolpho's beloved world of make-believe with the death of his father. He took the blow badly, weeping openly and unashamedly.

'You and your brother will have to look after your mother and sister,' he was told by the neighbours. 'It's time to start acting like a man and become responsible.'

This, confided the Maldarizzi sisters, was just so much wishful thinking on the part of the adults in Castellaneta. If anything, Rodolpho became an even bigger scourge than before, an undisciplined bully who fought other boys, continued to steal from his mother and his neighbours' homes, refused to study and was obdurately opposed to any kind of work, especially that connected with agriculture.

As he matured, sexual exploits gradually replaced Rodolpho's earlier wild, imaginative adventures, and the now darkly handsome youth graduated from childish hugs and kisses to sexual conquests of which he was to boast to friends.

On several occasions, he was soundly beaten by angry fathers of girls with whom he had been found in less-than-delicate situations, which only taught him to be more careful over the venues he chose for his amorous activities, but did not keep him away from girls.

Attempts by his local priest to dissuade the young Casanova from his sinful ways – even the threat of eternal hellfire – were a total failure. Friends Rita and Ada Maldarizzi – in whose home he spent more time than his own – would never forget the day he brought back a ravishing young girl, a roving gypsy singer, and paraded, impudently, with her through the streets.

Beatrice Guglielmi pleaded and threatened and begged him to devote himself more seriously to his studies, and even called in an uncle to apply extra persuasion with a thick leather belt. But it was useless. Rodolpho refused to work, refused to study and certainly refused to stop chasing girls. He was branded a troublemaker and a nuisance by almost everyone who knew him, an angry and wilfully disobedient youth who sometimes ended up in a police cell charged with vagrancy or petty theft.

Later, as a Hollywood star, he would claim to have attended a good boarding school and to have done exceptionally well with his studies, especially languages. But a picture of him in school uniform, produced for the fan magazines and press by the studio public relations team, was an obvious fake. A rare picture of the face of Rodolpho as a youth had been superimposed on the photograph of a schoolboy in uniform.

His mother admitted that she would have happily spent hours on her knees thanking God had Rodolpho shown even the slightest inclination to study. But he did not. His stock answer to her constant nagging and pleading for him to learn some kind of trade was that if she would only agree to give him enough money to go to Rome. or some other exciting city, then he would prove himself and make his fortune.

This frequently repeated scene usually ended with Beatrice reduced to tears of anger and despair, and Rodolpho feeling more than ever convinced that the only thing preventing him from making his fortune was his mother's refusal to finance his travels. Meanwhile, he filled his time stealing food from market stalls, lazing, dreaming or womanising.

To begin with, any big city was acceptable as a destination, but as he grew older, his preference gradually leaned towards America where, if the streets were not exactly paved with gold, they were reputed to be littered with opportunities to make plenty of money.

One cynical relative laughed at his plans. 'If every father of every girl you've pestered subscribed a handful of lire,' he suggested, 'there would be enough money to send you half-way around the world and set you up in business when you arrived.'

'Laugh as much as you want,' was Rodolpho's response. 'When I finally make my fortune you will all want to know me.'

Eventually, the shouting and the weeping became too much for everyone and Rodolpho's uncle, who had so often been called in to administer a beating to the boy, grudgingly gave him the support he needed to convince his mother.

If Rodolpho was to continue in his idle, selfish ways, he said, and follow the vagabond style of behaviour he had already begun, it would be better for the whole family if it manifested itself on the other side of the Atlantic. Rodolpho did not disagree. Years later in his secret diary, he wrote, 'My cousin said: "If he is going to be a criminal, he had better go to America and be one there, where he will not disgrace us and his name."

'It was painfully conveyed to me by my cousin and other members of the family that I was going by way of reform rather than anything else.'

As long as there were Italians in America who could be contacted and would agree to receive him and provide a roof over his head, and guidance, his uncle would support Rodolpho's pleas to leave home.

Under this added pressure, Beatrice relented, and letters were written to two young men who had emigrated to New York from Castellaneta and were alleged to be doing well. They replied that they would willingly have Rodolpho stay with them and agreed to 'teach him the ropes' about life in the big city. The American Dream was still there for the taking, they assured him. All he had to do was apply himself, have a good idea and be lucky. But Rodolpho needed no assurances. He knew that his personal fortune awaited him in New York.

Meanwhile, several neighbours, glad to be seeing the back of the scourge of Castellaneta, had added a few lire to the sum scraped together by his mother and uncle and a 'steerage' ticket, the cheapest possible, had been purchased on the Hamburg–America liner the *Cleveland.*

For Rodolpho, the days until his departure seemed to drag by, but to his mother they sped past all too quickly as the moment she dreaded approached.

Ada Maldarizzi remembered, 'She was very brave and made a huge effort not to cry when she said goodbye, even though she was convinced she would never see him again. Rodolpho was too excited to be sad. He could hardly wait to get away.

'After he had gone, Mrs Guglielmi broke down and sobbed. As far as she was concerned, another of her children was gone for ever – just like little Beatrice who died when she was eight.'

Two days later, on 9 December 1913, the *Cleveland* – with Rodolpho aboard – set sail for New York. His only achievement in Italy had been to leave it.

S NOW, THE first Rodolpho had ever seen, swirled about the steerage deck of the *Cleveland* as she edged her way past the Statue of Liberty towards Ellis Island, the main immigrant processing entry port into the United States. It was just two days before Christmas but there was little festive spirit among the Italian immigrants who were packed like cattle on to the tiny area of deck allowed them.

For two weeks, they had been crammed in the airless, windowless confines of steerage, their only escape from the odours and ceaseless din being this icy, windswept scrap of deck. Daily, since steaming north-west from the Straits of Gibraltar, the weather had deteriorated and, for the past week, they had been exposed to bitterly cold winds sweeping down from the Arctic across the North Atlantic ocean.

Rodolpho, like the majority of his fellow passengers on the lower deck, had never possessed an overcoat. His only protection against the cold was several layers of newspaper wrapped around his body under his shirt. He also wore his only suit and a jumper, hand-knitted by his mother. But his clothes, made for the climate of southern Italy, afforded little protection against the snow-laden wind, which tormented those who had braved the deck to catch a first glimpse of New York, with its towering skyscrapers pushing towards the winter clouds that covered the city like a dark grey blanket.

Yet no amount of cold could have kept Rodolpho from the deck, as the *Cleveland* nudged its way up to Ellis Island and, with straining tugs in attendance, nestled into its docking place there. Like those around him, his emotions swung from blackest despair at the prospect of being alone in the New World to burning optimism and faith in the future. It was claimed, and probably rightly, that no other experience could quite compare with that of a young man arriving for the first time in America.

Many years later, John F Kennedy, himself the descendant of an Irish immigrant, and who had attained the highest possible goal of the Presidency of the United States, would describe the Italians' lot in all its grim, graphic detail.

Most were peasants from the south. They came because of neither religious persecution nor political repression, but simply in search of a brighter future. Mostly farmers, their lack of financial resources kept them from reaching the rural areas of the United States.

Instead, they were crowded into cities along the eastern seaboard, often segregating themselves by province, even by village, in a density as high as 4,000 to the city block. Untrained in special skills, and unfamiliar with the language, they had to rely on unskilled labour jobs to earn a living.

They reached the new land exhausted by lack of rest, bad food, confinement and the strain of adjustment to new conditions. But they could not pause to recover their strength.

They had no reserves of food or money; they had to keep moving until they found work. This meant new strains, when their capacity to cope with new problems had already been overburdened.

Soon, Rodolpho would learn the terrible truth of those words. He stepped ashore on 23 December with little more than the clothes he was wearing, a threadbare canvas holdall with his meagre possessions, a single dollar bill sewn into the lining of his cap, and the New York address of former Castellanetans, written down for him by his mother.

Italian-speaking Customs and Immigration officials eased his entry into America and, on the ferry to New York, the company of other immigrants, some of whom he had befriended on the voyage, insulated him from the alien new world which now engulfed him.

But once alone, and no longer able to communicate with anyone around him, Rodolpho surrendered to terror, and for the first time realised the full enormity of the step he had so casually and impulsively taken. His family and friends, probably never to be seen again, were 4,000 miles away in the sunshine of Castellaneta, and he was in this cold, inhospitable ferry terminal with all his worldly possessions contained in the tattered holdall at his feet. There was little to distinguish him from the other young men jostling around him at the terminal exit. But they belonged here and, to Rodolpho, increasingly overcome with the desperate feelings of loneliness and inadequacy, they all appeared to have both purpose and knowledge. He longed to be back aboard the *Cleveland*, which, after a three-hour absence now appeared to him as a warm, safe and friendly sanctuary when compared to the busy, unwelcoming streets of New York which lay outside.

Eventually, cold and apprehensive, he plucked up the courage to leave the ferry building – his last contact with his old life – and, with the address on West 49th Street, given him by his mother, ever ready to push under the noses of passers-by, he set off in search of his new home and, hopefully, new friends.

At last, after hours of misunderstood directions and wrong turnings, his teeth chattering uncontrollably, and feeling colder than at any time previously, Rodolpho found himself amidst the slums of lower Manhattan on 49th Street, standing outside a five-storey building which bore the almost obliterated number for which he had been searching.

The dingy, third-floor apartment into which he was admitted seemed like a palace to Rodolpho and the welcome he received from the four Italians living there was so obviously heartfelt and affectionate that he was almost reduced to tears. As he answered their eager enquiries about family and friends in Castellaneta, Rodolpho marvelled at the luxuries of his new home. There were gas lights in every room and along the corridor, a stove and a gas boiler which actually produced hot water from a tap in the sink, and was so efficient that he soon found himself sweating and had to remove his jacket. Most amazing of all, in the corridor outside, there was a flushing indoor toilet, something unheard of in Castellaneta, shared only by the people on their floor.

Two of his new flatmates were from Castellaneta itself and the other two, brothers, were from a different area in the south of Italy. They laughed at Rodolpho's open-mouthed reaction to the apartment's modest amenities but readily admitted how amazed they had been when first exposed to what Americans considered to be bare domestic necessities.

Warmed by their enthusiastic reception, and delighted to be the centre of attention, Rodolpho talked far into the night – at first in answer to their questions – and then plying them with questions of his own.

He wanted to know about the girls, but of even more importance he wanted to know about his chances of finding a job. If all the wonders of New York he had just been told about were real, he would need money to enjoy them. There was no mother or family here to turn to for cash, however desperate he might be. For the first time in his life, Rodolpho was reluctantly forced to accept the necessity to work, and was equally forced to accept that, until he learned to speak English and was able to communicate with an employer, only the most menial jobs would be open to him. His English was non-existent and even after six months of applying himself to its study, Rodolpho was still barely able to make himself understood.

In that time, he performed a whole string of unskilled jobs as messenger, refuse carrier, dishwasher, laundry assistant and cleaner. He loathed having to work at all and particularly as the only jobs open to him were at the lowest end of the employment chain, providing endless opportunities for verbal abuse and disparagement and total job dissatisfaction.

His insolent response to criticism of any kind usually resulted in instant dismissal and he spent much of the time unemployed and looking for work. But, somehow, he managed to accumulate the mercifully few dollars needed to pay his share of the rent and food bills and provide a few litres of cheap imported wine.

Despite the cold, Rodolpho spent many hours walking the streets of Manhattan and wandering through the many department stores, usually tailed by ever-vigilant store detectives. He marvelled at the goods on display and that so many people should have the money to afford them. During those six months he became confident enough to use the elevated trains and subways which criss-crossed New York but his rides were infrequent because they cost money – he usually walked.

He also learned that the girls in New York, described in such lascivious detail by his flatmates, were every bit as independent, available and sensual as they had told him. But their favours were strictly off limits to an Italian immigrant – particularly a penniless Italian immigrant who could hardly speak English – and the daughters of his countrymen were guarded even more jealously in America than at home. The only way through those defences was a proposal of marriage, and no amount of frustration would wring that sacrifice from him.

When Rodolpho complained to his friends that Italians were so low on the social ladder that they were not even on the bottom rung, and that they were despised even by the Irish immigrants, they laughed and advised him to work for and socialise only with Italians, marry an Italian girl and raise a family. That way he wouldn't have to bother himself with what other ethnic groups were thinking.

But Rodolpho continued to be hurt by the daily regimen of insults, contempt and ridicule which seemed to be the Italian immigrant's lot and swore to himself that, one day, he would be in a superior position to all these people and would be able to repay and avenge his present suffering in kind.

As spring turned into summer, and the temperature soared above 70°F, Rodolpho's confidence seemed to grow in proportion and he determined to escape from the Italian quarter in the West Side slums and find work in a richer neighbourhood. He had sworn, on leaving Italy, that he would never accept work on the land – that, in part, was what he had been running away from. But in June 1914, he heard of a job going as an under-gardener on the Long Island estate of millionaire Cornelius Bliss.

Rodolpho rationalised it would give him a unique opportunity to study the rich and famous, whose ranks he felt destined, one day, to join. In addition, a stable garret went with the job and he would receive three decent meals a day on top of his pay – of $6 a week. It was the highest wage he had received since arriving in America and Rodolpho was cock-a-hoop.

He returned to New York the same afternoon and, after stuffing his still meagre possessions into the old holdall, he bid his flatmates farewell and became the sixth under-gardener to Mr Cornelius Bliss.

By this time, Rodolpho's suit was showing very definite signs of wear and, spurred on by the example of his employer and his regular house guests, whose sartorial splendour quite dazzled the young immigrant, he determined to spend his first month's wages replenishing his wardrobe.

It appeared to Rodolpho that the rich lived only for pleasure and the conquest of beautiful women, that they laughed easily and arrogantly accepted their superiority as a natural right. It became one of his greatest pleasures simply to observe his employer and his many friends, and though he believed his job to be way beneath him, he would make the most of this golden opportunity to study the rich at close quarters – and learn, and perhaps adopt, their mannerisms, tastes and tempting vices.

He knew his accent set him apart from most Americans but Rodolpho was convinced that if he could model himself on the rich, his foreignness would cease to be a handicap. Sadly, he became such a keen student of his superiors' habits that he began spending more time spying on and aping them than at his work, a fact that did not go unnoticed by the head gardener, who one day summoned Rodolpho to his office and summarily dismissed him.

Returning to Manhattan, he found his place in the old apartment had been snapped up by a more recently arrived immigrant and he was forced to rent a room of his own, in a small building owned by Italians, for $1.20 a week. Work was still hard to come by but, by exaggerating his experience on the Bliss estate, he convinced the Superintendent in charge of Central Park to give him a job as a junior gardener. His wage was almost as good as he had earned on Long Island, but this time he also had to pay rent and provide all his own food. His healthy young appetite was such that he soon found himself making inroads into the money he had set aside to buy new clothes.

His main jobs in the park were picking insects off the rose leaves and dead-heading the wilted flowers and this left plenty of time for a continued observation of wealthy New Yorkers who liked to stroll or ride through the park during the warm summer afternoons. He envied their style and self-assurance, but above all he coveted the beautiful women, whom many of the young men, of about his own age, escorted in the park, and in secluded areas often stopped to embrace.

The one real thorn in Rodolpho's side was his immediate superior, a beefy Irishman who, as a member of one immigrant group in the city, delighted in having someone of an even more contemptible group under his command. Each day brought its quota of jibes and sneers and orders to perform particularly menial and unpleasant chores over and above his regular work. It came to a head after two weeks when the Irish foreman ordered Rodolpho to collect a spiked stick and bag and pick up the rubbish from the grass.

The thought of wandering among the wealthy people he admired, gathering rubbish from around their feet, was too much for Rodolpho. In an explosion of temper he told his superior just what he could do with his pointed stick, and quit.

Within days, unqualified to get another job, he was broke and unable to pay his rent. After one hopeless day of tramping the streets, begging for work of any kind, he remembered, 'Drenched to the skin from the pelting winter sleet, foot sore, discouraged and tired out, I finally reached my room again. I dropped on to the bed and cried like a small and very homesick boy. I bitterly regretted in that hour all that I had done at home, all the valiant resolutions that had landed me in this far country where I could not even find my way about. I eventually sat down and wrote a long and rather desolate letter to my mother, repenting therein of all my follies and warning her that I was apt to return to Italy by the next steamer.'

His landlord may have been a fellow Italian, but he did not allow national sentiment to influence his reaction to Rodolpho's plight, and, taking his penniless tenant's holdall and contents in lieu of rent, threw him on to the street. Other landlords he tried were united in refusing him lodging the moment they learned he was broke and he was forced to wander the streets by night, as well as by day, a homeless vagrant dependent on goodwill and the pickings from restaurant and hotel dustbins to provide his meals.

What sleep he had was snatched in shop doorways or on a bench in Central Park, where he cursed his hot temper and would have willingly begged for a chance to recover his old job. Without even a change of clothes, he was again reduced to using discarded newspapers for linen, and his habit of sneaking into hotels to use their notepaper to write to his mother and their toilet facilities, had to be discontinued because, with his disreputable appearance, not even the most unconscientious doorman could be expected to let him slip past unchallenged.

He lived with the constant fear of being picked up by police, discovered to be a destitute alien and either jailed or shipped back to Italy in disgrace. The only work for which he was considered fit was washing dishes and sweeping the floors of bars, neither of which paid enough to afford him a room.

Four years later, when he again found himself at rock bottom, Rodolpho confessed to a caring friend on the West Coast that 4 August 1914 had been the lowest point of his life. He remembered the date because that night Britain and Germany had declared themselves to be in a state of war. But, at the time, the momentous occurrences in Europe did not concern him. The prospect of a million deaths across the Atlantic was unimportant compared to the one death he was contemplating bringing about – his own.

In just eight months, he had proved that he was one of life's failures. In this land of golden opportunity, he had won for himself less than nothing. He had, as his family had predicted, disgraced himself and his name. His achievements were nil, his prospects non-existent.

In the centre of the darkened bridge across the East River to where his wretched wandering had finally brought him, he stopped and leaned on a guard rail and stared into the black, swirling waters below.

He recalled the moment in his secret diary written years later. 'There came a day when I would have swept the streets for bread. When I thought again, and this time in that most bitter of all bitter ways, on an empty, aching stomach, of suicide, of all the peace and oblivion of the effacing waters.'

His mind raced, flooding with memories of home, his family, and his journey to this place which once held out such promise. Despairing, he thought that to take his own life here would be the best course. It was the easy solution, and he had always taken the simplest way out of every difficult situation.

Looking again into the dark, cold blackness beneath him, he saw the reflected lights of New York, the city he had dreamed he would conquer and make the stepping stone to a rich and distinguished new life.

Suddenly, he straightened his shoulders and lifted his eyes to the real city, back the way he had come. Angrily, he swore that a mere city would not beat him. He would not allow it to. I have the guts and I can take anything America can throw at me, he thought. What's more, I'll win.

He wrote in his diary, 'The man worthwhile hangs on though he hangs to a cross. I *had* to hang on.'

Thrusting his hands deep into his pockets, he turned and strode off back towards Manhattan, thinking, planning...

3

AT THE END of the first week of May 1915, America was rocked by the news that one of the world's largest liners, the *Lusitania*, had been torpedoed by a German submarine in the Atlantic and that, of the 12,000 passengers to have been killed, over 100 of their countrymen had also lost their lives.

Would this, people asked, shake President Wilson from his policy of strict neutrality and plunge America into what was already being described as the bloodiest war in history?

For Rodolpho Guglielmi, the significance of the *Lusitania* sinking, and the concern about whether his newly adopted country would enter the war in Europe, took second place to his own personal problems and ambitions. Besides, Rodolpho had already decided that, as a non-American citizen, he was not morally obliged to enlist in his host country's armed forces if they became actively embroiled in the fighting.

Of far more significance to Rodolpho was that, a few days earlier, he had toasted his twentieth birthday in champagne, surrounded by a group of attractive young women who were all willing to hand fairly substantial sums to the darkly handsome Italian in return for his sexual services.

After his near-tragic experience on the East River bridge the previous summer, Rodolpho had managed to find menial work as a bus boy in one of the popular Italian restaurants in mid-town Manhattan. From there, through the other bus boys and waiters, he had been introduced to the exciting new world of New York's dance halls and cabarets, which, over the preceding five years, had become firm favourites with the sophisticated New York social set.

Single and married women, and their actual or would-be lovers, used them as meeting places, knowing their afternoon or evening rendezvous would pass unnoticed under the cover of respectability these venues had established. The only news from war-beleaguered Paris which interested these gay young things was the unveiling of a new fashion, which sent women's skirts soaring to just below knee level.

Rodolpho, meeting the American women for the first time in such an intimate setting, was fascinated by them. He found their fierce sense of independence, provocative talk and daring display of flesh stimulating and exciting. Compared with them, the women of Italy – even those he had fumblingly seduced in their father's barns – were modestly retiring creatures who uncomplainingly accepted their role as second-class citizens.

In the cabarets of New York, the girls picked the men they wanted, men they had never seen before, boldly assuming male prerogatives of action, and did it on their terms. In America, women did not seek social equality, they expected and demanded it. A woman could pay a man to dance with her, to sit with her and, if he took her fancy, to make love to her in a room which she often arranged and paid for.

The name given to these male dancers was 'gigolo'. Used and enjoyed by the American female, to the American male they were a popular target for abuse, lavatory humour and even physical assault. With their heavily brilliantined hair and effeminate manners, they were anathema to the average American male, but to the sexually deprived and habitually work-shy Rodolpho, the role of gigolo presented itself as one of the most desirable and enviable professions he had yet encountered. The only problem was that he could not dance.

That in itself did not prevent him from going to the dance halls as frequently as his job allowed, and he was soon able to describe himself as 'one of the best wallflowers in the city of New York. I support more ballroom walls than any other man I've heard of.'

Finally, one of the older waiters came to his rescue and taught him the basic steps of the waltz and the tango, which had been imported from South America via Europe and was currently all the rage in America. The top cabarets had two orchestras, one for the professional entertainers and general dancing, and the other for the tango. The male tango dancers were the most sought after, and consequently earned the most money. It was to this specialist area of the profession that Rodolpho fervently aspired.

Within a few weeks, he was sufficiently proficient and confident enough to seek full-time work as a dance partner. With that and his striking foreign appearance, heavily accented voice and almost hypnotic eyes – which, when viewed from just a few inches while dancing, awoke, in most women, an unsuppresible sexual turmoil – he was set for success.

The cabaret owner he approached advanced him the price of evening clothes and offered some free advice: 'With your looks and manners, you're going to spend a lot more time in bed with your partners than on the dance floor. Make sure you do it in your own time and not mine.'

What Rodolpho soon began to term his 'love break' came between the end of the afternoon – or tea dance – session and the late evening activities, a period to give the dancers a chance to relax and change from their afternoon lounge suits to formal evening wear. But Rodolpho found little opportunity for relaxation. He was an instant success with the unescorted female customers, both young and middle-aged, and became the subject of frequent squabbles between sex-hungry society women who would dash to claim him as he made his entrance on to the edge of the dance floor.

Within a few weeks, he was earning a regular $6 a day – equivalent to his full week's money as a gardener – and by May and his twentieth birthday he was occupying a smart, two-bedroom apartment of his own on East 61st Street, and boasting a growing wardrobe of fashionable suits and jackets.

Success brought new problems. He found that most American men treated him with contempt and this made him angry. But he learned to retaliate simply by ignoring them and secretly laughing at them because their women preferred the services of an Italian gigolo to the all-American male. He also became more critical of American women, dismissing the majority as wilfully selfish and irredeemably unfaithful.

With success came also discrimination. As the cabaret owner had predicted, most of his admirers wanted him in their beds, moving in time to their own particular brand of music. But Rodolpho, his 18 months of enforced celibacy well and truly dissipated, became far more selective in his choice of companions.

Money was no longer the key which released the young Latin's passion. He detested being treated as a commodity, to be bought or discarded on a whim as a woman's fancy dictated. Beauty and breeding had become his main priorities.

Beauty there was in plentiful supply, but for genuine breeding and really high society, he had to look to one of the most famous cabarets – Maxim's, Bustanoby's or Delmonico's. For this reason, he began to concentrate less on the sexual side of a gigolo's life and more on the dancing.

His interpretation of the tango especially won him applause in the dance hall where he worked, and for several weeks the owner had paid extra for a demonstration of the dance, even providing a professional partner to perform with him.

At the same time as enhancing his dancing skills, Rodolpho worked on improving his other attributes. Hours spent in front of a mirror had enabled him to perfect the smouldering-eyed look which seemed to mesmerise his customers. He had the waist and hips of his evening suit trousers taken in an extra inch – and took to wearing a corset. He also honed his deep bow and kissing of hands to a well-choreographed excellence.

The moustache which he had grown the previous year was shaved off and he took to using generous applications of brilliantine on his thick, dark hair, so he could keep it slickly combed to his scalp.

His looks and manners, he knew, seemed effeminate to other men, but for Rodolpho Guglielmi they were all valuable tools of his trade. The director in charge of the exhibition dances and gigolos at Maxim's agreed, and hired the Italian on the spot.

The move to Maxim's successfully helped Rodolpho over another personal hurdle, a decision with which he had been struggling for some weeks. The ladies had always complained that they found it very difficult to remember his surname. Rodolpho, they told him, deserved to be coupled with a name suggesting far more romance. For the first time in his life, he was grateful for the many names given him at his baptism. Somewhere among them ought to be one that sounded romantic to American ears.

According to tradition, the name di Valentina was a Papal title bestowed on one of his ancestors for some long-forgotten deed of valour on behalf of the Holy Father. With very little embellishment, it was a story which could provide a highly romantic piece of nonsense to trot out if he were ever questioned about his name. If the ladies at the dance hall gave their approval, then di Valentina it would be.

As he whispered words of love into the receptive ears of his trembling partners, Rodolpho tried out his new name, and as the syllables rolled off his tongue, they smiled even more delightedly and hugged him closer. He had chosen well.

On his first night at Maxim's, as he took to the floor with his new partner to give an exhibition of ballroom dancing, he heard the name publicly aired for the first time by the master of ceremonies: 'Mister Rodolpho di Valentina.' Appearance, name and dancing skill all made an immediate impact, and half-an-hour later, when he became free to dance with the customers, he found himself at the centre of a group of elegant and bejewelled women of various ages who wanted to be the first partner of this arrogant and deliciously handsome, imported Continental who danced the tango as though it had been invented for him.

Almost overnight, Rodolpho became the most popular dancer at Maxim's, which meant the most popular on the New York cabaret circuit. Like a Broadway star, he began to receive bouquets, toilet waters, silk handkerchiefs and other small gifts from his admirers and, increasingly, he was invited by performers in other entertainment spheres to their homes and parties. One of these was a young actress who was already a major star on Broadway – Mae Murray. She visited Maxim's on several occasions and each time danced with Rodolpho, inviting him to see her own show from the theatre wings. Their fleeting friendship was quickly forgotten by

Rodolpho when she moved to Hollywood to star in the new feature-length movies that were now being produced in the tiny Los Angeles suburb. His wildest fantasies could not have predicted that one day, during a critical and desperate period in his life, Mae would pluck him from the gutter life of a penniless West Coast gigolo and make him her co-star in a movie. But all that was yet to come.

At Maxim's, Rodolpho was enjoying huge success with no hint of the desperately difficult days before him. In his letters to Castellaneta he no longer had reason to exaggerate his position in America. He was now earning $70 per week, good pay even by American standards, and in comparison to his old neighbourhood in Italy, a vast figure. But now that he had the means, he never thought to send money back to his mother, who had helped finance his passage to this new world out of her very limited widow's pension.

So popular had he become that, though some of the men still sneeringly referred to him as a lounge lizard or gigolo, and Maxim's expected him to dance occasionally with a favoured lady customer, he was no longer so receptive to offers of payment for physical acts of love.

If he did deign to dance with one of his admirers, it was universally understood that the minimum tip he would be prepared to accept was $5. 'Extra services' were priced proportionately. Highly sensitive to slights of any kind, temperamental and disdainful of his competitors, di Valentina was rapidly becoming the prima donna of the Manhattan cabaret set.

He accepted his immense popularity as his right and observers wondered if he would ever find someone to love as passionately as he appeared to love himself.

That moment came as he chatted to two Ziegfeld Follies girls who were out on the town with a pair of wealthy stage door 'Johnnies'. Rodolpho was beckoned to one side by the head waiter, who earned substantial tips from rich clients wanting to dance or even sit for a few minutes with di Valentina.

Nodding towards one of the ringside tables where three women sat, he whispered, 'The dark-haired beauty on the right is hot for you. And she has plenty. That's Jack de Saulles's wife.'

Rodolpho glanced across the dance floor and stiffened. The famous enigmatic smile, so carefully perfected in front of the mirror, slipped from his face. He was looking at one of the most beautiful women he had ever encountered, with large liquid eyes, full ripe lips and gleaming black hair which shimmered as she laughed at a comment from one of her companions. A glittering diamond pendant nestled in the honey-tanned V where a daringly low-cut gown exposed more than a promise of the sensational treasure within that seemed to be a direct challenge to every red-blooded male in the place.

Unconsciously, Rodolpho reached up a hand to pat his gleaming hair into place. For once, the head waiter noted smugly that the handsome dancer had been thrown off balance.

'Do you like it?' he asked.

'Sensational,' said di Valentina. 'You may present me to the lady.' And almost as an afterthought, he added, 'Tell the orchestra that I will dance the tango.'

It was to prove a fateful, fatal choice of number.

THE FIRST vibrant notes of the tango struck up as Rodolpho led Bianca de Saulles on to Maxim's dance floor, and as he took her into his arms for the first of many such meetings, the young Italian was already utterly infatuated with the beautiful South American heiress. This unfortunate proclivity of his, for falling in love at a first meeting, was to cause Rodolpho recurring problems and emotional distress throughout his life. This occasion was to be no exception.

Bianca, he knew, from the endless stories circulating about her, had, four years earlier, married Jack de Saulles, a well-known and wealthy New York celebrity and businessman.

The one-time Yale quarterback and star football team captain had met the former Señorita Errazuriz during a business visit to Chile, where she lived with her equally beautiful and fabulously wealthy mother, and the besotted American chased her to Spain, and then to France, and eventually married her in Paris.

But, within a year of their return to New York, the ex-football star tired of his exotic young wife. He was a man of limited intellect who craved variety in his sexual relationships and found it readily available among the chorus girls and bit players of Broadway's theatreland.

Bianca, young and vibrant, her passions aroused and her Latin temper fuelled by her husband's constant infidelity, decided to pay him back in kind. She had both the money and the friends to speed her plan to fruition, and together they had brought her on this night to Maxim's and into the arms of Rodolpho di Valentina.

Other couples gradually melted to the edges of the dance floor as the striking pair, seemingly oblivious to their surroundings, swayed, glided and writhed to the passionate and romantic rhythm of the tango. So immediate was their understanding of each other that the Italian and the South American might have practised this dance together since childhood.

As his lips brushed her cheek, Bianca answered with her whole body, from full breasts to trembling knees, holding tightly to her lover.

When the dance ended and, as the applause and cheers of the Maxim's clientele swelled about them, Rodolpho and Bianca arranged their assignation for the following day.

When he returned to the employees' table near the orchestra after escorting the dark-haired temptress back to her table and friends, one of the other gigolos slapped him on the shoulder. 'I envy you getting to grips with that little number,' he smirked.

Rodolpho froze and glared at the other dancer. 'How dare you even comment on her,' he snarled. 'She is the woman to whom I have given my love.'

In his apartment the following day, and on numerous other days during the following year, Rodolpho and Bianca gave full release to the passions which it had taken all their willpower to restrain on the dance floor. During these illicit meetings, she told him of her loneliness in the great mansion where she spent so much of her time, with only the servants as company, and of the vileness of her husband who had made not the slightest effort to conceal his adulterous affairs.

Rodolpho, in his customary, excessively emotional way, wept for her, sympathised with her and promised her his everlasting love. He said later of his feelings for her, 'I was dazzled by the radiance of her beauty. She was the princess I had rescued so many times in my boyish imagination. When we danced, she was very happy. But afterwards, her tears told me of the weight of her heart – loneliness for her homeland and bitter sorrow at the break-up of her marriage.'

She loved him in return, but in the end it was his relationship with Bianca de Saulles which was to trigger his hasty departure from New York, the move which would eventually bring him international fame and immortalise him as the world's greatest lover and the first Hollywood superstar.

Throughout the year of his affair with Bianca, Rodolpho claimed to have remained completely faithful to her, creating certain difficulties at Maxim's, where he was plagued nightly by well-bred, amorous females wishing to put him through his paces.

It was Bianca, too, who extricated him from what she finally convinced him was the sleazy world of the cabaret gigolo. The cabarets, she told him, were little better than camouflaged brothels with male prostitutes available on demand.

Her timing was perfect. Complaints of male prostitution had led to some of the gigolos being questioned by the New York Vice Squad and leading society figures were beginning to avoid the cabarets for fear of finding themselves at the centre of a scandal. She suggested that he consider showbusiness as an alternative career. 'You're as good as any professional dancer I've seen,' she told him. 'Why not team up with another professional and give exhibitions full time?'

It seemed like excellent advice to Rodolpho and, by chance, it coincided with him being invited to a showbusiness party by one of his admirers, a black stage dancer called Bessie Dudley. At the same party was another dancer, Bonnie Glass, and unwittingly acting as fate's broker, Bessie introduced her to Rodolpho.

Bonnie – whose real name was Helen Roche – was an attractive and shapely performer from Roxbury, Massachusetts, and had eloped with the son of a well-heeled local family and divorced him three years later. She was, she explained to Rodolpho, in the process of dissolving her dance act with Clifton Webb and was looking for a new partner. A quintet was playing at the party and Rodolpho simply opened his arms and invited her to dance.

After dancing only a few steps with the lean-hipped Italian, Bonnie made him a proposition. She was prepared to pay him $50 a week to be her new dance partner. It was well under half what he was getting at Maxim's, but Rodolpho barely hesitated. He recognised this as being probably the best opportunity he would get to 'turn legitimate' and become a recognised professional performer, and it would get him away from the clutching fingers of the barracuda-like sex-seekers in Maxim's cabaret.

He took her hand and kissed it and told her he would be delighted to accept her offer. But this delight quickly turned to disillusion and resentment when they opened at the Winter Garden and Rodolpho discovered that Bonnie, an established box office draw, was paid far more than him. Following their successful run at the Winter Garden, the couple appeared in a string of other New York theatres and proved a smash hit with the public wherever they went.

Egged on by Bianca de Saulles, who felt her lover was being exploited, Rodolpho repeatedly pressed his dancing partner for a more equal share of the earnings. But Bonnie was completely inflexible and told him that if he was unhappy with their arrangement then he could pull out of the partnership any time it suited him. She could easily find herself another, good-looking hoofer. Rodolpho was convinced she was bluffing – but he dared not put it to the test.

With typical contrariness, however, Bonnie abandoned the theatre circuit and took over the old Boulevard Café and reopened it as The Montmartre, doubling Rodolpho's wage to $100 a week.

An all-expenses-paid tour of the eastern seaboard cities followed, culminating in a memorable performance before President Wilson in Washington, which Rodolpho graphically described in a letter to his mother. If he had not yet become President, he'd at least danced before one.

Mrs Guglielmi was no doubt pleased to discover how successful her wayward son was proving to be in America but would almost certainly have much rather received a few of Rodolpho's easily-earned dollars than his boastful anecdotes. Right up to her death, she would remain disappointed at his failure to offer financial assistance of any kind to his family. Italy was now at war with Germany, and the Guglielmi family was suffering both financially and from a lack of food, in common with most of their countrymen in southern Italy. But the conflict across the Atlantic was not Rodolpho's concern and, if asked, he explained that he preferred to stick to the politics of his adopted country. Like himself, America was non-aggressive and strictly neutral. Italy must have been badly advised to enter the war on the side of the Allies, he said.

Spouting platitudes for his new country, gentle criticism of his birthplace and enjoying a smooth relationship with his partner, Rodolpho di Valentina was basking in his spotlit reputation and enjoying the rewards it brought him. He wanted nothing he did or said to upset this long-sought and deeply appreciated comfortable lifestyle.

His ambitions were truly satisfied, and had circumstances not so rudely dislodged him from his contented niche, it is doubtful if he would have made further efforts of his own to achieve greatness.

But the first of a series of shocks and setbacks was only days away as winter turned to spring of 1916. After their triumph on the Keith vaudeville circuit, Bonnie Glass decided to start yet another cabaret in New York. The Chez Fisher opened on West 55th Street to long queues and was a roaring success from the beginning. Yet unbeknown to her dancing partner, Bonnie was planning a partnership of a very different kind.

The news of her engagement to a multi-millionaire staggered Rodolpho. The new man in Bonnie's life – Ben Ali Haggin – had more money than he could possibly comprehend, but he understood enough to make him deeply jealous. This and the realisation that she was to quit dancing – and close the cabaret – floored him. Suddenly, when it seemed that nothing but success and good times lay ahead for him – even prompting him to have considered marriage to Bianca – he was thrown back among the legions of the unemployed.

There was, however unexpectedly, a silver lining to the dark clouds of misfortune which Rodolpho feared were set to engulf him. Although Bonnie had always been the star of their act, during the year they had danced together he had established his own, not large, but faithful following, among theatregoers. To his pleasant surprise a showbusiness agent with the fledgling William Morris agency offered to represent him, and had little trouble booking him into the Old New York Roof on

Broadway and then a tour with a string of unknown dance partners at $150 per week – far more than Bonnie had paid him.

Good fortune continued to smile on him. When the tour ended, he was approached by one of the most talented exhibition dancers and top box-office attractions, Joan Sawyer, who asked him to audition.

The audition went well and Miss Sawyer expressed herself suitably satisfied with his abilities as a dancer, but she was scarcely able to conceal her contempt for him as a man. Imperiously, she stated his terms of employment, which she quite clearly considered ridiculously generous to this Italian immigrant, and, on his meek acceptance, dismissed him from her presence.

Smarting under her calculated rudeness, but not so rash as to throw away the chance of linking his name with that of such a famous personality, Rodolpho turned for consolation to Bianca de Saulles. Their affair, which, throughout, had been conducted in great secrecy, burned with all the uninhibited passion of its beginning, more than a year before.

The ivory-skinned wife of the Wall Street lecher still held a great attraction for the young Italian. She give him her body willingly and as often as possible in a rite of love which never failed to carry him to indescribable heights of ecstasy. Afterwards, as they lay satiated and drowsy in each other's arms, she frequently raised the subject of her husband's bullying, drunken treatment of her and his revolting practice of boasting of his sexual exploits with other women.

Unable to compete with his lover's accounts of her husband's obnoxious behaviour, Rodolpho could only bitch about his dance partner's ongoing, contemptuous attitude towards him, and her scornful comments to him backstage. After one such griping session, Rodolpho devised a plan which might, simultaneously, he suggested, resolve both of their partnership problems. If they could contrive a meeting between the pair which could lead to adultery – the only grounds for divorce in New York State – then Bianca would gain her freedom and she and Rodolpho could marry.

As a senior partner in the prestigious Manhattan real estate firm of Heckscher and de Saulles, Jack de Saulles still needed, in public, to maintain the pretence that his marriage was working and, reluctantly, with boorish lack of grace, he occasionally escorted Bianca to one or other of New York's social events. If Bianca could persuade her husband to attend one of the city's nightspots where Rodolpho and Joan Sawyer were performing then he would guarantee, on his part, to present her to the ex-football star. The beefy degenerate's determination to possess physically every beautiful woman to whom he was introduced – and often to whom he was not – would do the rest.

By innocently mentioning that two of New York's most famous socialites were in the audience, and that he knew Mrs de Saulles slightly, Rodolpho ensnared his social-climbing partner, who was more than willing to be presented.

As predicted by Bianca, the satyr in de Saulles could be relied on to do the rest. Rodolpho could see him mentally licking his lips as he ogled the beautiful brunette dancer, and was not at all surprised when de Saulles reappeared later at the club – this time alone – and insisted on buying champagne for Miss Sawyer.

Three weeks later, papers were served on de Saulles for divorce, naming Joan Sawyer as corespondent. Within minutes, the dancer had been informed, along with the information that the name Rodolpho Guglielmi was revealed as one of the plaintiff's principal witnesses.

When she finally managed to get Rodolpho to the hotel suite where she lived, she informed him, white-faced with fury, eyes blazing and spitting her words like daggers, that he could consider himself a solo act once more. She had already cancelled their bookings and she hoped to forget quickly that she had ever known him.

In the divorce proceedings, which began on 27 July 1916, Rodolpho told how he had accompanied Joan Sawyer to de Saulles's secret 'bachelor' apartment, had seen the couple together at a hotel in Providence, Rhode Island and how they had shared a private drawing room car on the return train journey. The New York press, who described him as Joan Sawyer's former dancing partner, reported that he had volunteered to testify and did not think he was doing his partner a bad turn by doing so. Evidence from Joan Sawyer's recently employed cook and de Saulles's former valet, Julius Hadamak, clinched the case.

Rodolpho and Bianca congratulated each other on a highly successful operation. Their respective partners' reputations were in tatters while they had emerged from the hearings unscathed. But this held true for only five weeks after the divorce proceedings had ended.

On 5 September, acting on information suspected to have come from sources close to Jack de Saulles, detectives from the New York City vice squad raided an apartment on Seventh Avenue, a stone's throw from Carnegie Hall.

The lessee of the apartment was a Mrs Georgia Thym and the *New York Times* and the New York *Tribune* reported that she and a bogus count, Rodolpho Guglielmi, had been arrested.

Police had kept watch on the apartment for several weeks and it was believed the pair had been using it as a base for blackmail operations against rich New Yorkers who might find themselves in embarrassing divorce scandals. Mrs Thym had been discovered hiding in a bedroom and Guglielmi, when challenged by police, had denied his identity.

After questioning by the Assistant District Attorney and detectives, the two were arraigned and held as material witnesses. As neither could raise bail, they were sent to the House of Detention and spent three days in the cells before being released.

Eventually, on 15 September, the very day when Bianca de Saulles learned that her divorce had been granted, Rodolpho was charged with 'Misdemeanor – white slave investigation'. His police file, numbered E4127, is still on record at the Bureau of Criminal Identification in the New York City Police Department. Yet there is nothing in it. Both Rodolpho's file and that of Georgia Thym are empty. There is not even a notation to say if the pair were found guilty or if the charges were dropped, though these records were supposed to be complete before being filed in the archives.

The *New York Times Index* records Rodolpho's arrest in 1916 and lists it under 'New York City Police Department: Graft Investigation'. He claimed afterwards that he had been framed and that the charges against him had been dropped on the orders of the District Attorney, and that a retraction had been printed in the *New York Times*. But there is no record of this either in police or newspaper archives.

One contemporary writer recorded that in this period, according to the New York Police Department, Rodolpho picked up a reputation as a petty thief and blackmailer.

Five years after the incident, when he had achieved megastardom in Hollywood and had completely rewritten his biography with the aid of a studio public relations team, huge sums of money were spent on various, extremely questionable practices, to remove any records which might have caused later embarrassment to the studio or their prize actor.

The disappearance of his police record is almost certainly the result of one of these operations. But though he continued until his death to try to delete all mention of his arrest from the *New York Times Index*, all his attempts to do so were unsuccessful.

What the incident did succeed in doing was to sour any links Rodolpho had with the de Saulles name and, fearing further reprisals from Bianca's former husband if he openly resumed his previous relationship with her, he opted for another dance tour, with a group of comparative unknowns, outside New York and bade her a brief, far from fond, farewell.

In 1917, this tour was followed by a series of undistinguished bookings at theatres in New York, with an occasional exhibition at Maxim's. The number of theatres still able to book professional dancers was dwindling, and Rodolpho was now having to consider poorly-paid engagements to dance the prologue before the full-length feature movies now being turned out in Hollywood, 3,000 miles away.

'You'd be better off dancing *in* pictures rather than in front of them,' one theatre manager advised him. 'There's a heck of a lot of money being made by young fellows like you out there. Why not give it a try?'

The advice may have been sound but Rodolpho was undecided. Dancing exhibitions weren't entirely played out and it would be a big risk for someone, not noted for either his courage or his sense of adventure, to try to break into an industry of which he had absolutely no knowledge.

Then, as so frequently seemed to happen in Rodolpho's life, an event occurred which made up his mind for him and forced him into a new direction. On 3 August 1917, Bianca de Saulles shot and killed her ex-husband in an argument over custody of their child. She was immediately arrested and her trial was set for November.

Fearing that his previous rather sordid connections with his former lover could be dragged into the case, and far from confident over his position with the police, who could still deport him as an undesirable alien if they chose to, Rodolpho decided to head west. This decision was reinforced by Bianca's defence counsel who advised that the further Rodolpho moved from New York the smaller became the chance of his affair with the defendant prejudicing the jury.

It was a great come down for a 'top-of-the-bill' dancer but he allowed fear to overcome his pride and accepted a job as chorus boy in a lightweight musical comedy, *The Masked Model*, which was to tour the country, ending up in San Francisco. The pay was $75 per week, plus travel expenses.

The show played to miserable houses and finally closed in Omaha, Nebraska, mid-way between the two oceans. The producers had just enough money left to send the cast back to the east coast and everyone except Rodolpho opted for a return to New York.

He waved them off from the opposite platform, having exchanged his ticket for one to San Francisco, and headed west on his way to Hollywood.

LEAVING HIS single suitcase in the left luggage department at San Francisco railway station, Rodolpho asked a porter for directions to the nearest theatre, where the stage doorman was able to tell him the name of a local bar frequented by the town's theatrical set.

The doleful Italian barman Rodolpho talked to there initially criticised his strong accent in English, and then told him, in Italian, that he would find it easier getting a job in the Californian vineyards than landing himself work in showbusiness.

Fortunately for Rodolpho, not everyone in the bar was as gloomily pessimistic as the barman, and a young singer, who had warbled Irving Berlin's wartime hit 'Oh How I Hate to Get Up in the Morning' to a disinterested crowd of drinkers, tipped him off that a chorus job was going in the Bronson Baldwin musical *Nobody Home*.

Having collected his suitcase from the station, and after spending the night in a boarding house recommended by the singer, Rodolpho attended an audition for the chorus line vacancy, and by that evening he was part of the musical cast.

Three weeks later the show folded, but for Rodolpho it had already served its purpose. He had been mortified to discover that no one in San Francisco had ever heard of him. But Baldwin was impressed and so was Bryan Foy, one of Eddie Foy's Seven Little Foys, who were also appearing for a season in San Francisco. He had asked to be introduced to Rodolpho backstage and had praised his dancing.

The two men were of similar age and hit it off immediately. Foy suggested to the Italian that if he ever made it to Los Angeles, then he should look him up. Bryan might be able to put some work his way.

VALENTINO – THE FIRST SUPERSTAR

Lunchtime socialising with other members of the musical's cast had brought Rodolpho into contact with members of a motion picture company from Hollywood who were filming on location in San Francisco. One of these was Norman Kerry, who had already made a name for himself in this new branch of the entertainment industry. He, too, was about the same age as the handsome young Italian and they struck up a friendship which was to survive all of Rodolpho's years in Hollywood.

Kerry enthused about Rodolpho's strikingly good looks and personality; the greatest assets a screen actor could have, he said, when breaking into the movie business, and if Rodolpho could arrange his passage to Los Angeles, he promised him a warm welcome, a place to stay and introductions to the studios. Rodolpho di Valentina became very excited, for the picture painted by his new friend was one of easy living and huge rewards from success in an occupation where the repetition of short, simple-to-learn scenes would remove any mistakes a beginner might make. Mary Pickford had shown the way. From a $35-a-week extra, she now commanded, after eight years, half a million dollars a year. Other top stars, like Douglas Fairbanks and Charlie Chaplin, were earning more than $20,000 a week.

It was an insatiable industry. The public demanded more and more films and these, in turn, produced more and more stars. More mansions were under construction in the hills north of Hollywood than in any other residential district in America.

Two weeks later Rodolpho managed to secure a free berth on the Los Angeles train with the team from the Al Jolson production *The Passing Show*. He chose to ignore Norman Kerry's warning that Hollywood could also bring great disappointment

55

and a possibly miserable future of walk-on parts, which would scarcely pay enough to keep one above the breadline.

A few words from Al Jolson himself – delivered with a total lack of sincerity and without the accompaniment of a smile, to the effect that a glittering future could await him in motion pictures – had cheered him considerably, and he shrugged off the fear that this could be yet another journey to disaster and misery.

With wonderful dreams of stardom filling his mind, he sped southwards towards the dream-makers' capital, blissfully unaware that his fears were more than justified and that nightmare days were once more just around the corner.

* * *

After almost exactly four years in America, Rodolpho di Valentina stepped off the San Francisco to Los Angeles sleeper with only the clothes he stood up in and a small, battered suitcase containing his other belongings. Together, they represented the full extent of the rewards he had managed to accumulate since he had arrived on the *Cleveland* from Italy.

Feeling, if anything, more lonely than when, as a naïve and bewildered immigrant, he had found himself in the ferry terminal on the threshold of New York, Rodolpho wondered if another four years might find him entering another strange city with another threadbare suitcase in hand.

His name, shouted from beyond the ticket barrier, interrupted Rodolpho's melancholy ponderings and he spotted the grinning face of Norman Kerry, waving above the sea of waiting heads. Norman shook his hand warmly, insisted on carrying his suitcase and guided him to the street, where a new, four-door Ford saloon was parked directly outside.

'Jump in,' he said, 'and we'll get you home.' He raised his fingers to his mouth as Rodolpho began to speak. 'And no damned protests,' he laughed. 'You're staying with me, and that's all there is to it. If you want to break into pictures, you're going to need a decent place to sleep, a good address and someone to keep your things pressed. I have a small suite with a double room at the Alexandria Hotel and, if you don't object to sharing, then I sure as hell don't.'

For the first time in his life, Rodolpho found himself speechless, unable to thank Kerry adequately. They drove on in silence until they reached the outskirts of Hollywood, which seemed to Rodolpho to be not much more than a rather large, haphazardly put together village.

'Well, this is it,' said Kerry, taking in, with a sweep of his hand, a collection of ramshackle studio buildings, restaurants, shops and hotels. 'It offers the nearest thing to instant fame and riches in the world. If you've got half the talent I think you've got, then some of that is going to be yours pretty soon.'

How prophetically inaccurate those words turned out to be. They were words that Rodolpho would recall and increasingly sneer at in the months that followed. Not that Norman Kerry didn't try to find him work. He kept his word and introduced Rodolpho to dozens of directors, producers and agents, but none held out the slightest prospect of him getting a part in a picture.

At 5.00pm, every afternoon, Rodolpho would be downstairs in the Alexandria's marble-columned lobby bar which was a daily mecca for the movie fraternity. There was the added advantage that the management served free sandwiches with the cocktails and often this would be

Rodolpho's only dinner. Some of the men and women he met there even knew of his reputation as a dancer from New York, and their advice to him was to go back to dancing. He might, they added kindly, pick up the odd job as an extra, should dark-skinned, Latin heavies ever be needed, but as for landing a leading role, forget it. He didn't have what it took to make an impact on the ladies, which studio executives believed to be clean, American, apple-pie good looks.

With his meagre savings almost exhausted, Rodolpho was reduced to joining the thousands of other hopefuls who queued daily outside all the studios for bit parts, or simply to be an extra. The man who had once had the most beautiful women in New York queuing to dance with him at $10 a time now had to suffer the ignominy himself of standing in line hoping to be noticed – and all just to earn a miserable $5 a day.

As the weeks ran into months, not a single offer of work as an extra had come his way. 'It's useless. Nobody wants me,' he protested to Norman Kerry, the trader's son-turned-actor, who on most days was able to smuggle him into the studio canteen for a free, or very cheap, meal. He ate there so frequently that many of the regulars at the studio believed him to be a full-time actor.

At the start of 1918, in utter despair, Rodolpho eventually admitted defeat, and gave up the search for film work. Embarrassment, aided and abetted by poverty, drove him from Norman Kerry's suite and the Alexandria Hotel to a small room over a café in Santa Monica, on the Los Angeles coast. The meagre pay and small tips he earned as a dancer in a variety of the city's more dubious cafés forced him again to accommodate some of his female dance customers for afternoon sessions in his room. Most of them complained about their husbands, their children and the smallness of Rodolpho's ancient and unsteady single bed.

'Downstairs they pay to jump on me, and upstairs they pay for me to jump on them,' he lamented, but he found his employers and fellow dancers totally lacking in sympathy. In fact, several of the latter resented his popularity with the ladies. At the age of 22, Rodolpho seemed destined to live out his days in California as a low-grade male prostitute.

His spirit was battered, his ambition in tatters and his self-respect auctioned at $10 afternoon sessions in the café's upstairs room, when Norman Kerry appeared one day on an unexpected visit. Kerry urged him to have one more try in pictures, and Rodolpho, betrayed by his mercurial emotions, made a valiant attempt at refusal, then almost wept with gratitude.

Kerry explained that an old friend, the director Emmett Flynn, was making a picture for First National and looking for a dancer to work as an extra. 'It could be just the break you need,' Kerry told him. At least it would extricate him, if only briefly, from the seedy life which was gradually engulfing him in Santa Monica.

Emmett Flynn, who worked as an independent director, readily agreed to give his friend's protégé an audition and, to Rodolpho's amazement, not only gave him the part of lead dancer in the ballroom scene of his picture *Alimony*, but also appeared to take an immediate liking to him.

Rodolpho had hoped to meet the leading lady in *Alimony*, Josephine Whittel, but he never even saw her. His scene was completed in less than an hour, for which he received the standard extra's fee of $5 – barely equal to the tips he had received in the New York cabarets.

His actual début on screen lasted only a few seconds, but even this fleeting appearance and the pitiful financial reward could not dampen his enthusiasm. The moment he saw his face on the big screen, Rodolpho di Valentina was hooked. In those transitory moments in front of the camera, he had experienced an almost climactic thrill, which repeated itself when he watched the finished film on screen.

To describe the film as mediocre would have been to flatter it unduly, but to Rodolpho it was a minor miracle. He felt his whole life had been transformed and he assured the delighted Norman Kerry and Bryan Foy that, no matter what the obstacles, he intended one day to become a star.

His evanescent participation in *Alimony* may have impressed him, but no other person in the movie business, to whom he mentioned it, remembered seeing his unmemorable appearance in the film. So, after a further week spent tramping from studio to studio, without success, and flat broke once more, he was again forced to take up dancing to earn a living. The only flimsy prospect which kept his hopes of future stardom alive was a cheery comment from Emmett Flynn that the *Alimony* screen writer, Hayden Talbot, would seek him out when the script for his next picture was completed.

Feeling himself slipping back towards the twilight world of the afternoon dance sham, Rodolpho decided there would be no more sessions in seedy bedrooms in Santa Monica. But despite his many promises to himself, when Baron Long offered him a full-time dancing job at his newly opened Watts Tavern, a roadhouse on the outskirts of Los Angeles, he didn't hesitate. The pay was only $35 a week, but it was the best offer he had received in the nine months he had been in Hollywood, and he needed the money desperately.

It was comforting to find that the girl who would partner him, Marjorie Tain, was also an actress fallen on hard times. She told him Watts Tavern was rapidly becoming a favourite haunt of Hollywood producers and directors and added, optimistically, it was only a matter of time before one, or both of them, was 'spotted'. The word Rodolpho would have used was 'rescued'.

The pair were featured on the billboards outside the roadhouse, but despite this and their dancing themselves almost to a standstill five times an evening, no one from Hollywood appeared even to notice their existence.

As he left the tavern one night, exhausted and miserable as usual, Rodolpho was seized by a highly excited Emmett Flynn. The laughing director half-dragged the confused Italian along the pavement towards a waiting car. 'I've been looking for you for a week,' he said. 'Why the hell didn't you tell anyone where you were working?'

'Would you, in my position?' asked Rodolpho. 'What's this all about?'

Apparently, Hayden Talbot had finished his new script and had tailor-written one of the better parts for Rodolpho, explained the ebullient director. It was the role of a really nasty piece of work – an Italian count.

In the not-too-distant future, Rodolpho might have thought long and hard about accepting such a part. For he would learn about being type-cast and that being labelled a 'Latin heavy, dishonest, shifty, disreputable ...' would forever bar his way to stardom. But his feelings at this time were of ecstatic jubilation. He performed a high-kicking leap which almost carried him on to the bonnet of Flynn's battered limousine.

Clutching a copy of the script for *The Married Virgin*, Rodolpho went home and spent an almost sleepless night reading and re-reading his part. The following morning, accompanied by Flynn and Talbot, he arrived early at the Fidelity Pictures Studio and was introduced to the director, Joseph Maxwell.

Given Emmett Flynn's recomendation, Maxwell was happy to waive an audition and, after a brief stop in the production supervisor's office, Rodolpho walked out with a contract for $50 a week.

Convinced that he was now on the ladder to instant stardom young di Valentina was meticulous in putting every minute detail of Maxwell's direction into his performance. In addition, he had Emmett Flynn offering further guidance, away from the cameras, and a barrage of helpful tips from Norman Kerry and Bryan Foy. All went well, and Maxwell declared himself very pleased with the daily 'rushes'. Rodolpho could almost taste success. His name would appear on the cinema hoardings, admittedly not above the title with the picture's stars, Vera Sisson and Edward Jobson, but below, with the other featured actors. People would no longer be able to call him an unknown and pretend not to recognise his name.

But once again fate, this time in the form of a camera crew dispute over money, which quickly escalated to the court room, worked against him. The picture was shelved for almost two years – finally being released in 1920 – while financial squabbles with the production team and the studio were sorted out.

So Rodolpho began yet another round of the Hollywood studios. He had stood in line so often, hoping for bit-parts, that by now he was able to recognise several of his competitors for the hungrily sought-after scraps at the casting office windows.

Two of them, Beatrice Joy and Ramon Navarro, the man destined to become Rodolpho's successor almost a decade later, urged him to take a part-time job at the J Francis Smith school of art and design on Los Angeles's Main Street.

The pair of them were modelling for the students' life classes at night and chasing film bit-parts during the day. But to Rodolpho, with his Catholic peasant upbringing, this seemed even more immoral than selling himself to frustrated West Coast housewives who were habituées of the afternoon prod-and-pant sessions.

If he had to strip at all, reasoned Rodolpho, he would rather do it in front of one woman who had paid for his sexual services than in front of a group of degenerate art students. He was disturbingly aware of the way in which certain men in Hollywood had eyed his dancer's body and striking looks – their meaningful glances were not simply admiring – and he detested the idea of even being considered a possible target for their perversions.

Nursing his bitter disappointment at this latest hiccup in his film career, he agreed to a job at the Vernon Club, an off-beat cabaret-cum-dance joint beyond the lower end of downtown Los Angeles, which was nevertheless popular with elements of the Hollywood social set, who liked to appear daring by frequenting carefully selected places of ill repute.

In the Vernon Club, there were no fancy titles handed out to the dance instructors and demonstrators. They were just gigolos, pure and simple. They knew it, the management knew it and the customers knew it.

Each night as he danced, Rodolpho found himself half-longing for someone from a film company to recognise his latent talent and charisma and offer him a part, and half-fearing that he would be spotted by someone he knew, and lose any chance he might have had of future work in films.

One night, as he was earning $2 for an hour's savaging by a large, sweaty and heavily-painted society woman, whose hands kept straying, embarrassingly, to his buttocks, director Bob Leonard walked in with his wife Mae Murray, by now one of the most popular film stars in America and earning $5,000 a week.

Rodolpho recognised her instantly as the friendly actress who had occasionally danced with him in Maxim's three years earlier. As the couple were guided to their table, accompanied by a group of Hollywood friends, he wrenched the insistent, clutching hand of his dance-partner above waist height and hissed, 'You paid to dance. So dance, damn you, dance!'

With ramrod back, the mocking smile and the smouldering look he had practised so often before the mirror, Rodolpho whirled his befuddled partner across the tiny dance floor and began working his way back and forth in front of the star's table.

Twice his eyes caught those of Mae Murray, and a fierce surge of hope flooded his body as he thought he spotted a flash of recognition there. When she turned to a companion, nodding in his direction, and said something, he was almost certain she had remembered him from Maxim's.

Had he been able to hear the man's reply, he might not have felt so optimistic. 'He's just a house Italian gigolo called di Valentina.'

'He looks all right to me,' said the vivacious young actress, eyes gleaming. 'What do you think, Bob?' she asked her husband. 'He looks OK and he's a good dancer, too.'

'Well, Mae,' he said, smiling indulgently at his wife. 'If that's what you think, I'll go and get him for you.'

He made his way across the floor and tapped the dancer on the shoulder. 'If you've got a moment, my wife would like to dance with you,' he said.

'I'd be delighted,' said Rodolpho, and after hurriedly making an excuse to his partner and pushing her towards a table, he followed Leonard back across the floor.

After smiles and a brief and casual introduction, he found himself with Mae Murray in his arms and the focus of attention for everyone in the club. It was an exhilarating moment, for here was something he could excel at. On the dance floor, he knew, few men in the country could rival him.

After a few minutes, a little out of breath but completely captivated, Mae Murray was full of compliments. 'You dance like a professional,' she said, 'and you also look vaguely familiar.'

Rodolpho hid his disappointment that she had not remembered their previous encounters and told her, 'We danced together when I was the head dancer at Maxim's. he said. 'I'm working in pictures now but I like to come here to keep myself up to scratch.'

The young star smiled, not letting him realise that she already knew his real reason for being in the Vernon. 'I do remember now,' she grinned. 'It's been a pleasure to dance with you again. Perhaps I'll be lucky enough to find you here the next time I come.'

In the following two months, Mae and Bob Leonard became regular visitors to the club. At first, Rodolpho was simply invited to dance with the director's wife, but soon he was being invited to join their table and was even asked to accompany them to some of the more informal Hollywood gettogethers. To Rodolpho's relief, they confessed that they knew his real reason for being in the club, but assured him that it did not matter. He was neither the first, nor the last, young hopeful who had had to take on a menial or even unpleasant job, while trying to break into pictures.

By good fortune, and again with thanks to Emmett Flynn, who was proving a truly loyal, foul-weather friend, he was able to quit his job at the Vernon, though he still went there to dance, and to tell his new friends, the Leonards, truthfully, that he was appearing in another film, *Virtuous Sinners*, starring his other good Hollywood friend, Norman Kerry.

What he didn't say was that the part was that of an Italian Bowery tough, and that his scenes were completed in less than two days. Despite this, Emmett Flynn kept him on the payroll for the full production at the standard extra's fee, which had risen to $7.50 a day. At least now he was able to stand his round buying drinks for his new friends Bob Leonard and Mae Murray.

Hollywood in 1918 was rather like a gold-strike town of half a century earlier, just beginning to blossom from a hotch-potch of studio buildings, hastily-erected restaurants and shops and a handful of hotels. The community was small and nearly everyone in the film industry knew everyone else – at least everyone else who mattered. Rodolpho was resolutely committed to getting himself on the list of the latter.

The most popular eating place for many of the actors was Branstatter's, and lunchtimes would see a steady parade of film people, most of them in full costume and wearing make-up, strolling from the studios along Hollywood Boulevard to the restaurant.

The main dining room was upstairs and the food was so good that some of the biggest names in the movies would queue on the stairs to take their turn at one of the tables.

On Wednesdays and Saturdays, the stars would turn out en masse for the regular dance nights. The mid-week shindig would take place at the Hollywood Hotel, which many of the big names in the industry called home, and on Saturdays almost the same crowd would descend on their favourite weekend haunt, the Ship's Café in Santa Monica.

Rodolpho di Valentina became a regular at all three preferred venues, in addition to the Alexandria Hotel lobby bar which still remained the favoured afternoon choice for many in the movie fraternity. He would carefully position himself on the edge of important groups, ready to smile and join in if his opinion was sought, or swiftly moving away if someone appeared to be about to challenge his right to be there.

He was impressed at the way many of the top earners splashed their money around. That was the evolving Hollywood tradition and Rodolpho swore to Norman Kerry that when he achieved the astronomical earnings of these legendary stars, he would outspend them all. Equally, he vowed that he would never become dependent on drink or drugs as many of the most famous personalities of the day appeared to be. One star told him he had trembled so violently one morning after a night on the town, that he had to arrange for the props people to wire his arm to stop it shaking while he was being filmed with a glass in his hand.

Despite his regular attendances at all the main Hollywood watering holes, Rodolpho was unable to attract the attention of any of the better-known directors, several of whom were similarly 'showing themselves about' in the hope of attracting work.

It was Bob Leonard this time who came to the rescue with an introduction to fellow director Paul Powell, who was about to direct a picture with teenage star Carmel Myers for Universal, already one of the major Hollywood studios. Powell was looking for a newcomer to play the leading man opposite Carmel, and after meeting di Valentina warmly accepted Bob Leonard's recommendation of the young Italian actor.

Girls often became stars at 13 or 14 in silent movies, and were almost as often finished by the time they reached 18. Carmel Myers, who had started in the cinema when she was 15, was just 18 and Rodolpho di Valentina 23 when they made their first picture together. It was called *A Society Sensation*, and Rodolpho was paid $100 a week – only $50 a week less than his young co-star.

They met on the first day's shooting when he was brought on to the set by Paul Powell, and Carmel still remembered more than half-a-century later how she was bowled over by his quiet charm and staggering good looks. In her rest room at the studio, she told her dresser, 'He is wonderful. What style he has – and what personality. There is something about him I just can't explain. I guess it's sex. His voice is beautiful and deep and when he said I reminded him of his people, everything fluttered inside.'

The following morning, it was the turn of Rodolpho to have butterflies in his stomach, when he was told that a scene of the film, being shot on location that day, called for him to rescue Carmel from the sea.

It was unseasonally grey and overcast and a biting wind blew in off the Pacific on the lonely stretch of coast near Santa Monica. Carmel was in the water, clinging to rocks under a disused wharf and the director and cameraman were almost overhead.

'OK, Rodolpho,' Powell shouted through his megaphone. 'You run down to the pier and, as soon as you see Carmel, jump into the water.'

The clapperboard snapped shut and Powell yelled, 'Action!'

Wearing only a brief swimming costume, Rodolpho ran on to the pier, his eyes searching the water. Pretending to catch sight of the young heroine, he registered great concern. And froze.

'Cut!' shouted Powell. 'No, Rodolpho, I don't want you to pause. I want you straight in. Let's do it again.'

Again, di Valentina acted out his part perfectly until the moment came to leap from the pier. Once again, he froze. Powell's anger began to show as he screamed again for the camera to cut.

After a third attempt at the scene had failed, Carmel's mother, who rarely left the unit when her daughter was filming, began complaining that her daughter was in danger of catching pneumonia if she wasn't soon hauled out of the sea.

By this time, the director was furious. 'We'll give it one more try,' he warned Rodolpho. 'Then we'll pack up and start looking for a replacement.'

Looking utterly miserable, Rodolpho returned to his position on shore. 'It will be all right this time,' he promised.

'I sincerely hope so,' snapped Powell. 'Everybody ready? Action!'

For the fourth time, Rodolpho went through the pretence of spotting the now-shivering figure of Carmel in the waves. This time he didn't hesitate and leapt into the water beside her. Immediately, it became apparent to everyone why he had been so reluctant to go through with the scene. He couldn't swim.

As the nearest to him, Carmel struck out, grabbed him around the chest and hauled him into shallow water.

'What happened?' she gasped.

'I'm a dancer, not a swimmer,' panted the shivering and desperately humiliated Rodolpho. 'I thought everybody knew that.'

From that moment, they became good friends, and the on-screen romance between them might very easily have blossomed off screen, had it not been for the ever-watchful eye of Mrs Myers.

A few days after the life-saving incident, Rodolpho called on Carmel in her dressing room. Turning to her mother, he clicked his heels, bowed and asked, 'Madame Myers, may I have the honour of taking your daughter out to dinner?'

'I'm very sorry, Mr di Valentina' she told him sternly, 'Carmel is much too young for that sort of thing.'

Completely unabashed, he pressed on, 'Madame Myers, when I want something, I don't usually let anything stand in my way.'

It was said with great charm and great conviction, and Carmel, flattered and impressed by the Italian's words and manner, yet not daring to intervene, looked from her leading man to her mother.

'Even when what is standing in your way weighs two hundred pounds?' asked Mrs Myers. She smiled and Rodolpho laughed.

'Touché, Madame,' he said.

Regretfully, Carmel later confided, 'I'd have loved to go out with him, or have him back to the house, or for dinner, or for anything else you might like to imagine along the way. What a pity I was too young.'

Too young for romance, but not for friendship. During their working periods on set – with Mrs Myers always within surveillance range – the two talked for hours about themselves and their dreams. It was to Carmel that Rodolpho probably gave the most accurate account on record of his boyhood in Italy, and the many adventures and calamities which had befallen him since his arrival in America.

'He had nothing to lose then,' she recalled many years later. 'But after he became a star, he – or possibly the studios – didn't want the real story to come out. Between them they manufactured a ridiculous background version for consumption by his fans, which was quite laughable. Far better to have retained the truth, which made him a much more interesting and attractive character.'

At the time, Carmel tried to do everything she could to help her latest leading man – even to the extent of going to Universal chief executive Carl Laemmle and pleading with him to put di Valentina under contract.

Carmel, slightly taller than the affable 5ft 2in studio boss, who was known to all Hollywood as 'Uncle Carl', listed Rodolpho's qualities: 'He's going to be a big star. Grab him quickly, and put him under contract.'

Laemmle patted her on the shoulder. 'Don't worry about him, girl,' he said. 'We will always be able to get him at the same price and, anyway, I'm sure he's not going to be a big star like you.'

Uncle Carl did, however, admit that he liked the finished product of *A Society Sensation* and agreed with Paul Powell and Carmel that Rodolpho should be employed to do a second picture as her leading man. He even ignored his own judgement and sanctioned a wage rise, which brought Rodolpho's earnings up to $125 per week.

All Night was not the success everyone had hoped for, and the completion of this second picture with Carmel brought yet another reversal in Rodolpho's fortunes. After playing the second lead in two consecutive films, he had not unnaturally assumed that his worth as an actor had been recognised in Hollywood. Norman Kerry concurred enthusiastically, but directors and studio heads alike seemed collectively underwhelmed by his star potential. Only Carmel, he told Kerry plaintively, appeared to recognise his true worth.

But one other woman had her eye on Rodolpho and while not, perhaps, recognising his embryonic star qualities as an actor, she was fully aware of his very well-developed talents as a man and as a potential lover.

Over the months, Mae Murray had become increasingly involved with the one-time gigolo. But fearful of her reputation and the unpredictable temper of her fiercely jealous husband, she had not dared to suggest a private meeting with the hot-eyed, deliciously arrogant Latin.

That keenness to have him take her in his arms for purposes other than whisking her around a dance floor won him his first big role. Unlike Carmel, who was a relative newcomer to the Hollywood firmament, the volatile blonde star was one of the biggest box-office earners in the world, and what she wanted, she got.

What – or more correctly, who – she wanted was Rodolpho di Valentina and, in almost a repeat of their first meeting in Los Angeles, she sent husband Bob Leonard to fetch him.

Reluctantly, for by this time his suspicions of the dancer's attraction for his wife were already aroused, Leonard telephoned him and offered him the part of leading man in Mae's new picture, *The Big Little Person*.

It was clear to the whole cast and production team, as well as to the director, that Mae was putting a great deal more into the love scenes with the new boy than she usually did. Some of the kisses were so passionate that the couple's fellow actors were afraid to catch Bob Leonard's eye. Even Rodolpho seemed nervous of facing the director after one or two of his more scorching scenes with Mae.

During one of them, he appeared to become completely carried away and his hands began freely roaming her body. Many of his leading ladies were to experience this kind of physical proof of his arousal, but none of them, including Mae Murray, ever complained.

Indeed, she appeared to enjoy the experience so much that she demanded he be used again in her next film, *The Delicious Little Devil*. And, as always in Hollywood, what the star wanted, the star got.

Mae would play a luscious, night-club dancer and Rodolpho the son of an Irish millionaire. More important than the role, at this moment, was the $100 per week he would receive and the fact that his name would go on the placards second only to that of Mae Murray herself.

6

FOR THE FIRST time since arriving in Hollywood, Rodolpho di Valentina felt that he was on the brink of real success, and to meet it he decided on a dramatic change of personality.

From now on, the gregarious, eager-to-please hanger-on who had just completed his first two years in Hollywood would disappear for ever, to be replaced by a completely new and dramatically original model, a loner who would shun the crowd and thereby stand out as someone special, someone different from the rest.

As a first step towards this new image, he bought a pair of white Russian wolfhounds and a white bathing costume and at weekends, when the majority of people from the film colony gathered on the beaches of Santa Monica, he would stroll along the sands, alone except for the two dogs. People, he noticed, would point at him and whisper his name, the men with laughter or envy, the women often wistfully or with interest. Whatever they said did not worry him. The only thing that mattered was that they were saying *something* about him.

Convinced also by the new recognition of his talent that he had finally won for himself a place among the regularly employed, and wishing to further his new image, Rodolpho put a down-payment on a huge, second-hand Mercer automobile, agreeing to pay the balance of $750 monthly with $50 cheques.

He spent all of his spare time on the set of *The Delicious Little Devil* in his car or under it, for the second-hand giant frequently broke down. He was a very fast, but not very good, driver and other motorists in Hollywood soon learned to pull over when they heard the roaring engine of the Mercer overhauling them.

In the open front seat, and occasionally accompanied by a beautiful companion – there were an abundance of would-be film starlets eager to be seen with a budding star – Rodolpho was aware he cut a splendid figure. He had a flair for drawing attention to himself, a natural showman who boasted to Norman Kerry and Bryan Foy, 'It won't be long before everyone will be saying, "There goes di Valentina," whenever I appear in public. Even though no one will know the *real* me.'

The two smiled indulgently, but advised caution. They, along with most of Hollywood, had heard that in their second picture together, the love scenes between Mae Murray and Rodolpho were, if anything, even more hot-blooded than in the first and, although Bob Leonard's professional poise appeared to be unaffected by his wife's obvious enthusiasm for the lips and caresses of her new leading man, studio gossips predicted there would not be a third film involving these two.

Whatever the reasons, they were right. So were Kerry and Foy in advising caution for, after the Mae Murray pictures, the offers for di Valentina dried up and he was again reduced to accepting bit parts in a string of pictures, which were all that were offered to him in the following six months.

One of the first casualties was the Mercer. Reduced again to $50-a-time roles – when he could get them – Rodolpho could not keep up the payments and the finance company repossessed the car. He claimed that repair bills had cost more than the actual payments and that he was glad to see the back of it, but it hurt his ego not to be able to drive down Hollywood Boulevard in his gleaming success symbol. Girls, too, he noticed, were less willing to join him when he had no car and no starring role in a current movie. And, on top of all his other problems, he became very ill.

The worst Spanish influenza epidemic since the turn of the century had swept through California earlier in the year and, though many of his film and dance hall acquaintances had been stricken with it, he had come through unscathed.

He put it down to his tough Italian boyhood and the daily sessions of exercises and calesthenics with which he greeted each morning. Few people in his position – he had been eating badly again because of his reduced circumstances – managed to resist the bug for as long as he did.

When he did catch it, he got it badly. But even after six years in America, Rodolpho still retained the peasant's fear of doctors. Though his temperature soared to 104°F, and the fever raged day after day, he refused to see a physician or take medicines. 'I don't believe in doctors,' he told friends through cracked and burning lips. 'I am strong enough to fight any illness unaided.' They were words those friends would one day remember and recall with sadness.

Once recovered, he was forced to turn again to Norman Kerry for help. And Kerry, as always, was there to lend assistance to his friend. He introduced him to director James Young who offered Rodolpho a small part as an Apache dancer in his new film *Rogue's Romance.* It was an unimportant role but Rodolpho worked hard and James Young was sufficiently impressed by his diligence and commitment to recommend him for the part of a villain in Victor Schertzinger's film *The Homebreaker*. The part was reduced even further in the editing and in the final version Rodolpho was on screen for only a few seconds.

For three, to Rodolpho, interminable months, he was out of work and drifted steadily, but relentlessly, deeper into debt. Only a chance meeting with Paul Powell, who had directed the pictures with Carmel Myers, prevented him from quitting

Hollywood for good to escape his increasingly demanding creditors. Powell introduced him, with a favourable word, to the already legendary director DW Griffith.

Griffith was producing *Out of Luck*, which was nominally being directed by Elmer Clifton, and Rodolpho was given the part of a heavy to Dorothy Gish. His hopes of stardom were temporarily resurrected, because of working for Griffith, but quickly dashed when Griffith told him the only rebooking he would get after that picture would be as a stage dancer doing the live prologues to his future productions.

In no position to turn down the $100 per week offered, he agreed to team up with Griffith's latest protégée and mistress Carol Dempster, dancing the prologue to *The Greatest Thing in Life*, which featured for three months at the Auditorium Theatre in Los Angeles.

During this highly successful engagement, he auditioned with Griffith for the part of the Mexican hero in *Scarlet Days*, and for more than a week beforehand spent hours every night, after leaving the theatre, studying the script. It was a bitter disappointment when he lost the part to Richard Barthelmess.

The main reason, Griffith told him, was that Barthelmess showed a great deal more restraint in his acting of the character, and if Rodolpho could do less arm-waving and facial contortions, and learn to express himself with eyes and mouth in a far less obvious fashion, his acting career would stand slightly more chance of getting off the ground. At present, he acted as though he were a performer in the worst kind of music hall, melodramatic comedy sketch.

Never slow to accept advice, if the person dishing it out was an expert, he took the great director's words to heart and began putting his suggestions into practice during long sessions in front of a bedroom mirror.

His disappointment in failing to get the coveted part was made even more intense when Griffith offered him the job of dancing the prologue to *Scarlet Days*. Simply to warm up the audience for the star – the role should have been his by rights – almost reduced Rodolpho to tears. He was full of self-pity, but for $100 a week he was prepared to do almost anything that would prevent his having to return to his old stand-by job as a dance hall gigolo. At least this way he was working for one of the major studios, even if not on film.

In mid-June of 1919, Rodolpho was drinking one evening in the lobby bar of the Alexandria Hotel with Norman Kerry when Harry Reichenbach walked in. The introduction which followed was destined to be the most important in the Italian wannabe star's life.

Reichenbach had been the top media-manipulator for a circus and now worked for eminent and autocratic studio mogul Jesse Lasky. He was recognised as Hollywood's most brilliant publicity orchestrator. He told them that, as a favour to Herbert Sanborn, who managed glamorous Equity Studio's star, Clara Kimball Young, he had promised to look out for young actors to play opposite her in a new film. *The Eyes of Youth* had been a hit production on Broadway, starring Marjorie Rambeau, so Equity and director Albert Parker were transferring it to the silver screen with Clara in the main role. The part eventually offered to Rodolpho was of a clean-cut, boy-next-door character who is ultimately exposed as a treacherous imposter, being used by Clara's husband to engineer a divorce.

'Not another villain!' he wailed, but Kerry, ever alert to his friend's best interests, hushed him. 'You'll be doing a favour for Harry Reichenbach and he is a major influence on Jesse Lasky, who is one of the biggest film producers in Hollywood.'

Rodolpho reluctantly accepted the logic in his friend's argument and agreed to do the picture. He didn't make his first appearance until the third part and was on screen for only a few minutes, but it was enough. Those brief moments of screen exposure were to ensure Rodolpho di Valentina immortality as the greatest superstar in cinema history.

The Eyes of Youth was released five months later, in November 1919, and proved only modestly successful. But one person who did see it, again and again, was mesmerised by Rodolpho's performance.

She was June Mathis, one of the best writers ever to work for a Hollywood studio. The script she was writing for Metro was the most important to be produced in 1920 and, after seeing *The Eyes of Youth*, she was determined that only di Valentina could fill the leading role.

But the glorious future which fate had in store for him was of little benefit to the actor during that summer of 1919. Once more penniless – unable even to find work as a dancer – Rodolpho was reduced to circulating Equity notices to fellow actors for $1 an hour. Shelved, for the time being, was his carefully nurtured new image as a loner for, without work in pictures and with the possibility of stardom slowly becoming a distant fantasy, he sought regular contact with more of the people who might appreciate his acting ability, and who might be persuaded to offer him work. He had taken lessons in riding and fencing, and played tennis and bridge to a more than socially acceptable standard. He had worked hard to improve his English, although he still spoke with a pronounced accent. But he sincerely considered himself to be the equal of any other actor in town, and could not understand why the big break continued to pass him by.

People like Norman Kerry, Bryan Foy and actor-turned-director Douglas Gerard, who had also become a good friend, promoted him whenever an opportunity presented itself and were wonderfully supportive. All were there to console him at his most despairing moment, when a letter arrived from Italy with the heart-wrenching news that his mother had died.

Rodolpho wept bitterly, knowing now that he could never prove to her what a success he would be or alter her conviction, backed by his former neighbours and frequently expressed in her letters, that acting was akin to doing the devil's work. Filled with remorse, he thought of giving up his life in the States and returning to Italy – at least to visit her grave – and perhaps for ever. But his current – and, he acknowledged, his most persistent – problem, a severe lack of funds, made even that impossible, and he could only pray that his mother, in the end, had remembered him with love.

Now, desperate for recognition and to prove himself a success, if only as a posthumous offering to his mother, he avoided turning down any invitation which might involve a meeting with one of the powerful studio bosses or directors, and it was this urgent need which persuaded him to accept a casual invitation to a small dinner party being held at the Ship's Café in Santa Monica. It was one he would regret for the rest of his life.

It was a chance meeting with beautiful composer-conductor's daughter Dagmar Godowsky, whom he had met in New York while exhibition dancing in the clubs, which led to Rodolpho's most awful public humiliation to date.

Incredibly, in such a relatively tiny community, he had not known that she was now living in Los Angeles or that she had become a successful actress and was under contract to Metro.

Dagmar was delighted to learn that he, too, was now acting in the movies and impulsively asked him to drop in, that evening, at the dinner party being given to celebrate the completion of Nazimova's latest picture, *Stronger Than Death*. Several of the Metro bigwigs were expected to attend this tribute to the great Russian star, including one of the celebrated studio managers, Maxwell Karger.

It was too great an opportunity to miss, and Rodolpho promised to join Dagmar in the Santa Monica restaurant that evening. Hurrying home, he took out his best suit and, after half-a-dozen unsuccessful phonecalls, located a friend who would loan him a car to drive to the coast.

When he arrived, some 20 people were already seated at the large table, and the dinner was under way. Rodolpho checked his appearance in a mirror by the door and set his face in a warm smile before striding across the room to join them. Maxwell Karger had just proposed a toast to Nazimova and everyone had their glasses raised as Rodolpho reached the table and caught Dagmar Godowsky's eye. She smiled, beckoned him round and started to introduce him. Then Nazimova caught sight of the newcomer.

The beautiful young actress, who had invited Rodolpho, remembered the scene vividly, and recounted it in graphic and gory detail in her autobiography.

She lowered her head and froze. Her little frame was rigid and she looked as though she were having a divine fit. The whole table took its cue from her and, one by one, they, too, lowered their heads in this shocking form of grace. My voice tailed off and so did his.

Nazimova broke the tableau and thundered, 'How dare you bring that gigolo to my table? How dare you introduce that pimp to Nazimova?'

Everyone at the table was shocked into silence. Not a glass chinked and not a person moved as Rodolpho, face burning and eyes flooding, almost ran from the restaurant.

With no attempt to mask her victorious sniggers, Nazimova recounted how Rodolpho had been the centre of an unsavoury scandal in New York which had ended with Bianca de Saulles slaying her husband to be with the Italian gigolo.

Most of the guests knew that Bianca had actually murdered her husband while confronting him over custody of their child and had been acquitted at her trial, but no one chose, at the time, to challenge the Russian's interpretation of the two-year-old events.

Nazimova's outrageous abuse towards the good-looking young actor had, however, distressed a number of the people at the table. One of them, an attractive, dark-haired young Metro starlet called Jean Acker, was almost in tears when she asked to be excused from the rest of the party.

Dagmar Godowsky also offered her feeble excuses and walked out. Within ten minutes, the dinner party had broken up and Nazimova, already deeply regretting her hasty display of dramatics, was left to return to her home alone.

Unaware of this demonstration of sympathy for the churlish treatment to which he had been subjected, Rodolpho drove home to his tiny Hollywood apartment in tears of self-pity and shame. He knew that such juicy gossip as this would sweep the town in hours and that his disgrace would be a universal topic for days to come. He felt he would never dare venture out in public again.

Once more, he found himself facing the infinitely more attractive temptation of putting an end to his life, but the thought that he would be condemning himself for someone else's injustice stayed his hand.

It was, this time, Douglas Gerrard who came to his rescue. As Rodolpho had feared, the story had been repeated throughout Hollywood, but far from laughing at him, the whole community was outraged by Nazimova's infamous conduct.

Gerrard explained that actress Pauline Frederick, who until then had been barely aware of Rodolpho's existence. had heard about the incident and was waiting in the Los Angeles Athletic Club to invite him to a party at her sumptuous, newly-built mansion on Sunset Boulevard.

Thrilled by this unexpected reversal of fortune, the emotionally volatile Italian eagerly accepted Gerrard's offer to drive him to the Athletic Club to meet his new benefactress. He would accept her party invitation with the greatest pleasure.

It was Hallowe'en night and, as it turned out, the invitation might just as well have been the product of some malicious witch's curse, for it was to prove an invitation to further disaster.

8

JEAN ACKER had been the first guest to quit Nazimova's table, and had shed tears on Rodolpho's behalf when she feared he would become a laughing stock. Ironically, it was she who would ultimately be responsible for making Rodolpho a subject of ridicule and the pathetic butt of a host of Hollywood jokes.

Had he been able to foresee the result of going to Pauline Frederick's party, it is certain he would not have ventured within many miles of her home that Sunday.

But the rudeness of Nazimova, coupled with the lingering grief over his mother's death, made the emotional Rodolpho more than usually susceptible to a sympathetic companion, and when Pauline introduced him to Jean Acker and explained her distress on his behalf, he was deeply affected.

He noted that Jean Acker favoured a short, very masculine hairstyle, and wore a white blouse and tie under a rather severely cut suit, but it did not occur to him that the instant friendship which blossomed between them could just as easily have been of the type which can spring up between two compatible men.

Like most of the movie community he had heard rumours that Nazimova, whose English actor friend, Charles Bryant, posed as her husband, but was not even her lover, maintained an exclusive coterie of attractive young women – dedicated Sapphists – whom she exploited for her personal amusement and pleasure. But he was not then aware that Jean Acker was an occasional participant and that her more intimate friendships were also reserved for women. Indeed, at that time, for one particular woman, with whom she had quarrelled and subsequently rejected.

It amused some of the party guests to see the man who was so openly and fiercely proud of his virility and masculinity courting such a romantically improbable woman. Perhaps they thought he knew the stories about her and was simply amusing himself, or perhaps they delighted in seeing the arrogant young foreigner so hopelessly off course. Either way, the outcome was that no one bothered to set him straight, although it is very doubtful he would have believed the facts had they done so.

Rodolpho was genuinely enjoying Acker's company. He found her totally lacking in coquettishness and devoid of the fluttering-eyed insincerity of most Hollywood actresses. Their friendship had got off to such a promising start that he was eager to develop it further. To Rodolpho, forever true to form, that meant a private venue where he could demonstrate a more physical appreciation of the actress's effect on him.

Rarely slow when it came to exploiting a romantic situation, and unused to holding back his very basic and only superficially concealed passions, he insisted on arranging another, more intimate meeting, but the petite, hazel-eyed actress carefully side-stepped his heavily insinuated invitations, agreeing to meet him only in the restaurant of the Hollywood Hotel, where she maintained a permanent suite.

A mini-apartment at the Hollywood Hotel and a $200-a-week contract with Metro were a far cry from Rodolpho's couple of rooms on the poorer side of La Cienega and the few dollars scratched here and there which constituted his current income. But he was unabashed.

'I was already falling in love with this charming and beautiful young woman,' he admitted later. 'Even before I met her next day, I knew that I wanted her for my wife.'

It was the Bianca de Saulles situation all over again. The weak spot in his romantic armoury. Rodolpho would prove forever incapable of controlling his love genes, and with Jean Acker it would be no exception. After a single meeting and with a very sketchy knowledge of her background – and none at all of her sexual preferences – he believed himself to be irrevocably in love.

Following their meeting in the hotel restaurant, love-sick Rodolpho arranged to meet her on each of the ensuing two days – both assignations, at her suggestion, took place in public.

On the third day, convinced that he had found the woman who would be his life's soulmate, Rodolpho committed some of his few remaining dollars to hiring a pair of horses and insisted they go for a ride in the moonlight.

Judging by what happened next, his plan proved to be a runaway success. As they headed downhill from the ridge above Beverly Hills, Jean Acker gazed at the moonlight filtering through the branches of the tall trees and stretched lazily in the saddle. Local journalists who interviewed her the following day reported her own account of what was said.

'Isn't this romantic?' she remarked.

'Yes, but wouldn't it be more so if we rode to Santa Ana and got married?' he suggested.

She looked up, startled. 'You'd better not be serious about that, or I'll take you up.'

'I am serious,' he replied.

Twenty minutes later, when they reached her hotel, these casual exchanges had hardened into a definite resolve to marry. There would be no waiting period – a tragic error on both their parts – and they would marry by special licence the following day.

In the hotel, they bumped into Maxwell Karger and his wife, who told them a small party was being given at the home of the company's treasurer, Joseph Engel, for Richard Rowland, the Metro president and his wife, who were returning to New York. If the couple were serious about getting married, the party could double as a wedding celebration.

The following morning, Rodolpho took out a special licence and that evening they were married by an obliging local clergyman inside the Engel homestead. At the party, Rodolpho had two announcements to make. Although everyone knew him as Rodolpho di Valentina – which genuinely formed part of his real name – he had married Jean Acker under his family name of Guglielmi. However, henceforth, at his new wife's suggestion, he had decided to change his professional name to Rudolph Valentino.

'Sounds a bit like the Holy Trinity,' yelled one guest. 'Which name shall we toast?'

'All three,' laughed the new Rudolph. 'But when you see my name in lights, it will be as Rudolph Valentino.'

Ironically, the local papers, which carried the wedding story and knew all about Jean Acker, the Metro starlet, did not know Rudolph Valentino under any name, and referred to him throughout in their articles as Mr Balentino.

Shortly before midnight, the couple drove in Jean's car to the Hollywood Hotel, which she had designated their honeymoon home in preference to Rudolph's dingy apartment.

Valentino was almost beside himself with impatience to taste the delights which he had no doubt his beautiful young bride was just as eager to bestow on him. They had kissed only once, and briefly, since meeting for the first time five days earlier. That kiss had occurred a few hours earlier at the clergyman's instigation, after he had declared them man and wife.

They had left the car hand in hand and now they were just paces away from the welcoming privacy of Jean's apartment. The 5ft 11in Italian was almost dragging the diminutive actress as they crossed the hotel lobby.

'Slow down,' she said. 'You don't give a girl time to think.'

'This is no time for thinking,' laughed Rudolph. 'This is a time for action,' and placing his arm around her waist, he almost swept her the last few feet to the door of her ground-floor suite.

At the back of the hotel, several actors and actresses, including Norman Kerry, who had dashed ahead of the newlyweds, crouched by the window of Jean's bedroom, each clutching a tin can half-filled with pebbles, ready to spring up and shake their home-made rattles as the couple came in.

But instead of the soft, affectionate voices they had expected, they heard the cold, angry voice of Jean Acker, ordering her husband of a few hours to leave the hotel, where he was not registered.

It transpired that she had allowed him to turn the key in the lock and open the door, but as he prepared to carry her over the threshold, she had dashed inside and slammed the door in his face.

Through the door, she told him that the marriage had been a dreadful mistake. She did not love him; pitied him, perhaps, but loved him, never. There was no way she was going to allow him to touch her. The thought of his body on hers nauseated her.

Horrified, the listeners outside heard the bewildered, hurt bridegroom plead with her to give their marriage a try, but she refused to listen. She had been a fool, she said, to believe that she could see it through. She had wanted to be his friend, not his wife. Then she began to scream at him to leave the hotel. She had an early call in the morning to be at the studio for filming.

She did not want him then, or ever. He could not share her bed, her room or even the hotel.

Confused and unable to grasp fully what was happening, Valentino backed away under her onslaught, begging her to accept his love, until finally, recognising that his position was hopeless, he stumbled from the hotel and made his way home.

Here was the ultimate mockery, the final derisive blow, a farce of such absurdity that people would still be laughing at Valentino, the pathetic Hollywood clown, 50 years later. To be thrown out by his bride on their wedding night must make a man seem the most gullible and ridiculous of God's creatures. So many triumphs in illicit affairs to his credit wiped out by this contemptible failure to consummate his lawful union.

It was dawn before Rudolph Valentino – destined to be dubbed the world's greatest lover and to have the word 'heartthrob' coined by the fanzines to describe his devastating effect on millions of adoring women – could accept the fact that his wife had spurned him, and not even for another man.

9

RUDOLPH VALENTINO would not accept that his wife was a lesbian. Even when he learned that she had resolved her differences with her estranged girlfriend, actress Grace Darmond, and had gone back to live with her in their old apartment, he refused to believe that Jean could be anything other than a normal, heterosexual woman.

Norman Kerry's advice, far from trying to persuade Valentino to stick it out in the hope that Jean might suddenly come to her senses, was to get along to as many parties as possible, and go to town on the girls. 'You may be married, but there's no way they can accuse you of being unfaithful. You haven't had a chance to be faithful yet.'

Rudolph grinned at Kerry's straight-from-the-hip assessment of his marital status and promised to try to carry out his advice. Acknowledging, too, that he may have been a little hasty in proposing marriage to an almost complete stranger, he assured Kerry that, in future, he would make his head rule his heart. No doubt it was sincerely intended, but it would, predictably, fail to work when put to the real test.

Despite his eagerness to put a brave face on his wedding night rebuttal, Rudolph found it difficult to penetrate more than a handful of Hollywood shindigs. Jean Acker and her $200-a-week contract to Metro was much further up the pecking order than Valentino and was, therefore, far more acceptable to the hosts of the celluloid city's pre-Christmas festivities than her hapless spouse. He found himself limited to insignificant celebrations and the regular hotel and club dances.

At least on the dance floor, he reasoned, there was little chance of him making an even bigger fool of himself, and it was on one of these occasions, at the Screen Club dance, that he met another of the big name Metro stars, Viola Dana.

She was sitting at a large table with Jack Pickford and a group of other showbusiness friends. She had seen him dance before and, as she herself had been raised as a dancer, she readily accepted when he asked her to partner him for the inevitable tango.

Afterwards he escorted her back to her table and rejoined some bit-part actors with whom he had been talking – they to learn the truth about his split with Jean Acker, and he to pick up any information about forthcoming films.

At her table, some of Viola's companions gently chided her for so obligingly partnering Valentino. 'It's just not done to dance with that fellow,' said one of the studio executives. 'He's still little more than a gigolo.'

'I think that's rather an unkind word to use,' the young star snapped back. 'So he was paid for dancing with unescorted women. Well, I don't think there is anything wrong in that. It's nice for a single girl to be able to go along and partner a beautiful dancer like him, and not have some old guy stepping all over her feet. I think it's kind of ridiculous that people are not expected to dance with him. It's probably because all the guys are jealous of him.'

Support like that, from someone he had only just met, would have done wonders for Rudolph's flagging pride if he had overheard it. But little occurred in the next few weeks either to restore his self-confidence or make him more optimistic about the future.

He played bit-part villains in both *The Adventuress* and *The Cheater*, a Henry Otto-directed picture which was filmed at

Metro's Hollywood studio. Here, dressing-rooms for the casts of various pictures were all sited together in one part of the lot.

On Christmas Eve, when shooting ended, he found himself alone and with nowhere to go. He had secretly hoped that Jean Acker would, by some miracle, join him for the festivities, for despite Kerry's advice he had persevered with his attempts at a reconciliation. But Jean had ignored all his telephone messages and letters, which had become increasingly pleading and desperate. Finally, shortly before Christmas, from the out-of-town location where she was filming with Roscoe 'Fatty' Arbuckle, she sent a telegram: 'I cannot promise to visit Christmas. Heartbroken, but work before pleasure. Be a good boy. Remember me every second. Jean.'

Norman Kerry advised Valentino to ignore the telegram. 'Arbuckle is probably behind this. It's no doubt his sick idea of a joke,' he said. 'The public believe him to be a nice, kind-hearted comedian but the man is a disgusting and debauched pervert. These sentiments are not at all like Jean. Face up to it now. She dumped you for good. This nonsense is just intended to raise your hopes so they can have fun knocking you down again.'

It was hard for Rodolpho to acknowledge that Jean, however cruel she had been on their wedding night, could go along with such a contemptible and heartless deception, but by Christmas Eve, with no further word, he was forced to accept the unpleasant but undeniable conclusion that his estranged wife had been playing with his emotions.

As he trudged dejectedly past the Metro dressing-rooms he saw that one of them was still occupied – by Viola Dana. He rapped on the window of her bathing-hut-style dressing-room and called out, 'Merry Christmas!'

'Merry Christmas,' she replied. 'What are you up to tonight?'

'Well, the truth is, I'm not doing anything,' he told her.

'Why, that's awful. You mean it's Christmas Eve and you haven't got a place to go?'

He shook his head.

'Well, you've got some place to go now,' she said. 'Wait until I've finished dressing and you're coming home with me. I have a big house in Beverly Hills, which I share with my sister and her husband. My parents are going to be there to, so it will be quite a get-together.'

She paused and stepped out of her dressing-room and looked Valentino up and down. 'You'll do fine,' she said.

'For what?'

'As the leading man in our Christmas fun and games,' she told him. 'I want you to play Santa Claus.'

The role gave Valentino more genuine satisfaction than any of the film characterisations for which he was paid over the next six months. Wearing a long red cape and sporting a white beard and moustache, he belly-laughed, ad-libbed and waddled from guest to guest handing out presents.

'He was so happy,' Viola recollected, many years later. 'We always had extra presents in the house put aside for unexpected guests like Rudy, and we dug some out and wrapped them up for him. You'd have thought we'd given him some kind of treasure, the way he reacted. He couldn't get over us thinking enough of him to give him a Christmas present.

'When we found he didn't have a place to go on Christmas Day, I asked him to spend the night with us so we could have the next day all together. I could cry, afterwards, thinking about it, him being alone at that time of year.'

He stayed the whole of Christmas with Viola and it did much to dispel the gloom and unhappiness of recent events, though the arrangement over sleeping in her home did little for her reputation. Not that she cared a damn.

'He needed to be with someone,' she said. 'Rudy was always the perfect gentleman with me and I liked him very much. He often stayed over after that and I never had regrets about the great fun we had together.

'We were just kids trying to make movies. The least we could do was to give each other a little help and affection.'

Clearly, it was a sentiment with which Norman Kerry agreed, because he secured Rudolph a part as his villainous brother in *Passion's Playground*, which in turn led to an introduction to director Allan Holubar who was about to make *Once to Every Woman*, starring Dorothy Phillips, for Universal. His part as a shady Italian Count was boringly familiar but it did earn him $300 per week, plus a uniformed studio chauffeur.

Things were starting to happen again and, if friendship and open public recognition of Valentino could help them along, then Viola Dana was just the girl to provide it. Her parties were the envy of Los Angeles. As she said, 'When I give a party, it's in order to have a hell of a lot of fun. I've given some beauts.'

One 'beaut' she gave was for Winnie Sheehan, head of production at Fox Studios. Sheehan and his wife, former opera star Maria Jeritza, lived in opulent style, even by Hollywood mogul standards. The former crime reporter had a $1 million mansion in Beverly Hills and a retreat in the San Fernando valley. But even Sheehan was impressed by the party Viola organised in his honour at her home.

There was an outside and inside bar, with two extras in cowboy outfits guarding the connecting door. Guests who failed to down a drink at the outside bar were stopped from going any further by the gun-toting pair, who fired their weapons in the air and pointed the way back to the drink-littered counter.

Valentino, quiet, well-mannered and immaculate, was always a model guest at those parties, never intruding but always hovering within sight and earshot of any of the headliners and studio top brass. At one get-together in her home, Viola placed him at the bar with Lewis Selznik, the Kiev-born jewellery salesman-turned-movie pioneer, who was impressed with the Italian and steered him into a film being shot on location in New York by his own production company.

For his work on *The Wonderful Chance*, in which he played a leading role alongside Eugene O'Brian and Martha Mansfield, Valentino would again receive $300 a week. It wasn't equal to the kind of money Mary Pickford and Douglas Fairbanks were commanding – the two major stars of the early Twenties were each, by now, taking $1 million a year out of pictures – but it was on a par with some of the lower-league stars.

With his luck seemingly in, Valentino found himself in demand for another New York-based movie, shooting slightly earlier than *The Wonderful Chance*, and he was signed for that, too. His pay would be the same – this time for playing a heavy opposite opera star Margaret Namara in *Stolen Moments*.

Even Jean Acker's refusal to compromise over their separation failed to dampen Rudolph's spirits. He found New York slightly changed, though many of the cabarets and clubs in which he had worked four years earlier had survived the Vice Squad's investigations and were still doing brisk business.

'When I was here last,' he told his co-star, 'I found my friends among the showgirls and performers, who were completely ostracised by decent families. They wanted nothing to do with me, and certainly didn't want their daughters to have anything to do with me. But their daughters were more daring and had less scruples and, above all, they were searching for romance. So they didn't pay any attention to their parents.'

Valentino quickly set about renewing his acquaintance with as many of the 'delightful young ladies from both sides of the social fence' as made themselves available – as his co-star, Dorothy Phillips, would pithily recount to their mutual friend, Viola Dana. She was greatly relieved to discover that Rudolph was not only doing well, but was 'back to normal'.

It had been a triumphant return to New York, but an even more triumphant return to Hollywood was already being arranged for him.

As with all the momentous events in Valentino's life, this one was initiated by a woman – filmland's highest-paid scriptwriter, June Mathis.

On the strength of a five-minute sequence in an already forgotten film, *The Eyes of Youth*, she had picked out Valentino to play the lead in the most important movie production in Hollywood's history, the first million-dollar epic.

Some claimed she was secretly in love with the Italian and had proposed him for the most coveted role of the decade in a fit of madness induced by her overwhelming need to possess him. Others claimed simply that she was mad.

But in either case, the outcome would have remained the same. Rudolph Valentino, a comparative unknown – a pygmy alongside the huge and established celluloid heroes who had been passed over for the part – was to play Julio in *The Four Horsemen of the Apocalypse*.

ORIGINALLY WRITTEN in Spanish by Vicente Blasco Ibañez, *The Four Horsemen of the Apocalypse* had been translated and published in America at the conclusion of the First World War in 1918. It was instantly acclaimed by the critics as the best novel to come out of the four-year European holocaust, and within twelve months had seen over 40 printings. It was an immensely powerful and moving story, at that time unsurpassed in the modern warfare genre.

It told the tale of two Argentinean sisters; one was married to a Frenchman, the other to a German. When their father, a multi-millionaire dies, they travel to Europe and settle in their husbands' respective homelands.

The Frenchman eventually has a son, Julio, who becomes an extravagant and colourful figure of Bohemian Paris nightlife. He has an affair with a married woman, Marguerite Laurier, who frequently joins him in the French cabarets to tango, the latest dance craze to hit Europe.

When war breaks out, Julio, like his father before him, refuses to enlist, but when he follows Marguerite to the front, where her husband has been wounded, the sight of the German atrocities changes his mind. He joins the French Army, is promoted from private to lieutenant and awarded the Croix de Guerre for extreme bravery. Finally, the war brings him face to face with his German cousin and, as the pair join in combat, a high-explosive shell explodes nearby and kills them both.

The four horsemen of the Apocalypse are, of course, War, Conquest, Famine and Death.

In Hollywood, Metro executives – who blamed most of their current financial problems in the company on the failure of its war pictures, which had found an unreceptive audience in

America – refused even to consider an offer for film rights of the book.

But in New York, Metro chief Richard Rowland (whose farewell party from the West Coast had doubled as Valentino's wedding reception) was highly impressed by the book's soaring sales figures. He never did read this or any other novel, relying always on a one-page synopsis prepared by an assistant, but he began negotiations with the author's agent.

After a good deal of haggling, he agreed a contract for $20,000 against 10 per cent of the picture's gross earnings, a deal which appalled his associates in Hollywood. They would await a script, they wired him, but warned they were unanimously against making the picture.

By good fortune, the best screen writer of the day, June Mathis, was in New York, and Rowland entrusted her with the challenging task of turning the number-one best-selling novel into script form.

June's professional and sympathetic handling of the story won Rowland's unqualified approval, and so thrilled was he by her treatment of it that he decided to trust her even further. The film would need a first-class director and a promotable leading man, both of whom should be well known to the public and the picture industry. He charged June with this dual and vital mission, promising he would go along with her choice.

June Mathis ignored Rowland's advice completely and selected two comparative unknowns and, in so doing, was largely responsible for creating one of Hollywood's greatest directors and its most lasting, worshipped and legendary star.

Rex Ingram, a young, dynamic and highly creative director, was overjoyed at being chosen to transpose on to film the stirring and savage Ibañez masterpiece – which he had read –

but he was shaken by June's selection of Rudolph Valentino as his leading man.

He was aware that Rowland – and that meant Metro – was sinking the largest budget in film history into the making of this epic, and that the whole financial future of the studio rested on the success of this one picture. Casting an unknown instead of a big name with a proven box-office pedigree seemed, to Ingram, a risky method of ensuring Metro's future.

But he was also acutely aware that he owed his own presence on *The Four Horsemen* to June Mathis, and that she had endorsed his near-nepotistic choice of his fiancée, Alice Terry, as the female lead, without objection. After satisfying himself with a few personal and critical comments about Valentino, he gracefully gave in to her choice.

June had already started work on the script of *The Four Horsemen* when she spotted Valentino. She liked to break up her efforts at the typewriter with visits to the local picture theatre and, on one of these occasions, *The Eyes of Youth* was showing. Although he appeared only in the third episode, opposite Clara Kimball Young, and was playing the part of a heavy, Valentino's performance impressed the scriptwriter. He had the looks, the arrogance and the emotion to play Julio, she decided. But after completing the script, and before mentioning her choice to either Ingram or Rowland, she obtained a copy of *The Eyes of Youth* and studied again and again Valentino's interpretation of the flashy young divorce co-respondent before finally making up her mind.

This was the only possible Julio.

At first, she only knew the young actor as Rodolpho di Valentina, but after making cabled enquiries to Hollywood to track down his whereabouts and availability, she soon learned of both his name change – of which she approved – and the fact that he was working very close by, filming in New York itself.

The first Valentino knew of his selection was when he received a message, at the New York studio where *A Wonderful Chance* was being shot, asking him to call on Richard Rowland at Metro. When he arrived, he was escorted directly to Rowland's inner sanctum and introduced to June Mathis, whom he had heard of, but never met.

'I'd like you to play Julio in *The Four Horsemen of the Apocalypse*,' she told him.

Valentino looked open-mouthed from her to Rowland, who was nodding enthusiastically. In common with every other actor connected with the cinema, he knew that Metro was planning a mammoth production of the Ibañez book, and had even considered auditioning for the part, though he was already convinced someone like Barthelmess or Carlyle Blackwell would snap it up.

'I'd love to play the part,' gasped Valentino. 'But are you sure?'

'Quite certain,' said Rowland. 'But tell me, what are you earning at present?' he asked casually.

The ever alert and razor-sharp businessman had registered the Italian's temporary bewilderment at his sudden good fortune, and his consequent vulnerability, and recognised there to be a distinct financial advantage to be exploited

'Four hundred dollars a week,' said Valentino, automatically adding a hundred to his present wage.

'Would you be willing to take less than that? Three hundred and fifty, for example, to have the chance of playing Julio?' Rowland pressed home his advantage.

'Of course,' said Valentino, still dazed from the suddenness of being confronted with the promise of real stardom after so many years of waiting and hoping and dreaming. It was a shabby stroke to pull on the actor, considering the hundreds of thousands of dollars Rowland had already budgeted for the production but, as he commented later, 'Business is business.'

'Now you've settled the money side of things, perhaps you'd like to know why I chose you,' said June Mathis, eyes smiling behind large, horn-rimmed spectacles.

Still not quite fully able to take in the miraculous change in his fortune, Valentino sat and listened, with a rapt expression on his face, as she extolled his attributes and miming talents.

In a year from now, the fanzines would be explaining to countless new Valentino fans that it was, in fact, the Italian who had contacted Ibañez, and convinced him that he was the only actor capable of playing Julio. As a result of this, Ibañez had agreed to sell the rights, only on the condition that Valentino was included in the deal, and that June Mathis had sealed it by telling Metro she had always intended, through her script, to be the creator of the most important film star the world would ever see. Without Valentino no picture could be made.

This, and even more outrageous stories about his life and career, were to appear over the next five years, dreamed up by the studio publicity machine and, sadly, by Valentino himself, who would endorse most of these nonsensical tales as being genuine biographical anecdotes. But on that day in New York in 1920, his embryonic ego readily surrendered to his natural and genuine wonder and his reactions were still touchingly naïve.

When June Mathis revealed the identity of his leading lady, he jumped to his feet, spontaneously applauding. For Alice

Terry, then under her real name of Alice Taaffe, had been a fellow extra in his very first Hollywood movie, *Alimony*.

Half-an-hour later, clutching a Metro contract – turned out in record time at Rowland's behest – as tangible proof of his unexpected good fortune, Valentino hurried back to the set of *The Wonderful Chance*, where, standing on a chair, he excitedly announced to the whole film crew and cast that he was to be a star.

The director, George Archainbaud, who had grown to like Valentino for his enthusiasm, co-operation and punctuality during filming, congratulated him on winning the plum role of this, or any other, year and promised to speed shooting of the remaining scenes in which he was scheduled to appear, so that he could leave for Hollywood at the earliest opportunity.

TWO WEEKS after being told of his starring role in the intended Metro blockbuster, Valentino travelled in a first-class suite by train to Los Angeles. A studio chauffeur, who declared himself to be at Valentino's full-time beck and call, was at the barrier to collect him and his luggage, and drive him to the Hollywood Hotel, where a suite had been booked in his name. It was the first material proof of his change of status – and he revelled in it.

At the studio he was treated with rare deference by the other cast members and crew, even to the extent that when he suggested a technical adviser for the film, Paul Ivano, a Frenchman who had served as a photographer in the French Signal Corps during World War One, and who Valentino had befriended several months earlier after a chance meeting, his proposal was accepted without question.

He discovered, with scarcely concealed, childish glee, that he also now warranted a large dressing-room with its own bathroom and day bed. His first visitor there was June Mathis. She repeated her eulogistic appraisal of his talents and assured him that he was destined to become one of the greatest stars in Hollywood. Then came a serious warning. It was essential, she said, that he pay scrupulous attention to the direction of Rex Ingram.

Above all, she cautioned, he must show the greatest restraint in portraying the part of Julio. The usual grimaces and over-played gestures employed by the majority of movie actors must be forgotten. He must use his eyes to get across to the audience most of the character's inner feelings and emotions. Unless speaking, she wanted to see only a trace of movement of his lips.

Valentino remembered the advice he had received from DW Griffith and promised total obedience to her and the director and begged her to help him understand his part better by coaching him in the greatest possible detail with her interpretation of Julio's personality.

June Mathis was constantly on hand during filming, ever ready to offer advice or criticism. At the same time, Rex Ingram was determined that the film would be a sure-fire, box-office success, and spent many patient hours nursing the finest performance possible from his leading man, who, he maintained privately, had been unfairly foisted on him.

Valentino responded to their friendly assistance by redoubling his own efforts. His initial elation at being selected for the part remained undiminished. He was polite to everyone working on the picture and never once argued with Ingram, no matter how demanding the director was on occasions. Gradually, as filming continued, Ingram began to change his opinion of the Italian. It was becoming evident to everyone, from the daily rushes, that the scenes involving Valentino were more than just successful. They were incredible. So impressed was Ingram with his budding star's performance, his single-mindedness and his concentration during filming, that at the expense of his fiancée's part he asked June Mathis to rewrite the script, giving more of the story to Julio.

Even some of the hardy professionals on the film crew were roused to cheers by Valentino's tango sequences. First garbed as a *gaucho* in Argentina, then wearing tails as the Paris playboy, he was dancing his way into cinema history, in sequences that would be replayed to audiences into the next century.

There was nothing that even Rex Ingram's directorial skill could add to Valentino's fiery and uniquely personal interpretation of the South American dance and the naked emotion he conveyed to the screen through the camera lens.

In other scenes, Ingram, a perfectionist, rehearsed and re-rehearsed his actor until completely satisfied he could not extract even a fractional improvement from his performance. He alone, Ingram was fond of pronouncing, would be held responsible if the picture was a flop. The actors, however, would get most of the credit if *The Four Horsemen* was a smash success, but only the director could really be blamed if it was panned by the critics.

Valentino, with unquestioning confidence in his perceptive and brilliant director, prayed that the film would be the triumph they all needed, and endeavoured to be even more co-operative, willing and attentive both on and off the set. He was, agreed his fellow actors unanimously, one of the most easy-going but hard-working members of their profession they had ever had the pleasure of filming with.

Valentino had been born with a slightly cauliflower left ear, which had fitted well with most of the disreputable characters he had been called upon to portray until then. Ingram had spotted the defect early on, but expert make-up and camera angles which tended to capture more of Valentino's right side made the physical defect unnoticeable. Most of his fellow actors were not even aware of it. June Mathis would have left it undisguised. She told him it was in character with the daredevil Julio she had described in her script.

Their generous praise, together with the rave reviews from the editing room, were not lost on newspaper and magazine reporters who, almost daily, swarmed around the studio looking for tit-bits of information and gossip about the most important movie yet filmed. Many of them began to feature the name Valentino in their stories, and several predicted that he would become a major star.

He bought several copies of any publication in which he was mentioned and after agreeing with the studio publicity hacks that little was known about his background, he enthusiastically co-operated when they suggested sketching out a few biographical details to give out to the media. Between them, they concocted a fictitious story that was to become the blueprint for most Valentino biographers for more than half-a-century.

His father, it was revealed by the studio publicity department, had been a captain in one of the crack Italian cavalry regiments. When he died, he was given a military funeral with his coffin being transported in a coach drawn by six horses. The coachmen wore uniforms of black and silver, and his father's friends had walked beside the hearse holding large purple tassels, as a sign of mourning.

He had also been to a top grammar school, he was quoted as saying, and to the Royal Military Academy. As a teenager, he had travelled through France and enjoyed many amorous adventures in Monte Carlo and Paris, where he had fought a duel over a lady's honour. This, he told reporters, explained the scar on his cheek, the result of a lucky rapier lunge by his opponent.

He had travelled first-class to New York with a gift of $4,000 from his wealthy mother, and there he had worked as a superintendent in charge of laying out Italian gardens for a millionaire's estate before taking up dancing and acting professionally.

These hastily-invented details of his early life were embroidered even more by the studio publicity writers as press interest grew, and Valentino found that, at first, he had considerable difficulty remembering all the 'facts' about his pre-Hollywood history.

In what was to become the future pattern of his acting, Valentino took on the character of the part he was playing, away from the studio and even during his interviews with the press. Pleasant, philosophical and sensitive – as was Julio – he was able to recount those of his apocryphal early adventures he could remember with remarkable conviction, and one gullible female reporter was actually moved to tears by his heart-rending account of his father's death.

A new star was in the process of being born and Valentino resolved that he should emerge with all the right social connections and acceptable moral character.

Half-way through the picture's unprecedented three-month schedule, Metro executives, including the principal shareholder, Marcus Loew, and Richard Rowland, visited the studio. They watched the unedited footage to date, marvelled at the exquisite beauty of many of the scenes, and smilingly gave their OK to complete shooting, together with their endorsement to go to a full $1 million if the budget required it.

They sensed they had a sure-fire winner on their hands. A triple winner in fact, in the shape of Valentino, Rex Ingram and *The Four Horsemen*.

Twelve thousand people took part in the production, on sets constructed from 125,000 tons of materials, and the half-million feet of film were edited to two hours' running time for the theatres. Some of the symbolic scenes, with the four horsemen galloping across the sky, were described as truly spectacular.

Avidly, Rudolph Valentino continued to read every comment printed in the press and magazines, especially those articles or gossip snippets which mentioned him by name. Occasionally, a journalist would predict that Metro had thrown good money after bad in risking yet another war picture, and question the studio's wisdom in pinning all its hopes of success on two unknown leads and a little-known director.

It would be eight months before the picture could be premièred and those predictions proved right or wrong. Meanwhile, Valentino received approaches from other Hollywood studios, whose spies had reported back the birth of a phenomenal new talent. But taking the advice of June Mathis, he agreed to make at least one more Metro film before the release of *The Four Horsemen*. This, she said, would undoubtedly and dramatically change his bargaining position.

Content to remain with Metro and Rowland who, he believed, was treating him fairly, and hoping to reduce the horrendous back-log of debts which continued to plague him, Valentino signed to do *Uncharted Seas*, playing the lead opposite Alice Lake. Still waiting to get the public's reaction to an Italian romantic star Metro did not offer him more money, and Valentino, pleased to be so readily employed again, did not ask for it.

The new film, a trivial account of unlikely adventures in Alaska, finished early, and found Valentino still in his Hollywood Hotel apartment, still in considerable debt and steadily running up a new collection of creditors, including the salesman of a large and very powerful open sports car.

With regular money flowing in, albeit inadequate to meet his needs, and with his prospects at an all-time high, Valentino reverted to his old idea of presenting himself as a loner. Actresses and would-be actresses, with an almost uncanny instinct for picking out men who were on their way up, now vied with one another to partner the quiet, serious and impeccably-dressed Italian. But, in keeping with his image, most of their invitations went straight into the waste paper basket.

He preferred to keep his romantic activities out of the limelight, and the newspapers in particular. Unfortunately, this was not always possible, as Jean Acker, who had refused all his earlier written appeals to return to him, had been ditched by Metro and was now out of work and complaining to all and sundry that her husband was making no attempt to support her.

His sexual potency however, remained undiminished and he would sometimes sneak a girl into his hotel suite by a back entrance. These nocturnal dalliances frequently had to be aborted because of the relentless round-the-clock surveillance he was now subjected to by reporters. He found it hard to adjust to this lack of privacy and was grateful when his more judicious friends, like actress Gertrude Astor, with whom he had not, at this time, appeared in movies, but had met through Viola Dana, invited him to discreet and private parties in their homes.

Like the generous and gregarious Viola, Gertrude was a fun-loving party girl, with a large and luxurious home, to which, as a special favour to Rudolph, she would cautiously invite along attractive young companions for his amusement.

'He had very few girls that anyone knew about,' said Gertrude later. 'He would drive over to my house and I would have a girlfriend there, usually someone he knew, and he would pair off with her.

'I would play the piano and sometimes we would sing a bit. He liked quiet parties, but he certainly knew what to do with a woman. Most found him irresistible, and not just because he was a star in the making. He was very charming and good looking, and very damned sexy. I can vouch for that.'

I T WASN'T LONG before a dynamic, domineering and, eventually, destructive figure crossed the path – or rather, film set – of Rudolph Valentino, and drove thoughts of any other woman completely out of his head.

He first saw her on the Metro lot as she walked across a set for *Uncharted Seas*, and he was instantly, utterly and irredeemably captivated. His promise to Norman Kerry, after the Jean Acker débâcle, that he would let his head rule his heart in future, was instantly consigned to oblivion.

First, he remembered later, he saw Alla Nazimova, the 'incomparable' Russian whose cheap gigolo jibe had, a year earlier, reduced him to tears of anger and humiliation. He eyed her warily as she stopped to watch a rehearsal on his set. Then his gaze drifted across to the girl standing talking to her, and he could not take his eyes from her.

She was stunningly attractive, tall, graceful and very, very beautiful. Her oval face had strong, yet delicate, almost aristocratic features. Her eyes were brown, mysterious, searching, and her long, dark auburn hair was coiled in braids that seemed to form, he said, a halo. She looked to Valentino like some fairytale queen from a storybook. Even that was too meagre and mediocre a description.

'I saw before me no ordinary woman, but rather the reincarnation of some mighty goddess of the past.'

She glanced, for an instant, his way. Her eyes, which in seconds had him bewitched, swept over him as he stared at her, transfixed. Then, with Nazimova, she walked out of sight.

'Who,' he asked a member of the film crew, 'was that?'

'Natacha,' he was told. 'Natacha Rambova. A friend of Nazimova. Her set and costume designer.'

Within days, Valentino knew a great deal more than that. Her real name was Winifred Kimball Shaughnessy De Wolfe Hudnut, born on 19 January 1897, and her father, Colonel Michael Shaughnessy, a widower, married for the second time, had been a Civil War hero and millionaire.

Known to the family by the nickname Wink, Winifred was only three when her mother, also Winifred, divorced the Colonel and married Edgar de Wolfe, brother of America's first acclaimed interior decorator, Elsie. Winifred, who had also become a decorator, took over the running of Elsie de Wolfe's New York operation with Edgar, a charming but disinterested businessman, and became a millionairess in her own right.

Wink was sent to boarding school in England at the age of eight and remained there until she was 17. In common with many other little girls, she became a fan of the ballet and when the Russian Ballet visited London she was taken to a performance starring Pavlova and a young male dancer, Theodore Kosloff.

Her school holidays were usually spent with her aunt, Elsie de Wolfe, who had moved to France and lived in considerable splendour in the Villa Trianon, a virtual palace, in Versailles. It was Elsie who enrolled Wink in holiday ballet classes in Paris.

What Valentino did not learn was that Elsie showed a marked preference for the intimate company of women and was involved in a sapphic relationship with two other women, Elizabeth Marbury and Ann Morgan. Wink, who was a regular guest of the 'Versailles Triumvirate' as the three women were known, was aware at an early age of their lesbian relationship and concluded, even then, that she was being groomed for later initiation.

In 1914, shortly before the outbreak of war and before she could be absorbed into the Villa Trianon ménage, Wink returned to America and, against her mother's wishes, enrolled in a New York ballet school run by Theodore Kosloff, the same Russian ballet dancer she had seen on the Coliseum stage in London, who had emigrated to America to seek his fortune.

Kosloff believed Wink at 5ft 8in to be too tall to make a classical ballerina, but she showed a natural and quite brilliant talent for interpretive dance, was by far the most beautiful student to come his way and was from a wealthy family, the latter being the most essential prerequisite for enrolment.

Wink soon found that she had escaped one ménage in Paris only to be absorbed into another in New York. Kosloff insisted on his young protéges' complete fidelity, binding them to him by taking them – by force if necessary – as his lovers and, as their mentor, dominating their performance in the studio by a combination of artistic genius and explosive temper tantrums.

Wink was still a 17-year-old virgin when Kosloff first made love to her and added her to his harem. From then on, he was to control her life, and she became his willing slave, accepting without protest, and as his right, his decision to rename her after one of his dead mistresses – Natacha Rambova. She toured America with his Imperial Russian Ballet for two years and, in that time, and over the following difficult four years, the indomitable will and icy comportment, for which she would become best known, slowly emerged. She remained subjugated beneath the Russian dancer's callous indifference to her devotion, the sexual maelstrom within which they lived and his exploitation of her evolving talents as a designer.

For their ballet performances, Natacha had begun designing and making many of the costumes and, in 1917, when Kosloff accepted an offer from Cecil B DeMille to appear in one of his films, and moved his troupe and dance school to Los Angeles, she was indirectly hired as art director. It was Kosloff who negotiated this and future contracts in his own name and, when Natacha completed the sketches, he would present them to DeMille as his own work.

He still exercised a rigid control over all aspects of her life, but within a few years, as her designs began to win critical acclaim, and she received none of the credit, she began to resent bitterly his misrepresentation of her talents and accomplishments. She was also sickened to discover that the debauched dancer – in an attempt to stimulate his declining libido – was having sexual relations with two of his ten-year-old dance pupils.

It was almost inevitable in Hollywood that one Russian involved in movies would at some point meet up with another Russian who had won fame and fortune from the silver screen. Kosloff had already attended a 'Russian night' party at Nazimova's Mexican-style hacienda, a huge mansion built amid three acres of sculptured gardens on Sunset Boulevard. Therefore, he was hardly surprised when Nazimova showed up at his studio seeking lessons for a dancing role in one of her movies.

Nazimova's scandalous exploits as a bisexual were already well known in Hollywood, but she remained completely unresponsive to Kosloff's undoubted sexual allure. Though, she admitted afterwards, she did find some of the young female dancers to her liking and invited several to her house for intimate parties *à deux*.

She expressed a great liking for some of the costume sketches and set designs Kosloff showed her, and commissioned him to produce similar, innovative creations for her next film. It was all Natacha's work which he had shown the star, and it was the results of her artistic labours which appeared in *Billions*.

The sets and costumes in *Billions* impressed both the critics and Nazimova, who entrusted all the art work on *Aphrodite*, her planned next movie, to Kosloff. The exuberant dancer accepted this plum commission and ordered Natacha to begin her research and outline sketches immediately.

He then committed a most extraordinarily stupid and irredeemably fatal error. He sent Natacha to Nazimova with a sheaf of original sketches. The Russian actress was most complimentary about the art but suggested a few minor alterations for Kosloff to consider.

The current designs – and all previous designs, for that matter – were hers, explained Natacha, and quickly sketched in the changes Nazimova had requested, there and then.

The Russian was delighted, for she had discovered an instant rapport and attraction for the gorgeous younger woman, and offered Natacha a job as her full-time art director. To the 23-year-old, it was a God-sent opportunity – both to end her increasingly abhorrent relationship with Theodore Kosloff and to begin a new full-time career as a legitimate artistic designer.

Her escape from Kosloff proved more complicated, and far more dangerous, than she could have imagined. She chose the following weekend, when he would be staying with friends, to leave his house on Franklin Avenue. But as she prepared to leave, her suitcases packed and waiting in the hall and a taxi ordered, Kosloff returned unexpectedly. His colossal ego refused to let him accept that she was planning to desert him and his volcanic temper exploded.

He began to scream abuse at her and, when Natacha stayed seated in her chair in the hall, and would not retaliate, he became even angrier. To her horror, after disappearing into the rear of the house for a few moments, he returned with a narrow-gauge shotgun, and pointed it in her direction.

By now terrified, Natacha made to rise out of the chair and he fired one barrel, loaded with bird-shot, most of which struck her in the thigh. Blood splattered on to her body and face and, as she hobbled as fast as she could move, screaming, towards a ground-floor bedroom, Kosloff fired the second barrel. This time he missed completely, and was barred from chasing Natacha by other women – members of his harem – who had heard the commotion and had come to investigate.

Natacha finally escaped through a window just as the taxi arrived and, stumbling, blood-stained, through the door, she ordered the startled driver to 'get her the hell out of there'.

At the Metro studios, where she had fled to join Nazimova, Natacha collapsed in the star's dressing-room and sobbed out the bizarre story of Kosloff's attempt to kill her. It had only been Kosloff who had possessed her, she bawled, but he was, she believed, representative of his sex. All men were lying, cheating, unfaithful lechers. She would never again entrust her happiness to a man.

Distraught and exhausted, she spent the rest of the afternoon having bird-shot plucked from her thigh by a nurse.

Nazimova, although 41, felt no stirring of maternal instinct as she held the beautiful young American in her arms, but a rather more primitive passion. Her new art director might well turn out to be a more interesting catch than she had at first imagined.

Surprising Nazimova, who was a committed believer in revenge and retribution, Natacha chose not to make a formal complaint about the attack to the Los Angeles police. The inevitable media muck-raking which would surround a police investigation and probable trial – and the certain exposure of Kosloff's sex-slave dance troupe – would generate headlines which would wreck her début as an art director and permanently damage her reputation. It just wasn't worth the price she would have to pay, said Natacha, and the incident was never mentioned again.

Although Valentino complimented himself on discovering a great deal about Natacha – he knew, for instance, that her mother had recently married for the third time to American cosmetics millionaire Richard Hudnut, and that Natacha was beginning a new career with the Russian star who had befriended her – he had barely scratched the surface of her true background.

She was, although Valentino did not know it yet, wilful, determined, headstrong and dedicated to the success of that new career. She was also an exceptionally beautiful woman, whose dazzling smile hid a powerful will and a burning ambition to become a somebody in the film world, beyond being a ballet dancer's ex-mistress or the make-up magnate's stepdaughter.

Valentino wanted desperately to know her and to worship her. Yet she, it appeared to the love sick actor, regarded him as a mere nothing. Someone far beneath her. A low, uncultured actor who had no place in the life of the rich, artistic, generously gifted and talented girl which she, a true narcissist, without any self-deprecatory doubts, knew herself to be.

Whenever he saw her or tried to catch her eye and flash that previously always successful smile in her direction, she ignored him. Completely and absolutely. His Italian pride was deeply wounded, his confidence was shaken, and the only way he could get to know her, he decided, was somehow to arrange a formal introduction.

As it transpired no devious plots were necessary. The introduction, when it came, was through the last source he thought possible – from Nazimova herself, the internationally famous Broadway star who had established herself in Hollywood during the war years by appearing in a series of propaganda films.

Now hoping to bolster her sagging reputation with a box-office winner, she planned to make *Camille*. Nervous Metro executives had axed production of her erotic treatment of *Aphrodite* after public charges of obscenity and immorality in the cinema coincided with a move by the majority of states to pass new censorship laws in 1920.

For *Camille*, a modern version of *Lady of the Camellias*, Nazimova was looking for a dark, handsome and passionate type of actor to play the Frenchman, Armand, to her Marguerite. Valentino was the obvious choice from among the Metro men and, when she put the idea to him, to her great surprise, in view of their past history, he appeared overjoyed.

It was not, however, as she characteristically assumed, out of flattery for her and the pleasure of playing opposite a big-name star, but because it would give him the opportunity to get to know, and to work closely with, the woman he could not, and never would, chase from his mind.

Nazimova introduced him to Natacha shortly afterwards when Rudolph, in heavy fur costume, walked off the set of *Uncharted Seas*. Nervously, he bowed low and looked into her eyes and smiled. The smile which she returned, to his obvious and overwhelming delight, was, some would later remember, of immense satisfaction.

From that moment, he was completely under her spell and control – as she had been under Kosloff's – and Natacha, who was already realising that Nazimova's term of power in Hollywood had almost run its course, would use and dominate Valentino, the rising star, in her all-consuming ambition to become a power herself. He would become her new patron, whom she would enslave with her body and dominate with her mind. In a reversal of roles, she would become his Higgins and he her Eliza.

Through her, he would lose a third of those years left to him in his fast-rising career. Because of her, friends would shun him and top studios would bar his entry. She would bring him brief moments of happiness that he did not believe were possible, and depths of depression that were almost too extreme to bear.

For the time being, she said simply, 'Pleased to meet you, Mr Valentino.'

When shooting started on *Camille* – and for Valentino that could not be soon enough – it immediately became clear who was to be in charge. Although it was the first time Natacha had worked in a film studio, and she was technically responsible only for design, the fiercely independent loner from Salt Lake City used her influence with Nazimova to dominate the production. She treated established film-makers as her inferiors, and even director Ray Smallwood did not dare to block her. To an outsider, it would appear that she, and not he, was the actual director of *Camille*.

Paul Ivano, who had again been added to the production budget as a technical adviser, and who was himself a fervent admirer of Natacha, said, 'It wasn't hard to see why Rudy was crazy about her. I don't remember there being one red-blooded male on the set who didn't fantasise about her. It didn't matter that some of them thought she had some kind of unnatural bond with Nazimova. It didn't make her any less irresistible.'

She paid special attention to Valentino, to his hair, his costume and his style. If hers was a blatantly unsubtle approach, the entranced Valentino was only too willing to go along with her plans for self-glorification. This girl, he was certain this time, was the one who would at last bring him the romantic happiness he had searched for in vain. She would be his wife and the mother of the children he longed to have.

There was no one on the set to warn him that, with her untutored advice, usually voiced in opposition to the actual director, Natacha was undoing all the valuable work that Rex Ingram and June Mathis had invested to create the understated style which had then separated Valentino from the majority of other miming actors. She called for more eye-popping, mouth-distorting grimacing to portray Armand in the way she believed to be most effective.

Valentino heard the rumours that Natacha was romantically linked with Nazimova but chose to ignore them. To the amusement of most of the cast and crew he pursued his apparently unrequited courtship of the woman whose whispered nickname on set was 'The Icicle'.

It was all the more surprising to all of them, therefore – and, especially to Nazimova – when Valentino succeeded in penetrating Natacha's glacial defences in a classic seduction scene which took place within yards of the assembled company. In retrospect, however, the question most frequently posed in years to come would be: which of them actually did the seducing?

The afternoon began with Nazimova in a rage, which was not in itself unusual. She sat furiously upright on the elegant, richly-covered *chaise longue* and tapped her right, beautifully-shod foot on the carpet. She glared at the film crew who stood in a semi-circle around her on the set of *Camille*, amid a tangle of high-voltage cables, massive studio lights and hand-cranked cameras. They knew that someone was going to suffer for this affront to her dignity and professional pride, for nobody was allowed to keep the great Nazimova waiting – as she had now been doing for more than ten minutes.

'Where,' she suddenly snapped, 'is that damned gigolo?'

The director, Ray Smallwood, glanced nervously at the huge studio clock. If that idiot did not turn up soon, the Russian's notoriously evil temper was sure to explode in a snarling, spitting, spiteful solo, which would culminate in a walk-out and a stoppage of work for the day.

'Who the hell does he think he is?' he said, to nobody in particular. 'Find him, Harry, will you?'

Harry Grieve, a young technical assistant, who had worked on most of the lighting for the set designs, nodded and strode off in the direction of Valentino's dressing-room. He knocked and listened, but there was no reply. He knocked again, and opened the door.

He told me, 50 years later, that he had realised in an instant that it was not the best thing to have done. 'You wouldn't see it in the movies in those days but they lay there, on the day bed, with only her long, black, satin lined cloak for a blanket,' he explained.

A moan of torment and pleasure came from the lips of the beautiful, spoilt, headstrong and aloof young woman. Her meticulously manicured nails dug into the naked shoulders of Valentino and her long, white ballerina's legs entwined around his, contrasting sharply with the olive skin of the man who would, in time, become the world's first and most enduring sex symbol.

But this, as Harold Grieve's interruption indicated, was no time for love. Valentino twisted his head and nodded as Grieve quickly closed the door and went back to the set.

Five minutes later, Valentino appeared. He wore tails, a stiff-fronted dress shirt, patent-leather black shoes and a satisfied smile. Behind him, patting her hair into place, came Natacha Rambova. It was clear to some, from her satisfied expression that, in her eyes, it was she, and not he, who had won a significant victory.

Within hours, people all over the studio knew that the Italian's reputation as a womaniser was not based entirely on rumour. He had not only thawed, but brought to the boil, the icicle Rambova. This appeared to disprove the gossip that she was involved in a lesbian relationship with Nazimova. Yet days later, there was even more sensational tittle-tattle being discussed on set.

Harold Grieve, along with two other members of the art department, had peered down from their office in a gallery overlooking the lot, and had seen a group of girls, aged between 18 and 25, they thought, lined up in an enclosed, rarely-used section of the studio. Casually, to the amazement of the three men looking down, they stripped until they were naked to the waist. Then Nazimova, accompanied by Natacha, moved slowly along the line, smiling, talking and running their hands over the girls' bodies. 'It was,' said Grieve, 'like some sort of weird beauty competition and, eventually, from the line-up, five girls were chosen and told to report to Nazimova's Sunset Boulevard home that evening.'

Shocked and thrilled, the observers crept quietly from their vantage point to spread the word. Before long, it was common gossip, and the only man who refused to believe a word of it, said Harold Grieve, was Rudolph Valentino. Natacha, he swore, was the perfect woman, the girl who would one day be his wife.

And so he was proved to be right and wildly, tragically wrong. The obstinate, fiercely-independent, ambition-consumed Natacha, whose own agenda had taken her, almost certainly, to Valentino's day bed, would enslave, dominate and almost destroy him. Some people who knew them both would say that, because of her, he was still broken-hearted when he died; and that she, the smooth and sophisticated ballerina and artist from a millionaire background, was a disastrous match for the simple immigrant boy from Castellaneta.

THE ONE WOMAN with whom Valentino was not sure how to deal was Jean Acker. Having almost lived down the humiliation at being so shamefully treated on his wedding night, he could even begin to contemplate the idea of marrying someone else at some time in the future. But this would first of all entail obtaining a divorce from Jean, and June Mathis, with whom he discussed the problem, just as he did every other problem which beset him, advised patience.

The marriage had not been consummated. Let a few more months go by and then quietly divorce her, she counselled.

But Jean Acker had other ideas. On 17 January 1921, Valentino was served with court papers on a suit she had filed for maintenance.

She claimed he had refused to live with her, had never supported her and had deserted her. Now she demanded $300-a-month maintenance and asked for lawyers' fees totalling more than $1,000.

Valentino was, in turn, shocked, distraught and finally consumed with fury. He bellowed with rage, cursed her in Italian and then broke every item of crockery on a lunch trolley wheeled into his suite by a nervous, room-service waiter. How could she accuse him of desertion, he who had been dismissed so ignominiously from his bridal suite on his wedding night? He would confront her and give her the thrashing many true husbands have normally meted out to their miscreant wives at the first sign of disobedience.

Fortunately, Valentino consulted with June Mathis and Norman Kerry before rushing off to deal with his estranged wife, and they advised caution and a visit to a good lawyer.

William Gilbert, a civil attorney, advised a cross complaint for divorce, Rudolph's continued silence and an application to have the hearing set back at least six months. The actor had wisely kept copies of his many letters to Jean Acker and her replies. With these, the lawyer assured him, the money-hungry Mrs Guglielmi stood very little chance of succeeding in her infamous action.

Valentino was slightly comforted, but characteristically pessimistic about the outcome of the court case. Was it not a fact, he pointed out to his friends, that on every occasion when things appeared to be looking up for him, something happened to drag him down again?

Couldn't just one thing really wonderful happen without being diluted by disaster?

In March 1921, *The Four Horsemen of the Apocalypse* opened simultaneously in New York, Chicago and Boston and Valentino's prayed-for triumph became exhilarating reality. Without exception, the critics hailed the film a masterpiece and Valentino as a star. The following day, long queues formed outside all the theatres where the film was playing for indefinite runs, and audiences reacted with cheering and wild applause. As days grew into weeks, the queues grew longer as every theatre played to capacity audiences.

The critics had found a new star and tens of thousands of American women had discovered a new screen lover to fuel their fantasies and dominate their dreams.

The Four Horsemen proved an instant success throughout the western world, creating box-office records within weeks, and relegating Douglas Fairbanks's *The Three Musketeers* – its only adversary and a certifiable winner in any other year – to second place.

In Britain, the company with exclusive rights to American movies refused to accept it, because its chairman, Sir William Jury, believed it would be abhorrent to people who were barely recovered from the tragedy and horrors of the Great War.

Metro's answer was to rent the Palace Theatre in London where it played to packed auditoriums and set a new box-office record in the shortest time in British cinema history. The *Daily Mail* critic hailed it as a great advance in film production and praised the magnificent photography.

'But perhaps,' he added, 'we see rather too much of the hero and his lady love, for at times there are scenes so long drawn out that the story drags.'

On the whole, though, he advised, 'It is an excellent film. Last night it held the attention so closely that smoking or talking was indulged in by very few of the fashionable audience which filled the theatre.'

All this praise, and the film's immense success in Europe, did not please the German Government, and their Ambassador in Rome was ordered to ask the Italian Government to ban its showing. But the noises made by Germany generated far less interest than those made by the 18 sound-effects men specially recruited by Palace Theatre owner Vivian van Damm to bring the film noisily to life.

Working behind the screen, with rear projection to help them follow the story, they banged 23 drums of varying sizes and sounds, fired off rifles, revolvers and magnesium flares, splashed around in a shower bath, which splattered on to stretched tarpaulin to make rain, and released an enormous cylinder of compressed air to create the snorting of the mythical beasts of war. The highlight of their action-packed routine came, twice daily, when the Palace Theatre firemen gathered around a great tank in which maroons were let off electronically, producing, as the *Daily Mail* reported, 'noise, reeking smoke and general pandemonium, which made it appear like a visitation from the Four Horsemen themselves'.

Everyone agreed, it was an extraordinary motion picture.

TOWARDS THE END of filming *Camille*, Valentino and Paul Ivano moved in to live with Natacha in her tiny bungalow on Sunset Boulevard. It was a move prompted as much by financial constraint as by any wish on Valentino's part to share a bed with his new mistress. Ivano was there both as a friend and as chaperone, to counter any accusations of immoral conduct aimed against the high-profile couple.

Rudolph's debts had grown rather than diminished following his success in *The Four Horsemen*, and even after *Camille* was completed he was still paying off his tailors for outfits he had worn in *The Four Horsemen*. Unless the film was a period piece, in which case the studio would supply the costumes, an actor was expected to provide all his own clothes. Metro had produced only an officer's uniform and a *gaucho* outfit for *The Four Horsemen*, leaving Valentino to come up with some 20 other changes of clothes.

During this period, the lovers were habitually broke, but idyllically happy. That this was no brief and passing affair had soon become apparent to them both, and Valentino was sure he had met the woman he had been destined for. The bungalow had painted packing cases for furniture and a garage filled with pets, including a large snake and a lion cub named Zela, who was devoted to Natacha but occasionally escaped to terrify neighbours and any pedestrians who happened to be walking along Sunset Boulevard. On one occasion, they had the added excitement of seeing Natacha, topless and clad only in a pair of briefs, running along behind. She had been sunning herself in the garden when Zela made her getaway, and she instinctively gave chase. Not surprisingly, this time there were none of the usual complaints from the neighbours.

It was a time filled with much laughter and innocent joy and both would look back on these months as among the happiest in their lives. As they discovered more about each other, they realised they had much in common, despite the wide gulf in their backgrounds. Both knew and loved dancing and the film world; both were lonely and ambitious; and both would confront together the looming crisis in Valentino's career.

When *Camille* premièred, the only ones to come out of it with any credit were Nazimova, who dominated the screen throughout, and Natacha, for her designs, described by one critic as a haunting succession of mesmeric pictures. Some critics slated Nazimova's comedy pantomime performance and one called the picture 'an exercise in artificiality'.

Metro were not pleased with the finished product nor its mediocre performance at the box office, and used Nazimova's domineering and bullying tactics during production to cancel her contract with the studio. Even Natacha was appalled to discover that in the finished picture the Russian had arbitrarily edited out Valentino's presence by her death bed, probably his only decent scene in the whole of the film.

It failed to enhance Valentino's standing in Hollywood and, after the success of *The Four Horsemen*, there was a marked shortage of producers, or alternative studios, rushing forward with open cheque books, offering him either more money or a major movie deal.

Metro certainly wanted him to work and, confident of their authority over their easily-manipulated star, offered him the same money as before – $350 a week. With no other takers, Valentino felt forced to accept, the only consolation being that he was among familiar faces.

Alice Terry would again be his female lead in *The Conquering Power*, and it was June Mathis who had adapted Balzac's *Eugenie Grandet* for the screen. Rex Ingram was the director and *The Four Horsemen* crew had been lined up for the production.

It looked like a winner, except that Valentino's attitude to his career seemed to have changed. He was much more self-assured, a little less eager to please and ready to do what was asked of him. And he wanted more money – a rise of $100 a week – which Metro flatly turned down out of hand.

It was soon clear to Ingram, and several of the others, that the influence of the ambitious Natacha was already at work, pressing him to expect and demand better treatment and conditions and urging him not to sell his talent for the first sum that was offered. From the day they began filming, he questioned everything connected with the picture, from his make-up to the costume designs, and delayed Ingram's start by insisting on shaking the hand of every lighting assistant on the set. The electricians, Natacha had hammered into him, could enhance or ruin an actor's appearance. He must make them his friends.

Valentino's sudden belligerence on set grated with Rex Ingram, who did not initially understand how the charming, helpful and conscientious actor of a few months ago had suddenly transformed himself into this temperamental, arrogant and moody artist.

The crew noticed it, too. 'Valentino,' one of them said, 'should know better than to fight with Ingram. Actors don't impress him – he makes actors. He may be exacting but he's the best.'

The film dragged on in an atmosphere of almost constant hostility, and Ingram, who was known to loathe stars who insisted on behaving like stars and not like actors, eventually found Valentino's daily temper tantrums too much and walked out. He asked Maxwell Karger to fire Valentino and re-shoot the picture with another actor, but Karger placated him with promises of a disciplinary chat with the Italian.

His idea of a disciplinary chat was to offer Valentino $50 of the extra $100 a week he had been demanding, in return for an undertaking to make it up with Ingram and quit picking fault with everything and everybody on the set.

When they finally wrapped up the picture it was difficult to know who was the happier – the star or the director. Ingram was said to have threatened never to work with Valentino again, and Valentino felt much the same way. Despite the intervention of June Mathis as a peace-maker, their professional collaboration was at an end. June had failed to convince the Italian that he was putting more faith in Natacha's judgement and advice than perhaps her experience warranted. 'Be careful,' she counselled. 'You have so much to lose.'

When no decent follow up-film was suggested by Metro – and their only offer on a permanent contract was $400 a week – Valentino took Natacha's advice and quit the studio. Studio bosses, who had always considered Valentino a push-over, began to re-evaluate his girlfriend. They marked her down as a dangerous meddler and the word went round at executive level in Hollywood that Valentino was shacking up with a potential troublemaker.

It coincided with Paul Ivano, who could no longer tolerate sharing space with their exotic menagerie, moving out of the cottage, and the completion of Natacha's design work for Nazimova's *Salome*.

The Russian's first, independent movie production was a costly flop. It received predominantly scathing reviews after a private viewing, followed by a year-long hold-up in distribution, caused by a nasty dispute with United Artists over commission percentages. Some believed it to be a deliberate move by United Artists to deter independent film-makers.

The *New Republic* critic told his readers, '*Salome* was degrading and unintelligent. Try as she will Nazimova cannot be seductive – the physical handicap is insurmountable. She tosses her head impudently, grimaces repeatedly, and rolls her eyes with a vitrious stare. The effect is comic.'

The delay and the picture's reception by the critics seriously damaged and accelerated Nazimova's failing popularity with the cinema-going public.

Natacha's art direction received kinder reviews but did not attract further offers from the studios.

For several months, she and Rudolph did nothing, living almost like recluses in the Sunset Boulevard cottage, which was so small that when Natacha's mother arrived on a visit she mistook their home for the garage and asked where the actual residence was.

For a time, Rudolph was supremely content away from the squabbles and tensions of film production and able to spend his time making Italian meals for, and love to, his 'goddess'. Even Natacha seemed comparatively happy, and took on a couple of design students to eke out their dwindling reserves of cash.

They talked and loved and planned for the time they would marry. Though on this subject there was already a small, discordant note. Rudolph wanted a real home, a family home with children. Natacha, who had given a magazine interview admitting she was one of that minority of women who did not want children, and would never allow children to interfere with her career – 'babies are not for creative women,' she said – found it difficult to reassure him on this subject. 'We should wait,' she told him, 'until you are really established.'

As the months stretched out and no work was forthcoming, the impoverished couple were reduced to poaching rabbits together for their evening meal – Natacha driving while Rudolph took pot shots from the back seat with his shotgun – or gathering mussels from the beach. Natacha maintained her determined independence and refused to ask her wealthy family for money. Valentino, whose pride conveniently diminished along with their fortunes, would occasionally ask his friends for 'loans' to see them through the bad patch.

In time, the attractions of this hand-to-mouth, sex and spaghetti existence waned. They needed money, and money meant work. Natacha urged Valentino to visit the studios of Famous Players-Lasky (Paramount), already becoming the largest film-producing company in the world, and talk to the company's chief, Jesse L Lasky, who had written to Rudolph congratulating him on his performance after the première of *The Four Horsemen.*

Lasky was surprised but pleased to see the young star and, after ordering his secretary not to interrupt him under any circumstances, 'short of another war breaking out', listened with sympathy, and provided the occasional apt or reassuring word as Valentino poured out his complaints against Metro. Could Lasky actually believe it, he asked in amazement, that Metro had actually turned him down when he suggested he be put on contract at $450 dollars a week.

Lasky noted the flash of even white teeth, the wide sensual mouth, chiselled nose and compelling eyes and the almost panther-like animal grace of the actor, and didn't hesitate.

'Iniquitous,' he gasped, feigning equal amazement. But he knew how to treat a real star. He would give Valentino a five-year contract, on $500, rising to $1,000 a week, to start immediately if signed that day. 'Here we promise to treat you as a star should be treated,' he purred.

Flattered by this unsolicited and unexpected testimonial to his talent, a well-satisfied and jubilant Valentino signed the contract that afternoon, and left with Lasky's additional valediction of a week's bonus pay, in cash, in his pocket, a chauffeur to drive him home and an assurance he would call soon with news of a big picture.

Even Natacha, who had secretly begun to loathe their extended stay on poverty street, acted pleased, though she couldn't resist making one disparaging comment. It was her opinion that the contract should have *started* at $1,000 a week immediately, she scolded. At least the good times were back, and now all they had to wait for was Lasky's call.

It was not long in coming.

IN THE EVENING silence of her neat, well-ordered farmhouse, Edith Maud Winstanley patted her greying hair into place, pushed the granny glasses firmly on to the bridge of her nose and, with just a little more application than other women brought to the composition of their shopping lists, continued to create a worldwide sensation.

The shy, retiring wife of a gentleman farmer sent her imagination soaring beyond the bleak Derbyshire countryside to the shimmering sands of Araby where, under the blazing desert sun, her beautiful and pale-complexioned heroine, Diana Mayo, had been captured by a brutal beast of a sheikh, who was to force her – although she didn't yet know it – into sexual submission, again and again.

Diana's eyes passed over him slowly 'til they rested on his brown, clean-shaven face, surmounted by crisp, close-cut brown hair. It was the handsomest and the cruellest face that she had ever seen. Her gaze was drawn instinctively to his. He was looking at her with fierce, burning eyes that swept her until she felt that the boyish clothes that covered her slender limbs were stripped from her, leaving her beautiful white body bare under his passionate stare. She shrank back, quivering, dragging the lapels of her riding jacket together over her breast with clutching hands, obeying an impulse that she hardly understood. 'Who are you?' she gasped hoarsely.

'I am the Sheik Ahmed Ben Hassan ...'

Edith's husband Percy, who bred prize pigs and preferred not to talk too much about his wife's romantic scribblings, might not like her writing like this. The neighbours would, no doubt, be more than shocked to learn that they lived not a rapist's leap from a woman who wrote such things. But the money for books was good, and it helped eke out the family funds when times were hard. Edith would press on, no matter what they might say.

She looked, dry-eyed, she had no tears left. They had all been expended when she had grovelled at his feet, imploring the mercy he had not accorded her. She had fought until the unequal struggle had left her exhausted and helpless in his arms, until her whole body was one agonised ache from the brutal hands that forced her to compliance, until her courageous spirit was crushed by the realisation of her own powerlessness, and by the strange fear that the man himself awakened in her, which had driven her at last moaning to her knees.

People would, Edith knew as she wrote, call it sensationalism, sado-masochism, near-pornography. The very thought of a nice young English 'gel' being ravished by some nasty little Arab would appal and horrify them, and they would call it 'trash', fit only for under-house-maids. Yet they would read it, because it took them far away from drab reality to the distant desert where romance was rough and ready and very, very readable.

Stooping, he disengaged her clinging fingers from the heavy drapery and drew her hands slowly together up to his breast with a little smile. 'Come,' he whispered, his passionate eyes devouring her. She fought against the fascination with which they dominated her, resisting him dumbly with tight-locked lips 'til he held her palpitating in his arms. 'Little fool,' he said with a deepening smile. 'Better me than my men.'

The gibe broke her silence. 'Oh, you brute! You brute!' she wailed, until his kisses silenced her.

Edith smiled to herself. Her public would be shocked to learn that EM Hull, the pen-name she thought it best to write under, was not some widely-experienced man-of-the-world, but an ordinary farmer's wife from Derbyshire. Yet she knew, better than any man, what women wanted to read and a happy ending was an essential ingredient of her secret.

The sheikh, she would reveal, was no nasty Arab at all, but the son of a true-blue English peer – the Earl of Glencaryll, no less – who'd been brought up, through no fault of his own, by the old sheikh and had grown naturally into those disgusting, degrading, desert ways. And Diana would declare, on the last page, that she was deeply and desperately in love with the chap.

The colour stole back slowly into her face and a little tremulous smile curved her lips. She slid her arm up and round his neck, drawing his head down. 'I am not afraid,' she murmured slowly. 'I am not afraid of anything with your arms around me, my desert lover.

'Ahmed! Monseigneur.'

As she wrote the last lines, Edith was fairly certain she had a success on her hands, although even her wild imagination could not let her foresee just how massively successful it would be, and what a shattering effect her work would have on the world's standards and styles and fashions. And, especially, on the life of Rudolph Valentino.

It hit the public like a hard, unexpected slap in the face from a threatened, enraged woman. *The Sheik* (first published in

Britain by Eveleigh Nash and Grayson in 1919, and later in America) was a runaway success. Some critics called it 'tosh'. The public called it great and sat thumbing through its pages and panting for more as the wretched Diana Mayo suffered unspeakable torment at the hands of that beast.

It was read in tens of thousands of respectable homes, both upstairs and downstairs, by the servants and the served, the wealthy and the waiters-on, and they all loved every last ravishing word of it. Especially those last ravishing words.

Its success was repeated in America and it became an all-time best seller with 1,200,000 copies sold. Among those who devoured it at very few readings was a member of Jesse Lasky's staff, who urged him to make a film of the book. Convinced by her rave recommendation, Lasky bought the film rights for $12,500, wondering who could play the leading male role. Then he remembered Valentino's visit, and the actor's smouldering sex appeal.

A messenger was dispatched to the cottage in Sunset Boulevard summoning Paramount's latest star to the studio. There, Lasky told him he was to be given the title role in the best-selling novel of the year. And Paramount's top female star, Agnes Ayres, would play opposite him as Diana Mayo. George Melford would direct.

To Valentino, who adored the character he would be portraying, it was a gift from the gods. But to Natacha, it was merely a chance to appear in what would obviously be a cheap and nasty movie.

'The story is trash,' she told him. 'You can't do it. It will ruin whatever reputation you already have.'

Rudolph, disappointed that she was not as excited as himself about the offer, tried to argue its merits. 'It fits my personality like a glove,' he told her. 'This part might have been written for me. And they're paying me $750 a week,' he added, thinking that this would be the clincher to his argument.

It failed miserably. 'You will never become a true artist if you accept the first thing that comes along,' Natacha protested. 'And this is no good for you.'

She was, of course, wildly wrong, but Natacha Rambova was never one to be moved by rational argument.

As an excited and enthusiastic Rudolph prepared to make the film which he was certain would give him a dynamic and rugged new image, she constantly scoffed at the role, the script and the plot. Why didn't he hold out for the lead in the new Ibañez novel, *Blood and Sand*, which, she had heard, Paramount intended to buy. 'I'm to do that next,' he told her. 'Lasky has promised it to me.'

This slightly mollified Natacha, but she refused to give him any encouragement at all in his making of *The Sheik*. Her last comment before he left for location was that it would harm his image. He would be laughed out of the cinemas.

Because of these pessimistic predictions by his wife, Valentino became convinced that his deal with Paramount would not survive this one picture. She had so undermined his confidence that he believed they would scrap his contract when *The Sheik* proved a failure, as Natacha had repeatedly warned.

In that, some critics were inclined to agree with her. When the film was released, the reviews were cool. Valentino and Agnes Ayres, according to the general consensus of critical opinion, did well in what was an unrealistic, wildly romantic saga set in the sand. Pure hokum.

But if Natacha was about to say, 'I told you so,' she would be speaking too soon; the public, as they had with Edith Hull's book, ignored the critics and made up their own minds. And in their minds there were absolutely no doubts whatsoever. This was it!

This was primal chemistry, romance, excitement, passion and adventure. This was love, lust, sex and savagery served up just the way they loved it. And here, at last, was a virile, dominant and demanding hero, a man who knew what he wanted and made sure he got it. When Valentino moved those large, dark eyes until vast areas of white were visible, drew back the lips of his wide, sensuous mouth to bare gleaming teeth, flared his nostrils and ordered the captive Agnes Ayres to 'Lie still, you little fool!' women trembled and whimpered and sighed and simmered to the point of ecstasy. He demanded their attention and they gave it willingly, lovingly, longingly.

Whether intentionally or not, Lasky had used Valentino's sex appeal to its greatest possible advantage and unleashed an animal magnetism that women found irresistible.

Even men, openly professing contempt for a boyish-faced hero who lounged around the desert smoking scented cigarettes, had to admit that he had a certain style; that he could swash a nifty buckle. Coming clean, Damon Runyan admitted, 'He made me long for a fleet steed in the Sahara and the licence to capture any swell looking Judys I found running around loose on the desert.'

But Valentino – most probably after consultations with Natacha – dismissed the whole thing as nonsense. '*The Sheik*,' he said, 'was my idea of a poor performance. I hate it.'

Asked why, he pointed out that the sheikh was an Arab-Englishman. No Arab or Englishman goes in for that display of emotion. 'So why,' he asked of his questioners, 'all that eye-rolling?'

It was too late now for foolish questions like that. *The Sheik* bandwagon was beginning to rattle and roll. In all, some 125,000,000 people were to see the film. Sheikh fashions were to become the rage, for women and men. Vaseline, and other hair-care applications, would experience a significant sales-boost. A song called 'The Sheik of Araby' would be on everyone's lips. It tells of a mysterious Sheik, a great lover. 'Your heart belongs to me,' he sings. 'At night when you're asleep, Into your tent I'll creep.' It was a song, Valentino claimed often, which always set his teeth on edge.

There would be a spate of follow-up films and shows. And many would take to reconsidering seriously the techniques of courtship and love-making.

The only sour note came from Cecil B DeMille. He revealed later in his autobiography how he had written to Lasky, stating that *The Sheik* was a very stupid, uninteresting picture, with not a moment of reality, and it bores one throughout.

'There are some of the most beautiful shots of Arabs riding for so long that I would take little naps and wake to find them still riding.'

DeMille bet Lasky $50 that the picture would prove a flop! It was a bet Jesse took the utmost pleasure in collecting.

Even the English language would not be immune from the onslaught. From now dictionary definitions of 'sheikh' would not be merely 'Chief, head of Arabian or Mohammedan tribe, family, or village', but also 'masterful husband or lover, dashing or attractive man'.

And an entirely new word came into being. One raving magazine feature on Valentino's sexuality claimed he had set women's hearts throbbing across the world. He is, himself, a veritable *heart-throb*, wrote the journalist. This new noun, categorised as slang, quickly made its entry into English language dictionaries.

Eminent psychiatrists, noted psychologists and other assorted mental specialists would try to analyse and explain this curious social phenomenon with learned phrases like 'emotional vulnerability', 'sexual immaturity', 'public hysteria' and 'lack of inhibitory checks'. But to impressionable young girls and experienced mature women alike, as they sat in darkened cinemas transfixed by that flickering image on the screen, the secret was much more obvious.

It was the magic of that dark, dashing, desert devil, The Great Lover, the screen's first he-man sex symbol. It was all down to that one magnificent, marvellous man ... *and to one woman.*

In her neat, well-ordered farmhouse, Edith Maud Winstanley read the latest item about the new star called Valentino and then put the newspaper aside. There was a lot of work ahead of her: *Shadow of the East* (1921), *The Desert Healer* (1922), *Sons of the Sheik* (1922), *Camping in the Sahara* (1926), *The Lion Tamer* (1927) ...

Edith, a woman who knew what the world wanted, smiled to herself and sent her vivid imagination soaring, once again, beyond the bleak Derbyshire landscape outside.

THE HERO-WORSHIP by fans was not a new phenomenon to Hollywood studios. It meant, on the positive side, that the star involved became a bankable asset while only costing the company a modest, and wholly disproportionate, increase in salary, and the addition of a few more publicity men to the payroll.

The stars' lives were relatively unaffected. They bought larger mansions, faster and bigger cars and occasionally even yachts, but their social and personal activities remained much the same. The only real inconvenience was that, on occasions, they would be asked by fans to sign autographs if they were spotted entering or leaving a restaurant or bar or attending a theatre.

The deification of Valentino by his adoring fans, as the God of love, and their acclamation of him as the first male sex object, introduced an unprecedented and, to him, terrifying behavioural transformation in the fans' method of expressing their devotion.

He was the first person ever to experience this bizarre phenomenon – and it scared him witless. There was no one to whom he could turn to for advice, simply because he was the first of this new breed, the prototype role model for future generations – the first Hollywood superstar and sex symbol.

After *The Sheik* had opened on the West Coast on 30 October 1921, an entirely new type of fan evolved. The Los Angeles *Examiner* reported that 'Valentino, with his Latin subtlety and verve, blazes to sudden rage with impressive conviction and as readily flashes white teeth in nomadic frankness. His performance is vibrant and responsive to every innuendo of his role.'

Strong words from a reviewer, but tame compared with the reaction of millions of women when they saw the film – some of them dozens of times, with friends vying with one another to see who could notch up the most attendances. Valentino was the first man to cause international mass hysteria among women who were exposed to his smouldering sex appeal and raw animal magnetism, through the mass communication media of the motion picture.

Theirs was a physical reaction. When he threw Agnes Ayres across his saddle and rode off into the desert, virtually every woman, in audiences across the world, was as one with her. When he kissed and raped her they experienced it, too, felt it happening to themselves, and they adored both the feelings and the man who engendered them.

To these women, Valentino was an all-powerful cocktail of sex and danger and genuine passion, of secret desires being fulfilled and daydreams brought to life, albeit on the big screen. He was the heady release valve on millions of grey and romantically barren lives and they craved what he appeared to be offering them.

When they saw their superstar idol in the flesh, the need and desire to touch him and possess something of his became overwhelming.

The first time it happened he was quite unprepared for the sheer hysterical ferociousness of their attack. It was in mid-November and he was shopping with two of his most valued friends, Norman Kerry and Paul Ivano. They were strolling from shop to shop on Sunset Boulevard, as they had done countless times before, and were just entering a clothing boutique when a woman passer-by recognised Valentino and screamed his name.

Within seconds, other women gathered and suddenly they had him surrounded. Some just clung to him, sobbing his name, others tried to climb on to him, and most just wanted to touch him or to stroke his hair. The three men, especially Valentino, were stunned by the speed of what they all believed at the time to be an attack on the star, with intent to do him harm. His surprise quickly escalated to fear when the women who could not get close to him began reaching past others to tear at his shirt and jacket and even his hair.

As the two friends struggled to haul the women off him and began calling for help from the boutique sales staff Valentino yelled that they were trying to kill him – and started punching and kicking. He said later, 'I know they were women, but I thought I was fighting for my life. They were acting like wild beasts.'

Kerry and Ivano, with help from the boutique staff, eventually managed to free him, half-carrying, half-pulling him into the shop, and bolted the front door. The whole incident was over in less than a couple of minutes and, apart from a minor scratch on his cheek, a torn shirt and a missing pocket from his jacket, no serious harm was done. But Valentino was trembling with fear.

It took several glasses of water and the soothing words of Norman Kerry to restore him to something like his normal composure – and then he was even able to laugh at the incident. But all three men agreed that they had never seen or heard of any similar occurrence involving fans. 'Your sheikh antics seem to have affected women in a way that nobody else ever has,' said Kerry. 'On the brighter side, one thing is certain – you are never going to lack for female company ever again in your lifetime.'

VALENTINO – THE FIRST SUPERSTAR

Although he was able to smile about the experience in retrospect, Valentino recognised that it was unlikely to be an isolated reaction. Other such mobbings would almost certainly occur, and he began taking precautions to protect himself. Thereafter, he would only appear in public when accompanied by some of the studio publicity men or when there were good security arrangements at the venue. Eventually, he hired an ex-New York cop, Luther Mahoney, as his full-time personal bodyguard. Mahoney moved with his family to Los Angeles and remained with Valentino until his death.

The Italian's days of wandering freely around Hollywood were over. The world's first megastar was already having to face the drawbacks of his unique status.

ON 23 NOVEMBER 1921, just a little over two years after their tragi-comic wedding, Rudolph Valentino and Jean Acker faced each other across a Los Angeles court room before Judge Thomas Toland. Each sought a divorce from the other, and their evidence was expected to clash on almost every headline- making point. The Hollywood journalists and gossips were not to be disappointed.

Giving evidence first, Jean Acker claimed that, two months after marrying her, Valentino had entered her apartment, invaded the bathroom while she was naked in the bath and hit her. Then he had told her he did not want to remain married to her and asked her to help fabricate evidence for a divorce.

Appearing both sick and miserable, she sat in the witness box and in a faint voice explained that she had started work at the age of 18 and by the time she filed suit for maintenance in January she had been earning up to $200 a week.

When a man married, she declared, she thought he was in a position to take care of his wife. She had not known in advance that Valentino was so broke. To have had him in her hotel would have embarrassed her and she did not want to support him until he found work. She had given him money, clothes and underwear. But marrying a man like that? 'He was unknown then,' she said.

Her girlfriend, Grace Darmond, appeared, and swore that Jean Acker's version of Valentino's assault on her was true.

Rudolph's lawyer, WJ Gilbert, then asked Miss Acker why she had banned her husband from visiting her on location six weeks after their wedding when he had spent $100 on telegrams begging her to see him.

She quoted an unwritten rule, which no one else in Hollywood had heard of, that husbands and wives should not visit each other on location. Then she admitted that, at that time, her girlfriend, Grace, had been visiting her at the location hotel.

She agreed with Gilbert that she had not, in fact, given Valentino money or clothes and the only real support she had given her husband was that he used too much of her perfume.

Valentino had expected that, when called as witnesses by Jean's attorney, Metro executive Maxwell Karger and his wife would speak against him, because he had walked out on the studio.

Surprising both Valentino and his wife's attorney, the Kargers swore that Jean Acker had told them, within hours of the wedding, that she was sorry she and Rudolph had married. In tears, she had remarked to Karger that she thought it best if they separated.

Highly nervous, and speaking with a distinct stammer, Valentino was sweating badly when he took the oath on the witness stand. He told of his confusion on the night of his wedding, how he had pleaded with his wife to admit him to the bedroom. There had been no question of his forcing her to marry him and he was completely unable to explain her behaviour, he said. He had believed Jean Acker to be a normal woman.

He did admit striking her, under extreme provocation, when she insulted him after agreeing to meet him and discuss a reconciliation.

'I took her to be my wife for better or worse, whether I be rich or whether I be poor,' he said. He had loved her and always hoped that she would agree to live with him.

The defence attorney then tried to embarrass Valentino and trick him into talking about his sex life with Natacha, by producing nude pictures of the star.

The truth was that Natacha preferred Valentino naked to clothed and enjoyed posing him for sexy photographs. The ones produced, copies of which became valuable and coveted collectors' items among fans, were taken in a San Francisco studio where Natacha applied make-up to his body, added points made of wax to the tips of his ears and teased his hair into devil's curls. This 'lascivious faun', as she dubbed him, was photographed wearing only a fig leaf and carrying a flute.

Under oath Valentino lied and stated that the snaps were a study for one of his future film roles.

Douglas Gerrard told the court, 'Every day I was with him he would call her up but she always declined to meet him.' He revealed that Jean had moved back in with Grace Darmond only days after the wedding.

Gerrard's most telling evidence came when he produced a telegram which Jean Acker had sent him from location on the Arbuckle picture. After receiving shoals of messages from Valentino pleading to visit her she had telegrammed Gerrard: 'Rudolph threatens to see me. Keep him away. I don't want him up here. Jean.'

When Jean took the stand again, she finally admitted to the packed court room that the marriage had never been consummated. She had spent one night with her husband in his apartment, to discuss a reconciliation, one month after their wedding. But she left him again the next morning and they did not make love.

Having adjourned the hearing after five days of evidence, Judge Toland announced his decision on 10 January 1922. There was desertion on the part of Jean Acker, and Rudolph Valentino was entitled to a divorce on those grounds. The interlocutory divorce would become final on 4 March 1923.

Jean left the court in tears, the sympathetic arm of Grace Darmond around her waist. Valentino exuberantly hugged his attorney, friends and reporters and invited them all to celebrate his victory in illicit champagne at the secret premises of a friendly local speakeasy owner.

That evening, during dinner with Natacha, Valentino's happiness was lifted to new heights when she accepted his proposal of marriage.

But Natacha, ironically, in view of the scandal and legal quagmire into which they were soon to become entangled, insisted that before they could marry he must rid himself entirely of the problem of Jean Acker.

The judge had made no order regarding maintenance. Now Natacha, backed by Mr Gilbert, insisted that Valentino make a single, once-and-for-all payment to his former wife. He agreed and in May was able to sign legal papers with Jean Acker contracting to pay her $12,100, in return for which she agreed to release him from all future claims for alimony and legal fees.

He was quoted as saying, 'Jean had always claimed that she wanted to be my soul-mate, when, in fact, all she wanted to be was my cheque-mate.'

Still broke, he borrowed $5,000 from Paramount and agreed to pay the balance in further instalments at fixed intervals.

With his head out of one matrimonial noose, Rudolph Valentino felt he could begin to breathe more easily, unaware that the strangling threads of another were already insinuating themselves, garrotte-like, about his throat.

D URING THE preparation for his court appearance and the divorce hearing, the all-important question of Valentino's future film career had also to be answered.

Friends like director Douglas Gerrard, Paul Ivano and Norman Kerry urged him to take Paramount's advice and, unless the studio appeared to be deliberately down-grading him with their choice of pictures, stick to the schedule they laid down for him.

Natacha, on the other hand, believed that only she could successfully and meaningfully guide her lover's advancement in Hollywood. Certainly, she agreed, *The Sheik* had brought him enormous popularity – 1,000 letters a week were flooding in to Paramount's publicity office – but he now owed it to himself, and to her, to take only those artistic roles which would win him the critical acclaim he deserved.

Valentino reminded her that she had dismissed *The Sheik* as rubbish, pure and unmitigated, and had predicted that it would finish his career. Far from that, he pointed out, it had established him as a superstar and lifted his salary to a level that was almost keeping pace with their spending.

Even so, he was apprehensive as he approached their bungalow on Sunset Boulevard, after agreeing with Paramount Vice-President, Jesse Lasky, to appear in *Moran of the Lady Letty*, based on the Frank Norris novel.

Natacha's reaction was just as explosive as he had feared. For almost an hour she berated him, cursing his gutter-level taste and lack of manliness in not facing up to Lasky.

'He is making a fool of you!' she screamed. 'How can we inject art into this putrid garbage? It is just another low-budget, gutter culture film about dockside brawling.'

Valentino drew himself up to his full 5ft 11in and played what he believed to be the winning hand in their argument.

'He also raised my salary to $700 a week – without my even asking,' he announced.

'Fool!' yelled Natacha, with renewed fury. 'He would have given you $1,000 if you'd asked for it. If you've agreed, I suppose you will have to go through with it ... and I'll have to make it as artistic as possible.'

Valentino's bewildering eagerness to accept her advice on all aspects of film-making exasperated his friends and tried the patience of director George Melford who, after his triumph with *The Sheik*, had been assigned to the Italian's new picture.

Though his criticisms lacked enthusiasm, and clearly did not originate in his own head, Valentino constantly questioned the quality of the interior designs, costumes and camera angles and brought the lighting team almost to the point of strike action.

This preoccupation with artistry was all very well, said Melford, who privately admitted the sets were some of the cheapest he had worked with, but audiences were paying to see Valentino in action, not to admire his clothes and the sets. This realistic piece of advice from the director had no outward effect on his star actor but, to the intense relief of everyone associated with the picture, *Moran of the Lady Letty* was completed without a major studio row.

Natacha, by designing and making Rudolph's costumes herself, had ensured that he contrasted, more than favourably, with the tawdry quality of Paramount's cut-price wardrobe.

Meanwhile, *The Sheik* continued to break all box-office records and Paramount, determined to keep their petulant young star happy, offered to raise his salary to $1,250 a week and cast him opposite Gloria Swanson in the screen version of

Elinor Glyn's novel *Beyond the Rocks*, which they had recently bought.

Elinor Glyn, whose chief claim to fame had been coining the word 'it' for sex appeal, was an English writer whose work tended to concentrate on her own passionate support of more emancipation for women.

Beyond the Rocks had been panned by the literary critics and its theme dismissed as depraved and unsavoury. Valentino's agreement to appear in the screen version provoked yet another contemptuous and vituperative harangue from Natacha. If his ambition was to ruin his career before it became firmly established, she said, then starring in this trashy society drama was one of the quickest ways to achieve it.

The news that Gloria Swanson – one of the most famous of the original Mack Sennett Bathing Beauties – was to co-star with Rudy slightly mollified his outraged fiancée, but she informed him that the only possible way he could contemplate going through with this 'insult to his talents' was by insisting on her full-time presence on the set.

The addition of his friend Gertrude Astor to the cast helped to ease tension for Valentino, who found himself under constant crossfire from Natacha and the man on the megaphone, Sam Wood. Quite naturally, Wood had believed he would have full control of the picture when Jesse Lasky invited him to direct. He knew Natacha by reputation, but no one had warned him about her temper, her determination and her almost hypnotic control of the man recently acclaimed the world's greatest screen lover.

Valentino used the pressure of fan mail to escape most of their highly defamatory and roasting exchanges, but when roped in by his fuming mistress, he invariably sided with her against the unfortunate director. Paramount had by this time assigned two secretaries to Rudolph to cope with his correspondence, and he kept them just off the set, ostentatiously dictating to them during every break from shooting. Natacha's presence also did little to smooth the somewhat cool relationship that developed after the first few days between Valentino and Gloria Swanson. There were no hostile scenes, but it was clear to the whole cast and crew that the two stars were hardly enamoured of one another.

Valentino's habit of taking on the character of the part he was playing was partly to blame for the tense situation. In *The Four Horsemen*, while playing Julio, he became pleasant, philosophical and sensitive; as Lord Bracondale in *Beyond the Rocks*, he became indecisive, superior and jealous, criticising the script and the plot and protesting that some of the best scenes were going to lesser players.

He never seemed to let the character go and this irritated Gloria Swanson, one of the most glamorous and highly-paid stars in the country. To her acting was something you did in front of a camera and nowhere else, and in this way she would go on to earn, and spend, $8 million in the Twenties alone.

The chief reason for her animosity towards her co-star stemmed from his brusque rejection of her famous 'come on', which would snare her seven husbands before her death in 1984. 'I don't fool around with other women,' he told her. 'I'm in love with Natacha.'

At 22, and at her most beautiful, Gloria was not very happy to be classed with 'other women'. It was a new experience for her to be turned down and, in revenge, she thereafter went out of her way to upstage him during shoots.

Once again, Jesse Lasky was besieged by angry and frustrated technicians, from the director down, complaining about the non-co-operation and hypercriticism of Valentino and the wilful arrogance of the female Svengali who manipulated him. Lasky pleaded for patience and understanding. The divorce hearing had placed a considerable strain on the Italian, he said. It was a difficult time for all of them, but the picture was what counted. The studio's newest fulgent personality was cursed and despised by the crew, but Lasky's appeal prevented open disruption of the schedule, and *Beyond the Rocks* was finished on time.

Valentino's victory in the divorce court had restored his customary Latin ebullience, and even Natacha was elated when Lasky summoned his star to the studios and revealed, finally, that he was to feature in another Ibañez adaptation, *Blood and Sand*.

He broke down and wept in the Vice-President's office. But they were tears of joy. The part of Juan Gallardo was the one he wanted more than any other.

Not since *The Sheik* had he considered a role so perfectly suited to his particular talents. 'This will be the greatest performance of my career,' he promised. It was the kind of exotic costume role in which he excelled, and Lasky's additional news that his friend George Fitzmaurice was to direct the picture lifted Rudolph to new peaks of happiness.

Excitedly, he told Natacha that, as the film was to be shot on location in Spain, he planned to precede the crew there to take special instruction in bullfighting and so bring added authenticity to his portrayal of Ibañez's matador hero.

Therefore, an announcement from Paramount that Fitzmaurice was not available to film *Blood and Sand*, and that it had been decided to shoot the picture in Hollywood rather than Spain, provoked such a monumental rage in Valentino that Lasky fled the studios and refused to meet him until staff assured him that Rudy's temper had subsided. He agreed to see him only after Valentino was told that Paramount had obtained the services of Fred Niblo, considered universally within the profession to be one of the top directors in Hollywood.

This sop to his ego somewhat appeased Valentino, but once face-to-face with Lasky he complained bitterly about the switch of locations. To achieve the authentic atmosphere it needed to be filmed in Spain, he said.

Sensing the voice of Natacha behind Valentino's protestations, Lasky swore that the sets in Hollywood would be exact reproductions of actual Spanish constructions, faithfully copied down to the last dab of cement and, stupidly, as he later confessed, he encouraged Natacha to visit the set as and when she wished. It would help to contain Valentino's tantrums, he reasoned, remembering, too late, that it was she who was the cause of his hostile and unco-operative behaviour.

But what about his instruction in the art of bullfighting? Rudolph finally broached the subject about which he felt most strongly. He would require the exclusive services of a top matador, who must be on hand throughout production.

Happy to concede this small point, after having overcome Valentino's other major complaints, Lasky promised that such a man would be found. A fortnight later Rudolph had the services of a new dresser, an ex-matador who, for the exorbitant fees demanded for him by the actor, was delighted to school him in all the traditional and flamboyant arts of bullfighting.

Valentino even won a concession from Lasky to be allowed to practise his newly-acquired skills in a portable bullring – although he was limited to facing only young bulls or horned cows, and an armed guard stood by to intervene and shoot the animal should their valuable human property find himself in difficulties.

Despite his childish delight in strutting the sands of his personal arena. Valentino was far from ready to capitulate to all the studio's other demands. Taking upon himself many of the arrogant characteristics of Juan Gallardo, and more than adequately primed by Natacha, he treated the film personnel and director Niblo with calculated contempt. At the slightest sign of opposition he would storm off the set. Work on the picture was painfully slow.

To his great surprise, he discovered that his big-breasted co-star, Nita Naldi, was firmly on his side and more than willing to support him in his frequent clashes with authority. Surprisingly, she also became a close friend of Natacha's – one of the few friendships Miss Rambova formed in Hollywood. They would fall out only after Natacha and Valentino divorced and Nita Naldi replaced her by crawling into his bed.

Even the choice of dressing-room allocated to him turned into a slanging match between Valentino and Lasky's minions. Knowing perfectly well that a dressing-room with a private bathroom was unavailable, Rudolph nevertheless demanded this as his right. Filming ceased for a whole day and, in the end, Lasky had to intervene to get the cameras turning again.

Natacha, whose experience of film-making was negligible compared to that of Niblo, insisted on being present at all times and, in her aggressively self-opinionated way, challenged the famous director on virtually every pronouncement he made.

Still believing that his star would perform more willingly if Natacha was there to support him, Lasky argued in favour of her continued presence. But Fred Niblo, resenting the flagrant manner in which she was presuming on his role, finally delivered an ultimatum: if Natacha wasn't taken off the set, he would quit.

Valentino retorted that if Natacha was barred from the studio, he would consider himself barred, too. Almost at his wits' end, and complaining to anyone who would listen that never before had a studio executive been plagued by such an intolerable, pretentious and over-bearing pair, Lasky called in the warring trio and managed to negotiate an uneasy truce.

In fairness, Valentino was justified in many of his complaints. The studio business manager, Eyton, had taken against Rudolph from the outset and seemed determined to belittle him whenever an opportunity arose. Valentino said that during the period when the bullfight scenes were being shot under a scorching sun, and during a windy, dusty day, he was compelled to make as many as eight complete changes – and because Eyton had refused to provide a dressing-room, he had to make them in full view of everyone.

After three days like this, Valentino threatened to walk off if a dressing-room wasn't forthcoming. Eyton's response was to have a three-sided partition 'room' put up, open at the fourth side and with no roof. 'The burning sun continued to shine in,' said Valentino, 'directly on to the only chair they had provided for me in my so-called dressing-room. My costumes were such that I could not use underwear and was naked underneath, so when I sat on the chair between changes I burned my backside. It was not the right way to treat a star.'

Incredibly, despite all the tantrums and stoppages – notably because of Niblo's patience and genius – Valentino fulfilled the promise he made to Lasky at the outset and turned in one of the finest performances of his career.

His portrayal of sexual passion and exotic virility dominated the picture and was guaranteed to provoke an ecstatic reaction among his fans.

Viewing the first rough cut of the picture, Lasky forgot about the feuds, ordered an even larger team of Paramount publicity men into action to swell further the Valentino legend and took his recalcitrant star and his fiancee out on the town to celebrate.

Shortly before Christmas 1921, Valentino managed, mainly by borrowing from the studio, to scrape together the deposit on a rather dilapidated, eight-room house on Wedgewood Place, Whitley Heights, on the edge of Hollywood. It stood in an acre of garden and lacked any form of power or heating.

He and Natacha moved in with their pitiful scraps of furniture from the bungalow and a borrowed camping stove. Their menagerie was distributed among various zoological parks, except for Zeta who was given to a recommended local trainer who supplied animals for movies.

As a consolation – Natacha was heart-broken at losing her beloved pet – Valentino's present to her on Christmas Day was a Pekinese puppy, which he popped in her stocking.

They were cold and unable to have a hot bath and had to light their way to bed with candles, but it turned out to be, probably, the happiest Christmas of their time together.

If they were happy, then Lasky was almost deliriously so, for Paramount had another multi-million box-office blockbuster on its hands. Valentino, the man who had saved Metro, would single-handedly establish the newly-formed Paramount as one of the giants of the film industry.

Sadly for future generations of film-lovers, Lasky ordered his editor to cut several vital scenes in order to keep the picture to Paramount's standard feature running time. These emotive scenes explained his character's dramatic fall from bullfighting hero to hopeless alcoholic. Natacha fought hard to have these scenes restored for, without them, the character loses the sympathy of the audience, going from successful celebrity to hopeless drunk apparently by choice and not through circumstance. But Lasky was adamant. The actor's wishes were completely unimportant, he ruled. The studio always knew best.

Already envisioning the fortunes to come, and before their confrontation over the cuts, Lasky declared himself delighted when the happy couple told him they planned to marry.

The Vice-President, like them, was not fully familiar with the vagaries of Californian law, and was therefore unaware that he had toasted a proposal which could terminate his money-making star's Hollywood career, and was destined to land him in jail as the key figure in a major scandal.

19

FOR HOLLYWOOD and for Rudolph Valentino, 1922 was a bad year.

It was the year that filmland's capital earned itself the title of Sin City and the Olympians of the dream-making industry were exposed as mere mortals with very basic weaknesses of the flesh. Rape, orgies, murder, perversion and drug-taking provided running scandals that kept the tabloids in a frenzy of lurid disclosures which were to tarnish the image of the Golden People for a decade.

The first cataclysmic event was the arrest of popular comedian Roscoe 'Fatty' Arbuckle for the rape and murder of starlet Virginia Rappe. Eventually he was charged with manslaughter and acquitted – but his career was irredeemably wrecked.

Then came the murder – still unsolved – of Paramount's leading director, English-born William Desmond Taylor. It was an outrageous and depraved business involving drugs, sexual perversion and an unofficial harem of Hollywood starlets.

Taylor, it transpired, was the main practitioner of the 'casting couch' technique, a notorious profligate who collected items of underwear from his starry-eyed conquests and filed them, labelled with names and dates, in a special chamber in his home.

To add to the juiciness of the scandal, it was revealed that two of the lustful director's mistresses – he pursued affairs with them at the same time – were movie heroines Mabel Normand, a Mack Sennett star, and Mary Miles Minter. It was even suggested that Minter's own mother had succumbed to Taylor's lewd approaches.

Shocked but fascinated film fans had barely taken in these sordid disclosures when it was announced that matinée idol

Wallace Reid had died in an asylum while undergoing treatment to cure his drug addition.

Hollywood moguls, anxious to correct this degenerate image, and fearful that public reaction would manifest itself in a box-office boycott, approached a member of President Harding's Cabinet, Postmaster-General Will H Hays, and invited him to become their 'czar', with far-reaching powers to stamp out any evils in motion pictures or, more importantly at the time, among those who made them.

In May 1922, Hays arrived in Los Angeles and was greeted by Jesse Lasky and United Artists President Joseph Schenck. The thin, abstemious mid-westerner announced that his first task would be to probe the off-screen conduct of the stars and force them to meet the high standards of respectability he intended to introduce as a matter of extreme urgency.

Lasky, whose company distributed Arbuckle's movies, and had had Taylor under contract at the time of his murder, squirmed uncomfortably as Hays recounted the disturbing effect on public morals that these squalid affairs were having – and then volunteered his full co-operation in stamping out immoral practices in the film capital.

But this spontaneous offer was to cause him untold anguish just a week later, when Hollywood's latest scandal swept all other items from the nation's front pages: Rudolph Valentino, the first honest-to-goodness sex symbol of the screen, and with a following of millions of impressionable female fans, had committed bigamy.

A phonecall from Will Hays followed the newspapers into Lasky's office within minutes. To prevent accusations that the industry condoned this kind of blatant immorality, he told the agitated studio boss that it might prove necessary to blacklist Valentino.

Hay already had Valentino in his sights because of the incredible sexual turmoil the actor's performances generated among women, which the new 'czar' found both offensive, unnatural and very disturbing. He was also concerned that in projecting himself as a woman's sex object, Valentino had provoked a very conflicting, and Hay believed potentially dangerous, response among men. Most men, while being secretly envious of the actor's looks and sex appeal, were in public more likely to abuse and ridicule him and see him as an adversary.

In 1922, with three major, swashbuckling box-office hits to Valentino's credit, this male envy had begun to find more vocal expression. Just what would the news of Rudy's bigamy have on the men and women of America?

As Lasky clapped his palms to his forehead in despair, 100 miles away in Palm Springs the newlyweds were having their first doubts about the wisdom of their romantic gesture.

Both had been aware that the divorce from Jean Acker would not become final until the following year, but Valentino was convinced that if they married in Mexico they could not be charged with violating Californian law. Airily, he explained that other impatient couples, some in the film business, had married in Mexico or in another state without legal repercussions.

He ignored – or chose to overlook – the fact that those others had been protected by a certain degree of anonymity. But when he and Natacha drove across the Mexican border on 13 May, with Douglas Gerrard and Paul Ivano, they were spotted within minutes of arriving in the small town of Mexicali.

By the time the mayor had been consulted, and agreed to perform the marriage ceremony, several thousand inhabitants had gathered around the old, stone-built town hall. While the mayor's deputy hurriedly gathered together the Mexicali military band, his wife recruited half-a-dozen other women, wives of the town's most prominent citizens, and began planning the special wedding feast her husband had decreed necessary to mark this singular honour being accorded his community.

Valentino and Natacha, who had planned a brief and preferably quiet wedding, were nevertheless flattered by this spontaneous gesture of goodwill, and the bridegroom agreed to make a speech to the several hundred people who turned up.

That evening, the mayor and four carloads of cheering, exuberant admirers of the Hollywood newlyweds accompanied them to the border and bid them an emotional farewell. From there, the couple drove north to Palm Springs to begin their honeymoon, which they planned to spend in the desert resort and in San Diego.

But two days later, the newspaper headlines shocked them out of their euphoria. Reporters, wise in the ways of the Los Angeles courts, and sensing a far better story than the simple announcement that Valentino had married, checked with judges and court officials whose opinions were unanimous: the wedding in Mexicali had been a bigamous one.

Valentino's first impulse was to flee and put as much distance as possible between himself and the Californian officers of justice. Arrangements to depart that day for New York were well in hand when an anguished Jesse Lasky called them on the telephone. Running away could only make matters worse, he yelled. The legal position was bad enough, but the opinion of Will Hays and the question of Valentino's film future was of paramount importance. If the lovesick star could bluff it out and return to Hollywood immediately, advised Lasky, Hays might be convinced that no serious case of immorality was involved.

'As far as you were concerned, you had been granted a divorce,' Lasky bellowed down the phone. 'You didn't understand the part about the interlocutory decree.'

'He is right,' Valentino told Natacha. 'After all, I am supposed to be the great lover. The public might understand that I was blinded to these minor legal details by my love for you. We must go back to Los Angeles immediately. My public will forgive me.'

In the almost bare rooms of the house in Whitley Heights, which the Valentinos intended to furnish after their honeymoon, they held a council of war with Lasky, studio lawyers and Rudolph's own attorney, Mr WI Gilbert. All agreed that the less the couple were seen in each other's company the better, until the whole sorry mess had been sorted out, and it was decided that Natacha should leave for New York that very afternoon.

On the Sunday morning of 21 May, at the request of the District Attorney. who had already publicly stated his intention to prosecute for bigamy, Valentino went to the Los Angeles municipal offices and entered a plea of guilty before a Justice of the Peace. Bail was granted on production of a surety of $10,000!

But it was a Sunday, pointed out Valentino's attorney. To find that amount of cash quickly would be difficult, if not impossible, although he could promise it would be produced the following morning. In that case, so would the defendant, snapped the DA, and ordered Valentino to the cells.

Thrown in among the normal weekend round-up of drunks, pimps and petty thieves, he screamed non-stop abuse at his jailers who had, as laid down in police regulations, emptied his pockets and removed his tie, braces and laces before putting him behind bars.

That Paramount did not have $10,000 in cash, even on a Sunday, appeared inconceivable to the outraged actor. He believed, almost certainly correctly, that the studio were deliberately holding it back to teach him a lesson and swore that, when extricated from this position of injust persecution, he would teach Paramount and Jesse Lasky a lesson. Friends questioned how the studio could possibly pretend to be looking after the best interests of their biggest star if they were content to leave him locked in a cell.

Meanwhile, Douglas Gerrard, who had been a witness at the wedding, was one of the few people actively seeking a solution to Valentino's predicament. He contacted a close friend, San Francisco Chief of Police Dan O'Brian, who was visiting Los Angeles, and explained about the exorbitant bail fixed for Valentino's release.

O'Brian sympathised but said he was unable to raise that kind of money on a Sunday. By chance, actor Thomas Meighan was with the police chief and overheard the telephone conversation.

Unaware of the identity of the person in trouble, but with the generosity for which he was famed, Meighan interrupted O'Brian and told him, 'If this friend of yours is in a jam, how much does he need?'

'Ten thousand bucks,' said O'Brian. 'Have you got it?'

'No, but I can get it soon enough,' replied Meighan. 'Who is it needs the dough?'

'Rudolph Valentino,' said the police chief. 'Still want to put the money up?'

'Yeah,' said Tommy Meighan, 'I think he's all right,' and hurried from the hotel, returning half-an-hour later with a certified cheque for $10,000. How he had managed to obtain the cheque O'Brian did not ask, but called Douglas Gerrard and told him he now had the means of getting Valentino out of jail.

By this time, news of Rudolph's imprisonment had swept through Los Angeles and a small army of reporters and photographers, together with several hundred fans, gathered outside the police headquarters. His attorney advised keeping to a brief, prepared statement, in which Valentino admitted he may have erred, but only because of his deep love for Natacha. To the American people, who had called him the greatest lover of the screen, he wished to say that the love responsible for his actions was prompted by the noblest intention that a man could have.

With only ten days to prepare their case, and instructed by Lasky that on no account must the hearing be allowed to drag out, or adjourned to a later date and thus preserved in the public eye, lawyers for Paramount and Valentino's personal attorney advised that his only hope of being cleared of the charge was to plead non-consummation of the marriage.

Valentino, who only four months before had used non-consummation as grounds for his divorce, wailed that his pride as a man could not let him submit to this kind of public humiliation again. Did they want the whole world to believe that he never went to bed with his women, he demanded. Patiently, the lawyers explained that the only alternative to their suggestion was to accept the very real danger of a prison sentence. The bigamy case against him would be the first of its kind in California with international overtones. The State sentence for bigamy was from one to five years, and with this much publicity surrounding the case, no judge could do less than impose the minimum jail sentence. That was the best they could hope for.

Deeply embarrassed, Valentino acquiesced.

At the June hearing, he sat beside his lawyers, unsmiling and for the most part head bowed, as seven witnesses who had been around during his alleged honeymoon in Palm Springs swore that he had never spent a single moment alone with Natacha after signing the marriage register in Mexicali. A court packed with schoolgirls, matrons and outrageously dressed flappers, stared fixedly at the star as they heard how he had never occupied the second single bed in his wife's room.

Natacha, it was stated, had been taken ill after their return from Mexico and a doctor had advised that she should sleep alone. Despite highly sarcastic questioning from the Deputy District Attorney, the witnesses maintained that Valentino had slept in a room with two men on the first night and on a couch on the porch on the second night of their stay in Palm Springs. The marriage had not been consummated, said his attorney, and thus could not be considered to have taken place.

The judge agreed. On 5 June, he announced that there was insufficient evidence to support the complaint. He felt that evidence of cohabitation could not be sufficiently shown to bring in a verdict of guilty from a jury. To save the county the great expense of a trial, he had decided to clear Valentino of the charge of bigamy.

Grudgingly, Rudolph agreed with Lasky that the advice from studio attorneys had been well founded and reluctantly accepted their further advice that, for the time being, Natacha should keep away from Hollywood. The judge's ruling had cleared Valentino of immediate threat, but the District Attorney could still ask for Grand Jury action.

Even so, said Lasky smoothly, in terms of publicity the court hearing had been worth a million dollars, and it was planned to start work on his next picture immediately. Once again, Valentino agreed, but this accord with his employer was short-lived.

Rudolph wished to make *The Young Rajah*, scripted by June Mathis, a work which Lasky considered trite and lacking in any kind of entertainment value. He proposed several alternative subjects, but Valentino was intractable. Either Lasky would agree to *The Young Rajah* or he could cancel the company's contract with him.

Lasky capitulated. At least he did not have Natacha Rambova to contend with, he reassured himself. But he was mistaken. In voluntary exile from Hollywood, Natacha was quite determined not to resign her control of her 'almost' husband. To the utter despair of director Philip Rosen, Valentino telephoned her daily and did his utmost to follow her advice, which was generally contradictory to that handed out by the man on the megaphone. Each morning, he appeared at the studio clutching copious notes and sketches forwarded to Los Angeles from the Adirondacks home of Natacha's stepfather and mother.

Valentino insisted that Natacha's designs and script changes be incorporated into the picture, even though some of the costume designs were so outlandish that Lasky, called in as an arbiter, completely lost control of himself and collapsed into a chair with tears of laughter rolling down his cheeks.

Idly, Valentino waited until the paroxysm was over and then reiterated his decision to use the costume designs. Lasky replied that if he wished to deck himself in baubles, bangles and beads and make a public laughing stock of himself, he could go ahead. As long as the damned picture was finished quickly, he could appear in skirts if he wished. Huffily, Valentino retorted that Paramount and artistry were poles apart. He found it degrading to work for a company so reluctant to recognise the fruits of real artistic genius – for this was what he considered Natacha to be.

It was Lasky's turn to get angry. The studio had stood by Valentino throughout all his difficulties, he said. They had made him a star and, incidentally, advanced him more than $50,000 over and above his salary to settle his first wife's maintenance and make the first payment on the Whitley Heights house. Perhaps it was Valentino's turn to do something for the studio in return? There was no conspiracy against him or Natacha, but Paramount were in the business of making pictures, not flattering egos. And pictures which, in future, would be chosen by the studio and not by the actor.

Seething, Valentino returned to the set, where he savagely criticised the long-suffering director's every comment – a tactic he maintained until the final scenes on *The Young Rajah* had been shot. Then, primed by Natacha, he again confronted Lasky and announced that he would not be attending the Los Angeles or New York premières of *Blood and Sand*. He had no intention of suffering the indignity of having his clothes torn off him by hysterical women of low intelligence. He suspected, he told him, that Paramount's security men would deliberately let the women at him just to get more column inches in the press.

Lasky, who was quite capable of organising such a riot, said nothing.

In July, Natacha had reason to remind Rudy that it was Lasky who had betrayed them by letting *Photoplay*'s Dick Dorgan back on to the lot after Rudy had insisted he be barred. This man wrote the worst kind of lying gossip and scandal and Valentino had been his target on several occasions.

Dorgan's retaliation was the most critical of Rudy in print so far. Natacha telephoned and told him to buy a copy of July's *Photoplay* where a piece by Dorgan, entitled 'A Song of Hate', featured a disgusting attack on him:

I hate Valentino. All men hate Valentino. I hate his Oriental optics; I hate his classic nose; I hate his smile; I hate his glistening teeth; I hate his patent-leather hair; I hate his Svengali glare; I hate him because he dances too well; I hate him because he's a slicker; I hate him because he's the great lover of the screen; I hate him because he's an embezzler of hearts; I hate him because he's too apt in the art of osculation [kissing]; *I hate him because he's a leading man for Gloria Swanson; I hate him because he's too good-looking.*

Ever since he came galloping in with The Four Horsemen, *he has been the cause of more home-cooked battle royals than they can print in the papers. The women are all dizzy over him. The men have formed a secret order (of which I am running for president and chief executioner, as you may notice) to loathe, hate and despise him for obvious reasons.*

What! Me jealous? – Oh, no, I just hate him.

Hurt and upset by this unprovoked attack, Valentino again complained to Lasky who dismissed it as 'harmless fun'. Just look on it as more publicity, he told the fuming actor.

For Valentino, it was almost the last straw. Resolutely, he defined his conditions for remaining with Paramount, the chief of which was the right to approve all scripts for his future films. If the studio denied him this right, he would consider them in breach of contract and take his services elsewhere.

The following morning, without advising Lasky, he boarded the Eastbound train and headed directly for Foxlair Camp, the Hudnuts' home in the Adirondacks, and a reunion with Natacha. On 2 September in New York, he read out a statement, which she had helped him prepare, which revealed that he was dissatisfied with Paramount and intended to leave the studio. Seemingly oblivious to the fact that Natacha's advice invariably landed him in trouble, Valentino had again acted on her counsel, without taking expert opinion.

Two weeks later, Paramount retaliated with an injunction restraining him from entering into any contract with any other film production company. In December, the Appellate Division in New York heard evidence from both sides. An attempt by Paramount to patch up their differences with the star, with an offer of $7,000 dollars a week and the right to consultation over the choice of films and director, had failed.

Natacha had refused to accept anything but total capitulation on the part of the studio. 'We will not even consider it,' she told Valentino. 'It's just an attempt by them to bribe us out of our principles.' In his heart, Valentino believed the studio's offer to be an exceptionally generous one, particularly as once again he was being besieged by creditors, and his financial resources were painfully non-existent. But, wary of showing any sign of weakness before his strong-willed 'wife', he agreed with her decision and told Paramount that there could be no deal.

Paramount, in a prepared brief, listed many of Valentino's more hysterical demands and stressed his temperamental nature. Regrettably, reviews of *The Young Rajah* were poor and the film was doing only modest business compared with *Blood and Sand* and *The Sheik.*

This, pointed out Lasky's lawyers, provided excellent proof of what happened when an actor was allowed to choose his own films. In this case, Valentino's judgement had been utterly wrong. The studio had been proven correct in wanting to keep full control.

Valentino countered with accusations of insufficient and improper billing and poor dressing-room facilities. He had been shadowed by detectives, he claimed, and Paramount had been cruel and insulting to Natacha, who was his wife in spirit, if not in fact.

Natacha weighed into the battle by granting a candid interview to a woman columnist on *Photoplay*, for their Christmas 1922 edition, in which she accused Paramount of using dirty tricks in an attempt to ruin her relationship with Rudolph.

The studio's lawyers had told her, she revealed, that Rudy was likely to get a ten-year jail sentence and urged her to go to Europe and join her family.

She said, 'Because they kept urging it, I nearly went to Europe as they requested. I realise now that they were only trying to get me out of the way as they believed that would improve Rudy's box-office value. They declared that I would be

The face that made a generation of women swoon – Valentino, the first superstar.

In addition to his many lovers, Valentino took two wives. They are pictured here: Jean Acker (*left*) and Natacha Rambova (*right*).

The Latin Lover and three of his leading ladies. (*Top left*) Vilma Banky –
'The Hungarian Rhapsody'. When her lover accused Valentino of having an affair with
her, Valentino challenged him to a duel. (*Top right*) The sultry Alla Nazimova.
Although Valentino admired her as an artist, he disliked her as a woman. Her lesbian
affair with Valentino's first wife scandalised Hollywood. (*Bottom*) Agnes Ayres,
Rudy's leading lady in *The Sheik*, the film that turned him into a true sex symbol…

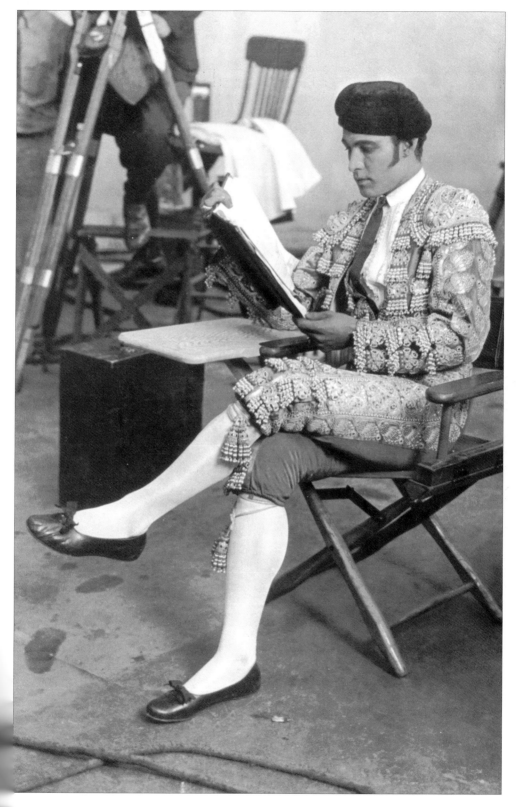

Rudy checking his lines on the set of *Blood and Sand*.

A rare publicity poster for the 1924 movie *Monsieur Beaucaire*.

Top: A still from *The Four Horsemen of the Apocalypse*. Valentino's leading lady was Alice Terry.

Bottom left: Pola Negri, the Polish beauty with whom he had his last big affair.

Bottom right: The beautiful Gloria Swanson. At the age of 22, Swanson was earning $500,000 a year, but she was less than thrilled when Valentino rejected her 'come on'...

The mysterious, rugged good looks that made Valentino the most lusted-after man in the world.

the ruin of his career and then, finally, they told me Rudy had already forgotten me. I knew Rudy, so I didn't sail to Europe. I knew my job was right here.'

In addition, she told *Photoplay* that the studio had betrayed Rudy as an actor and herself as a designer by putting minimal money into *The Young Rajah.* 'They gave Rudy cheap material, cheap sets, cheap casts, cheap everything.' The idea, she alleged, was to make as much money as possible for the studio by exploiting her husband's personality, with the least possible outlay.

The court was sympathetic but could not rule in Valentino's favour. He must either agree to work for Lasky at Paramount or retire from the film business until February 1924, the date when his contract was due to end.

At a New York Press conference, Natacha answered for them both. 'Most of the films being selected today are an insult to the public's intelligence,' she said. 'If we are not to be allowed to alter this state of affairs by selecting our own pictures, then Mr Valentino is better off removing himself from this artistic desert. He must at least be allowed to share artistic control with a director he trusts.'

Rudy stood grimly by, nodding his head sadly. In answer to further questions, he said he intended to write his autobiography and then embark on a visit to Europe, during which he would return to his birthplace and spend time with his brother and sister, although he did not explain where the money to finance the foreign jaunt was coming from.

News that Jean Acker was petitioning the courts to have her name changed from Jean Gugliemi to Jean Acker Valentino did not bring any comfort. Rudolph wearily instructed his lawyers to file an objection. They accepted the brief and, at the same time, tactfully pointed out that, unless legal fees of more than $40,000 could be paid quickly, their client might find himself involved in another court action – with themselves on the opposing side.

It was during his court battles with Paramount that Valentino first became involved in spiritualism.

Natacha, who would gain international renown as a spiritualist after Valentino's death, had been fascinated with the occult since her teens and frequently attended séances. Rudy had always dismissed her beliefs as fantasies, until he witnessed a series of strange happenings at the West Sixty-Seventh Street apartment that Natacha and her aunt, Teresa Werner, had taken so they could be near his rooms in the Hotel des Artistes.

The 'happenings' – mysterious tapping in various parts of the apartment – were psychic attempts to establish contact, said Natacha, and they became more frequent whenever a particular friend of hers was paying a visit. The friend's mother was dying, and she believed the spirit messages concerned her ill health. The tapping reached a crescendo on the night the woman died, and then abruptly stopped.

A few weeks later, the friend contacted Natacha and begged her and Rudolph to go with her to the home of a New York medium who, she said, had been receiving messages from the dead woman and from Valentino's mother. Excited, somewhat scared and with, on Valentino's part, a degree of mistrust, they accompanied Natacha's friend to the medium's apartment.

When they arrived, Valentino was handed a sheet of paper which drove out all his suspicions and left him shaken and impressed. The paper contained, he believed, a message from his dead mother and mentioned details of his childhood unknown to anyone in America. No further communications were received that day, but the Valentinos became regular visitors to the séances, where contact was allegedly established with people from the Castellaneta area who had died after Rudy had left home.

Under instruction from the medium, the fascinated couple were gradually taught how they could 'communicate directly with the spirit world', and soon claimed to have built up a circle of regular contacts who had passed over.

Among them were Meselope, an Egyptian born many years before Christ, and Black Feather, an Indian who nominated himself as Valentino's personal 'spirit guide'.

Most of the messages he received were optimistically phrased. One prophesied that his difficulties with Paramount would be resolved before the expiry date of his contract. In another, Black Feather prepared the Valentinos for an extended tour of America, which would bring many new friends and great financial rewards. Both predictions were destined to come true, engineered by a man who, at the time, was unknown to either of them.

It would have taken more than an army of mediums to convince hard-headed public relations man Sidney George Ullman of the existence of spirits. But had he been consulted, he would have unreservedly endorsed Black Feather's verdict on the Valentinos' immediate future – great financial rewards were just around the corner and he was the very man to help the impoverished pair grasp them.

Convinced that the glamour of the sheikh would bring women in droves to catch even a glimpse of Hollywood's Great Lover, George Ullman had already approached the Mineralava Beauty Clay Company with a startling proposition.

Valentino, he said, may be prevented by the court injunction from appearing in pictures, but there was nothing to stop him going on tour as a dancer. And if the woman who partnered him was Natacha Rambova, and they could be persuaded to endorse the product publicly, it could be the greatest sales gimmick in promotional history.

The directors of the ladies' toiletries firm enthusiastically agreed. The first part of Valentino's heavily fictionalised autobiography, serialised in *Photoplay*, was creating record sales for the February edition of the magazine and, as a result, Paramount, lacking any current titles because of their dispute with the star, had rebooked his three early blockbusters – *The Four Horsemen*, *The Sheik* and *Blood and Sand* in hundreds of theatres around the country.

A personal tour by Valentino, argued Ullman, could not fail to be a smash hit with his fans. He left Mineralava's offices with a firm commitment in his pocket. They would pay $7,000 a week to the couple, the same weekly fee which had been offered by Paramount and rejected. It was the highest fee ever paid to a dance team – for a four-month cross-country tour of the United States.

Having done his homework well, and knowing the Valentinos' financial position, Ullman anticipated little difficulty in persuading the couple to accept the deal. In early March, he boarded a train for Chicago where, now that the California divorce decree was final, Valentino and Natacha were planning to marry. But when he arrived, the public relations man heard that this arrangement had been postponed: Illinois required one year's waiting period after a divorce became final before a marriage licence could be issued.

Despite the turmoil brought about by this latest, unexpected setback to their wedding plans, Valentino and Natacha agreed to see Ullman in their hotel suite. For Ullman, it was an impressive meeting and was recorded, like a press release, in his diary:

Naturally, I was familiar with his pictures and thought of him as a handsome boy. I had no idea of his magnetism, nor of the fine quality of his manhood. To say that I was enveloped by his personality with the first clasp of his sinewy hand and my first glance into his inscrutable eyes is to state it mildly. I was literally engulfed, swept off my feet, which is unusual between two men. Had he been a beautiful woman and I a bachelor, it would not have been so surprising. I am not an emotional man. I have, in fact, often been referred to as cool-headed; but in this instance, meeting a real he-man, I found myself moved by the most powerful personality I had ever encountered in man or woman.

Valentino, for his part, was greatly interested in Ullman's proposal and impressed by his business shrewdness in arriving with a ready-signed offer from the sponsor. It was a much harder task to convince Natacha that such a promotional tour would not be beneath her dignity. But Valentino had two strong points he could argue in favour of the deal – the company they were to promote was in the cosmetics industry, as was her stepfather's; and second, Ullman had cleverly included in the contract that it should be an all-expenses paid tour. This way, they could use the $7,000 a week to clear their debts and still end up with money in the bank. Enough, he said, to pay for their belated honeymoon to Europe. Natacha surrendered, almost gracefully. The financial argument was one she clearly understood and she had recognised the need to keep her husband-to-be in the public eye until the Paramount injunction expired.

A few days later, on 14 March 1923, in the presence of Natacha's aunt Teresa Werner and George Ullman, the couple were married in a secret ceremony at Crown Point, Indiana, where the judge assured them it was perfectly legal and binding.

At least now they could end the sham of pretending to sleep in separate rooms, laughed Valentino.

After the ceremony, they travelled to Chicago once more and boarded the private and luxurious railroad car Ullman had engaged for the tour. It was furnished with gilt mirrors, Turkish carpets, original paintings and tastefully-selected furniture. There was a private bathroom for each of them and two guest bedrooms in addition to the newlyweds' main honeymoon suite. The staff included their own chef and waiter for the small dining salon and a woman to look after their costumes and clothes.

Valentino was deeply impressed by Ullman's obvious concern for their comfort, and even Natacha grudgingly admitted that it bettered her expectations by a considerable margin.

Bad weather was predicted for the first stop on their tour, and Ullman was privately concerned that, now the moment of truth had arrived, his glowing prediction of the quality of reception the Valentinos could expect might have been overly optimistic. True to the forecast, a fierce blizzard was raging in Omaha, Nebraska, when their train pulled into the main town station. Some of the streets were deep in snow and a police escort reported that outlying suburbs were virtually cut off from the town centre. While the couple rested in the honeymoon suite of the main hotel, Ullman anxiously waited at the large auditorium.

He need not have worried. Over an hour before the performance was due to begin, the theatre was packed to capacity. Hundreds of people, braving the elements to see the Great Lover in person, had to be turned away. As it was, when the orchestra struck up the overture, every aisle in the theatre was packed with standing fans, who cheered wildly as the curtain rose and revealed Valentino in *gaucho* costume and Natacha in a Spanish flamenco dress, gliding across the stage in the first steps of a tango.

This initial success was repeated in every town on their itinerary. Huge crowds gathered at the stations for their arrival and departure, theatre managers all reported record attendances and several city mayors even closed schools to allow the children to see Valentino. Often, when their timetable was published in sufficient detail in advance, admirers lined the railroad track to wave to the couple as their train passed by.

The theatre programme, agreed between Ullman and Valentino in Chicago, never varied. After the initial dances, Rudy would call for silence and thank the Mineralava Company for making his visit to the town possible. His beautiful new wife used the company's beauty products, he declared, and he hoped ladies in the audience would do the same and discover just how helpful the toiletries could be.

A popular feature of the show was a beauty contest, conducted by Valentino, which promised the winner the chance of a movie contract. At the start of the tour, the contest was judged solely by Rudy, but there were so many complaints of favouritism and 'fixing' that Ullman advised a change of format. For the rest of the tour, the contest winners were decided by the audiences themselves and judged on the volume of applause. Each performance ended with Valentino and Natacha re-enacting the scene from *The Four Horsemen* which had made him famous, and gliding off to the film's theme music, 'Tango of the Flowers'.

The live performances, and the reissue of his old movies, attracted the largest audiences in history in many towns across America, and the press reacted by devoting endless pages to the couple's movements, comments and clothes.

Photoplay reported new record sales for their March edition in which Rudolph's increasingly improbable autobiography unfolded. He claimed to have tried to join Italy's airforce at the outbreak of World War One, but had been turned down because of a rare eye defect. The fact that Italy did not have an airforce during that war did not seem to occur to anyone. He had then tried to join the British Flying Corps, but with the same frustrating result, he claimed.

But the response which brought most pleasure to Valentino was the public's acceptance of his book *Day Dreams*, a volume of love poems said to have been written by him for Natacha during the year that marriage was denied them. It sold in hundreds of thousands.

Outside cinemas, huge placards urged women to enter and thrill to the exploits of the greatest lover of them all, and *Day Dreams* was an extension of that exotic and seemingly irresistible enticement. For while a female admirer had to share her idol with other members of a cinema audience, with *Day Dreams* she could retreat to the privacy of her bedroom and read his words, imagining that he was there, speaking them just for her.

In the preface to the book, also allegedly penned by Valentino, they could read:

To you, my gentle reader, I wish to say a foreword of warning before you peruse the contents of this book. I am not a poet nor a scholar, therefore you shall find neither poems nor prose. Just dreams – Day Dreams – a bit of romance, a bit of sentimentalism, a bit of philosophy, not studied, but acquired by constant observation of the greatest of masters! ... Nature!

While lying idle, not through choice, but because forcibly kept from my preferred and actual field of activity, I took to dreams to forget the tediousness of worldly strife and the boredom of jurisprudence's pedantic etiquette.

Happy indeed I shall be if my Day Dreams *will bring you as much enjoyment as they brought to me in the writing.*

Convinced that Valentino was a natural medium, Natacha later maintained that many of the pieces in the volume were inspired by Walt Whitman, Robert and Elizabeth Browning, and other romantically-minded poets. Her husband admitted to being 'mildy psychic' and did not deny that the inspiration for his writings could have come from the spirit world. Whether dictated from 'the other side', emanating directly from Valentino's own thoughts or penned by an anonymous collaborator, the end result was the same – *Day Dreams* was an epic and best-selling publishing success. Three pieces achieved special popularity and were frequently quoted.

In 'You', Valentino seemed to speak directly to the mortal object of his affection, whom his adoring fans immediately accepted as themselves:

You are the History of Love and its Justification.
The Symbol of Devotion.
The Blessedness of Womanhood.
The Incentive of Chivalry.
The Reality of Ideals.
The Verity of Joy.

Idolatry's Defence.
The Proof of Goodness.
The Power of Gentleness.
Beauty's Acknowledgment.
Vanity's Excuse.
The Promise of Truth.
The Melody of Life.
The Caress of Romance.
The Dream of Desire.
The Sympathy of Understanding.
My Heart's Home.
The Proof of Faith.
Sanctuary of my Soul.
My Belief in Heaven.
Eternity of All Happiness.
My Prayers.
You.

His 'A Baby's Skin' is one of the pieces Natacha claimed was dictated by one of the dead writers who were regular communicants with Valentino:

Texture of a butterfly's wing
Coloured like a dawned rose,
Whose perfume is the breath of God,
Such is the web wherein is held
The treasure of the treasure chest,
The priceless gift – the Child of Love.

It was after another message-gathering session with the old Egyptian, Meselope, and his Indian spirit guide, Black Feather, that Valentine approached George Ullman during a stop in the tour at San Antonio, Texas, and asked him to become his personal manager. He was, he said, very impressed with the smooth handling of the Mineralava contract, and the resourcefulness shown by the public relations man in the day-to-day organisation of the tour.

He also admitted, quite coincidentally, that his financial affairs were in a hopeless mess: he owed more than $60,000 – $48,000 of which was owed to his lawyers – had put his future film career in jeopardy by his wilful and cavalier treatment of Lasky and Paramount, and felt he was being exploited on all sides. Not unnaturally, George Ullman refused to give an immediate answer but, after further begging from Valentino, assured him he would seriously consider the proposal. On one point though he was adamant – if he accepted Valentino's offer to become his manager, he must have exclusive rights to guide his career and business affairs. There must be no interference from others, especially from Mrs Valentino.

Valentino considered the implications for only a moment. The immediate problem was to get his affairs in order. What mattered was that his films were gathering in millions of dollars, of which he was not receiving a cent, and his debts were growing daily. Lawyers alone were costing him $2,500 a week and they were achieving nothing. If Ullman wanted to operate independently of Natacha, he would have to learn to control her in his own way. Whatever Rudy said now would be invalidated by Natacha's own actions later. He nodded his head.

The one side-effect of this arrangement which Ullman had not anticipated, and which would bring him countless, sleepless nights of worry, was that in yielding financial control and responsibility of their affairs to him, both Valentino and Natacha would never again be aware of their financial status or feel any kind of responsibility themselves. They would simply spend freely whenever a whim or a desired object took their fancy. And that was exactly how things worked out.

As soon as the tour ended, the Valentinos and George Ullman headed back for New York. Ullman's first task was to pay off Rudy's lawyers and engage someone a good deal cheaper and much more effective. He also settled the debt to Joseph Schenck, head of United Artists, and other prominent film executives in Hollywood, who had loaned Valentino money during the lean period after his break with Paramount.

Having lifted some of the financial pressure from his new clients, Ullman turned his attention to Valentino's film career.

Ritz-Carlton Pictures, a new movie company with a group of millionaire backers, had already approached Rudy to star in a series of films, and JD Williams, the President, told Ullman he was prepared to leave the choice of films and director to the star. He had talked with Jesse Lasky at Paramount and, provided Valentino was prepared to make two further films for his contractual employers in the autumn, they would willingly release him to Ritz-Carlton.

Lasky and Paramount boss Joseph Zukor travelled to New York to negotiate the return of their prodigal star.

His new salary of $7,500 a week would commence immediately and he would have absolute freedom to choose the scripts, writers, co-stars and directors. The films would be shot at the company's Long Island studios and Natacha would act as technical adviser. It seemed like a total victory for Valentino.

In ebullient mood, Rudolph agreed to make a recording for Brunswick Records, something they had been negotiating with Ullman for many months. He sang two songs, one in Italian and one in English. It is the only recording of Valentino's voice in existence and is still available today, nearly 80 years on. One can hear how heavily accented was his English, a point also made by famed showbusiness columnist Louella Parsons who interviewed him in New York. 'Mr Valentino speaks with an accent,' she wrote. 'He looks Spanish, but he is Italian.'

On the day he signed the contract with Lasky and Zukor, the evening newspaper announced the great lover's return to the screen, and a crowd of several thousand, mainly women, massed outside the Valentinos' hotel. It was almost dawn before police reserves managed to clear the streets.

In their suite, Rudy toasted George Ullman's prowess as a manager and then lifted his glass to his wife: 'I am once more the complete Rudolph Valentino,' he said. 'Now, at last, we can begin our honeymoon.'

WHEN THE CUNARD liner *Aquitania* slipped into Southampton on the penultimate day of July 1923, Rudolph Valentino stood on deck and looked out on England for the first time with mixed emotions of excited, almost childlike, anticipation dulled by a gnawing apprehension.

This was, in theory, to be the triumphant voyage, the storybook return of the prodigal, culminating in the homecoming of the hero, with his beautiful new bride, to the town from which he'd set off to find fame and fortune. It was, in fact, to become a journey of minor disasters, major disappointments and domestic squabbles – and a 'belated honeymoon' on which the bride would refuse, point-blank, to continue, and insist on going home to mother.

The start had gone well, if judged by Hollywood standards. Hundreds of screaming women, hoping for even a momentary glimpse of their love god, had mobbed the Valentinos in New York eight days before when, with Auntie Teresa Werner in tow, they arrived to board the ship and had to fight their way up the gangplank, surrounded and protected from the hysterical fans by burly sailors. The voyage had passed smoothly, with the couple receiving star treatment, attentive service and the privacy they demanded as honeymooners. The Valentinos were permanent guests at the Captain's table and retired each night to a sumptuous first-class suite; a far cry indeed, reflected Valentino, from the slave ship-like conditions he had experienced on his last Atlantic voyage.

Yet, as he prepared to land in England, confessing to a fellow traveller that he had not slept properly for three nights, Valentino found himself constantly worrying about the reception he would receive from the British public. Would they be as dedicated and enthusiastic as those he had left behind in America? Had his screen-projected charisma been enough to win over the allegedly reserved English women on this side of the Atlantic, and did the men here regard his screen cavortings with as much cynicism as their American counterparts?

His doubts were partially answered by a small but enthusiastic group of admirers who had gathered on the landing pier in Southampton to greet him, and by the number of photographers who rushed aboard to take pictures of him, smiling and waving his grey felt hat in welcome, and of Natacha, wearing a bored and disinterested expression above a long, fur-collared coat to protect her from the British summer weather, which she remembered well from her schooldays in Surrey.

The reporters seemed genuinely interested, too. 'I have come over entirely for rest and pleasure,' he told them, and added a phrase he was to regret the following day: 'I have not had a decent suit made in ten years, and now I am going to try London for some.'

It was after midnight when their train pulled into its London terminal, and his fears about an apathetic reception were instantly dispelled when he saw the more than 1,000 people who had waited hours in almost torrential rain for him, and Valentino, as delighted to see them as they were to set eyes on their idol, declared it 'the most spontaneous and thrilling greeting I've ever had'.

Then he and Natacha drove off to the Carlton Hotel where, arousing more boyish excitement than historical appreciation, Valentino was told that the suite in which he would sleep had once been occupied by the King and Queen of Belgium.

The next day, and each morning which followed, hordes of journalists descended on his hotel armed with questions, cameras and curiosity. They eyed the already legendary Italian movie star with cool, professional interest, missing nothing about this strange new superhero, from his neat, dark suit, cornflower-blue shirt with matching silk socks, to the grey-and-cream check tie, held in place by an emerald pin. And his wife, sitting quietly by his side, rarely smiling, seldom talking, yet, despite that determined set to her jaw, undoubtedly attractive in a currently-fashionable 'Polly' dress made for her in New York.

Valentino, knowing the ways and waywardness of the American press, treated their English cousins warily. 'I'm very glad to be in London,' he announced, to nobody's surprise. 'I've been wanting to come here all my life, and I'll be here for 15 days. Then, when I've bought some clothes, we'll go to Paris so that Mrs Valentino can buy some.'

Natacha allows herself a smile. Next question ... How many suits will you buy here?

Valentino waves a hand, on which, one reporter notes and scribbles down, are three platinum rings, one with a huge emerald, and reveals his flashy amethyst cufflinks. 'Oh, say a dozen or so.' And, just in case that sounds a little overly ostentatious: 'As many as I can afford. There's nowhere in the world like London for men's tailoring and, as I have to play well-dressed Continental parts, I look upon the suits as an investment.'

Next question. Will you dance, as has been rumoured, in public in Britain?

Valentino grimaces. 'I have received several offers to dance in London, but I'm not accepting any of them. We can't bear the sound of the word dancing. Who could, after dancing the tango for many months throughout the United States, every night? To dance when one has to dance is not the same thing as dancing when one wants to dance.'

Natacha breaks her silence. 'Ever since we were married we have been acting and dancing together and going about in a private car without any privacy. Now I think it's quite time we had our honeymoon.'

How about all that jazz? It is a subject Valentino has often sounded off about in America.

'Jazz, unfortunately, has not yet started to die in the States. Over there, I suppose, they must have something to excite them, since they no longer have liquor.' Rudolph pauses for the obligatory chuckles. 'I believe that the dances of the future will have the grace and dignity of the old-fashioned ones. There will be a general return to the beauty of the waltz, the dance that will never go out. But, at present, I consider that the tango, properly danced, is about the best of the modern dances which, on the whole, are not lovely at all.'

How long will your honeymoon last? Surprisingly, Valentino ignores the opportunity to give a romantic answer.

'I must be back in New York in October for my law suit against the Famous Players,' he says seriously. 'I am dissatisfied with my contract which I signed when I was new to business. I don't like the way my latest pictures have been treated and I want the right to choose my own stories. And there is a clause in the contract which I consider unfair. It states that if my manner, bearing or form changes detrimentally, the Famous Players can suspend me for a year without salary, and with a ban on working for anyone else. Then, if my manner, bearing or form changes back again, they can add the period of my suspension to the period of the contract. I want to break that contract, and sign another with a different firm.'

With that, the first press conference was over and the reporters dispersed to write their pieces.

These were, on the whole, complimentary. 'Mr Rudolph Valentino,' wrote the *Evening News* reporter, 'whose face and figure on film have attracted letters by the hundred thousand from girl admirers in America ... is tall and very handsome, in the dark, aquiline, iridescent-eyed manner of Mr Ivor Novello. He appears to be strangely modest and restrained in the popular conception of screen heroes and sat and talked of clothes and contracts and the dedicated art of the cinema, while Mrs Rudolph Valentino listened with intent expression, and lips gently parted.'

Parted lips also fascinated the *Daily Mail* man. Intrigued by the silent star's voice, he revealed exclusively for the benefit of cinemagoers who'd never been given the chance to hear it, 'Mr Valentino speaks English more like an Englishman than an American – or rather, an Italian, for he is Italian born.'

Whatever the language or the accent, Valentino swore feelingly and at length, when he was confronted with his next visitors, for no sooner had the pressmen left his suite than it was invaded by what seemed to be representatives of every tailoring and men's outfitting establishment in the capital. Reading that morning that he wanted to clothe himself in London and knowing that their cloth on his frame would be a worldwide walking advertisement, they swarmed in with samples and suggestions, statistics and smooth talk.

The silent star sent them packing with a few well-chosen words presented with a tired smile, and then slipped out of the hotel to try to become just another tourist. Despite more press interviews, business calls and suit fittings, he managed to do just that during his London stay. He and Natacha followed the tourist routes to Windsor Castle, the Tower of London, Hampton Court and made two visits to the theatre, where they received standing ovations. They lunched with Mr Benjamin Guinness, purveyor of Irish stout to the populace, at his Cumberland Place home and there met government minister Lord Birkenhead and his wife and young daughter, Lady Pamela. They had never heard of Valentino or he of them, but they reportedly got on famously.

Finally, they visited Natacha's old school, Leatherhead Court in Epsom, and a country breeding kennels, and when they left Britain, flying from Croydon to Paris, Le Bourget, on 15 August, the new Valentino family was considerably enlarged by three Pekinese, which Natacha just could not resist. It was, she told Valentino, a family obsession picked up from Elsie de Wolfe during Natacha's holiday sojourns at Villa Trianon.

The spending and the dog-collecting continued in Paris where, apart from picking up more praise, invitations and free meals, Valentino competed with his wife's cash investment in Paris fashion by ordering another new wardrobe of clothes and a superb Voisin open tourer to take them to Natacha's parents' home on the Riviera.

Because it could not be made ready in time for the start of their journey, he graciously accepted the loan of another car from the company. And he was also happy to accept, from Jacques Herbertot, owner of the Theatre Champs-Elysées, another dog, a Doberman-Pinscher.

So, with more luggage and more dogs than they comfortably knew what to do with, the Valentinos set off on the next stage of their journey south, during which they would experience the first serious quarrel of their marriage, brought about by his reckless driving.

For Valentino, his newly-acquired car was a thrilling, beautiful toy and he was determined to test it to the full by driving to Nice over the Alps through Grenoble and Dijon, rather than the simpler route through Lyons. Exhilarated, he sped round the snaking, constantly-curving Alpine roads, smiling at the car's performance and laughing at Natacha's pleas to drive more slowly. For her, the flat-out drive along primitive roads was a nightmare journey, most of which she spent with her eyes tightly closed. Had she been aware that he had never had a formal driving lesson, and had been stopped or fined for speeding on several Californian highways, she might have been even more terrified.

Valentino, too, enthralled by the macho demonstration of his driving skill, refused to listen to his genuinely frightened passenger. 'I know what I'm doing – I have a distinct flair for speed,' he tried to reassure her.

But as he swerved the car around yet another treacherous bend, misjudging speed and distance badly, Natacha screamed in terror as they left the road and Valentino, frantically stamping on the brakes, came to a halt with one front wheel of the tourer over a steep precipice.

It was, they would tell friends back in Hollywood, a rather tense moment. Valentino, ashen-faced, his hands gripping the steering-wheel so tightly that his knuckles showed white, and Natacha shaking with anger, relief, fury and fright.

'Did you notice,' he asked his wife after a while in a quiet, nervous voice, 'that when I wrenched the wheel round, it wasn't only me? Black Feather leaned over to help give that pull that saved us.'

Natacha was not impressed. 'The gods have nothing to do with driving,' she informed her husband, and once again begged him to drive more carefully. He did, and they completed this leg of their journey safely.

The reunion with Natacha's mother and stepfather lasted ten days. At the 20-room château near Cannes, the Valentinos, both on the brink of physical and mental exhaustion after their difficult journey, recovered quickly and Rudolph announced, to his not altogether delighted in-laws, that he might easily live there for several months each year in future.

It was with great reluctance and serious forebodings, which she voiced aloud, that Natacha finally agreed to leave her beloved Pekinese puppies with her mother and get back in the car for their trip to Italy. To keep her company, they took with them Aunt Teresa, who had left the *Aquitania* at Cherbourg to travel to the Hudnuts' home by train.

From the outset, it was not to prove one of the happiest of journeys. At the Customs post, Valentino was disappointed to realise that officials did not recognise him. Hardly surprising, as none of his films had yet been distributed in Italy, where it took five years for Hollywood output to reach the theatres. There were no smiles or handshakes and no welcoming greetings for the returning hero.

Only a long delay, while the Customs officers at Ventemiglia inspected every item of baggage, and then charged them an exorbitant fine for taking in too many cigarettes.

When they reached Genoa, it was after midnight and Natacha, exhausted and tired, and hoarse from pleading with Valentino to slow down during the long drive, succumbed to a minor nervous breakdown.

'I'm afraid she won't be able to come with us all the way,' Valentino told Mrs Werner. 'All this dirt and dust and my driving are a little too much for her to cope with.'

The following day, however, she felt better, and the journey continued. Their next stop was in Milan, where Valentino's sister, Maria, was to join them for the rest of the trip.

But Maria, worried when they did not turn up on time, had taken a train to Genoa, and they missed each other. After a dozen telephone calls and messages, she eventually returned to Milan and met up with them for an emotional, tear-filled reunion.

The women eyed each other with guarded interest. Natacha, meeting her husband's sister for the first time, saw a plain, shabbily-dressed young peasant woman, devoid of make-up, who had clearly never enjoyed the better things of life. Maria, on her side, was astounded to discover that her brother had taken this – admittedly very beautiful, but gaudily dressed and painted – worldly-wise girl as a wife. She was visibly shocked by Natacha's appearance, for, dare she whisper it, such liberal use of lipstick and rouge and such bright clothes were normally only to be seen on ladies of ill-repute and not on a respectable wife.

Biographer Michael Morris, in his biography *Madam Valentino*, recorded Natacha's words following the meeting. 'I am afraid I was a terrible shock to her proprieties. Not only did I use powder, but lip rouge and kohl as well! Not to speak of the brilliant colouring of my clothes and an extensive use of perfume. All of which, according to Maria, was simply not done except by an unmentionable class of persons. She was frightfully concerned over her brother's reputation and could not refrain from the suggestion that I, at least, should not wear a glove over my wedding ring.'

Amused by his sister's very provincial attitude, Valentino assured her that things were done differently in America and soon they were talking excitedly of childhood days, of America, of films and of his success. Natacha and Aunt Teresa, neither of whom spoke Italian, were forced to sit in silence as the journey continued on its precarious course.

It came to a sudden halt as they drove into Bologna at sunset – and into a telegraph pole. 'Look out! Look out!' Natacha screamed again. It was too late. The grey pole had merged into the colour of the road and Valentino had not seen it. 'I was only driving slowly, too,' he cursed, as he examined a damaged fender.

Swearing again that he would drive more carefully, Rudolph carried on, across the Apennines and even more treacherous roads, to Florence and Pisa and, eventually, to Rome.

Here, at least, the movie fraternity knew of Valentino's success. He was invited on to the set of *Quo Vadis* and was wined and dined by studio chiefs, though Valentino sulked when a promised meeting with Benito Mussolini did not materialise.

It was in Rome that Natacha ultimately decided that enough was enough, and that her nerves would not stand another mile of her husband's crazy and inconsiderate driving. 'I have had enough of risking my life for a diet of bumpy roads, beggars, poverty and disease,' she told Valentino. 'I am going no further,' and, despite protests and repeated promises of slow, crash-proof driving, she left her husband and went back to France and her mother.

So it was only Rudolph, Maria and Mrs Werner who left Rome for Campo Basso and the next emotional reunion, this time with brother Alberto, his wife and son. Once again, there were long hours of reminiscences, memories, talk of childhood days. But Rudolph was impatient to be on the way to Castellaneta, and home.

Alberto was far from keen to join him on the pilgrimage. He was sure there was nothing in their home town for him. 'The roads are terrible,' he told his brother. 'Anyway, there's nothing up there to see, not many people you'll want to meet.' He and Maria both opted not to join him on the journey home.

But nothing could stand in the way of Rudolph Valentino and the homecoming to his birthplace. Nothing except a couple of burst tyres and a hotel in Taranto, where his angry complaint that there was no bath bewildered the manager, who explained that most other guests used the Turkish bath around the corner. Infuriated still that his name did not carry any weight in Italy, outside of Rome, and embarrassed in front of his remaining companion, Mrs Werner, that the best attention was not automatically forthcoming, he set off on the last stage of his sentimental journey depressed and increasingly uncertain of the reception he would find in Castellaneta.

He wrote in a letter to a Hollywood friend, 'I was as I had been when I left Italy, as unknown to films as films were unknown and unexpected to me.'

If the journey so far had been stressful, Valentino found his final homecoming infinitely more so, and bitterly disappointing.

From the start, his grand, gleaming automobile impressed the townsfolk more than he did. It was the most beautiful and exciting thing many of them had ever seen, in a community where horse-drawn carts and donkeys or a stout pair of legs were still the generally accepted means of transport.

The man who stepped out of the automobile and stared about him with a strange look on his face, both sad and somehow lost, looked quite absurd in this impoverished, rustic setting. Standing there, in the middle of the dusty town, beside his magnificent machine, with a huge, almost comical cloak wrapped around him, he looked to at least one of the observers, a local urchin, like something out of a circus.

Laughing excitedly, the boy ran to the nearest house, where Don Angelo Maldarizzi and his family lived.

Inside, Don Angelo was pottering and his wife, Donna Vincenza, was in the kitchen with their two daughters, 17-year-old Rita and Ada who was four years younger. The girls heard the commotion and, curious, ran to the front door to see the 'circus clowns' the boy was shouting about.

'I was dumfounded when I saw who was there,' recalled Rita, who says she felt her legs go weak and feared she might even faint. For when she looked at the man in the cloak she saw the teenage boy from next door she had once known well, but had almost forgotten – Rodolpho Guglielmi.

'One by one, the family hugged and embraced the man and looked curiously at the elderly lady sitting in the car, who made no attempt to alight. 'The aunt of my wife,' he explained. 'She can't understand what we're saying.'

Eventually, they went into the house. Donna Vincenza brewed coffee and brought out cakes, a local speciality Rodolpho had loved as a boy, and he lounged back on a divan, smoking, talking, explaining. 'I was in Italy,' he said, 'and I knew I dare not leave without coming back home. I had to see it. But everything is exactly the same as when I left.' He kept repeating, 'Nothing has changed at all. Everything is exactly the same.'

He talked of his life, his wife, his films. Rita was dazzled and confused. She had never seen a film, or heard of Hollywood. He seemed, she thought, to live in a fairyland world. He had changed almost beyond recognition from the boy she had known, becoming a wholly and totally different person – an alien almost. He didn't belong in Castellaneta any more.

Her father saw that, too, and was clearly unimpressed by the changes. He began to scold their visitor. 'Why did you have to run off from home, gallivanting abroad? Your place was to remain here, with your family and the people you were raised with.'

Rodolpho sat forward, waving his arms in emphasis. Everything he does, Ada thought, seems to be theatrical. 'But, Don Angelo,' he protested, 'you must understand that America has given me millions. Do you realise that? Millions! And I have to be where there are millions. Millions of dollars! Can't you see that?'

Don Angelo shook his head. 'I suppose you know best. The young always do. But it's sad to see young men like you leaving our town. Some of them never come back ...'

'But I'm back,' Rodolpho laughed. 'I've come to look at the house and visit the cemetery. That's where I'm going now.'

He went alone, through the siesta-silenced streets, to stand quietly at the family graves where his father and mother and little sister Beatrice were buried, and on to the whitewashed house, looking much smaller than he remembered, in which he'd been born and where, with tears and grief he thought would break his heart, he had kissed his mother for the last time before leaving for America. But he had been right to go. To get away from this place. He knew that now. This was a distressing, depressing, unchanging town. He could never have found happiness here.

When he returned to the Maldarizzis' home, Rita sensed that he was restless. 'It hadn't made him happy, coming here,' she said. 'The word had gone around that he was back and people were gathering in front of the house – including some of his cousins. But few recognised him as someone famous or were fully aware of the success he had made of his life. None of them wanted to talk to him, they just wanted him to give them money, and when he refused they became belligerent and some even spat at him. More than resenting his wealth, they were jealous that he had escaped and that they could not. Next to him, they seemed uncivilised yokels, dirty and raggedly dressed. It was an impossible gulf to bridge and he knew it.'

Rita recognised it and knew he couldn't wait to drive away from this hostile town of his youth in which he had become an unwelcome stranger.

Only Donna Vincenza's inherent hospitality endured. 'You will stay and eat with us?' she asked. 'We don't know when we will see you again. It may be years ...'

'No, no, thank you,' he said, moving towards his car. 'We really must be off ...'

'But you will come back, soon ... some day?' Rita asked.

Rudolph smiled. 'Who knows?' he said, and he said it, Ada thought again, like an actor in a drama. And then, with more kisses and embraces, he was gone.

As he climbed into the car, the sisters cried. They knew they would never see him again. 'What,' Rita asked, 'does the great

Rodolpho want with a little country town with dirt roads and carts?'

Back at the Hudnut villa, Valentino told Natacha, 'It was a mistake to go back. I'm glad you didn't have to suffer it. They were rude and uncaring. They resented my success.'

It was time to go home. Not the nostalgic, never-to-be-rediscovered fantasy home of his childhood but his real home, which he would furnish from the rewards of fulfilling other people's fantasies. In Hollywood.

WITH THE FREEDOM, at last, to make any movie of his choice, Valentino was adamant. It would be *Captain Blood*, the swashbuckling tale of a daring English pirate who terrorises the Caribbean, defeats the French on behalf of his king and sweeps the governor's daughter off her feet. It was, he said, what he wanted, and what his fans demanded.

Lasky could scarcely believe his ears. Had he been consulted he could not have picked a better Valentino vehicle. It would have the impact of *The Sheik* and *Blood and Sand* combined. It would take Paramount's profits into the stratosphere.

But in their excitement, both had ignored, or forgotten, that Valentino's choice did not have Natacha's blessing. He may be the superstar, but she was about to demonstrate once again that it was she who called the shots – both in their marriage and his career.

She had her own, inflexible ideas about just how that career should develop, and her plans did not include the making of *Captain Blood*. Valentino protested, but was told to stop being so cheap and unartistic and to raise his standards. It meant, as usual, that he was quickly overruled.

Captain Blood would have to wait a further two decades before resurfacing to confirm the heart-throb potential of another screen hero – Errol Flynn.

The story Natacha had chosen, and the only fitting one for her husband's dramatic comeback, she told him, was *Monsieur Beaucaire*, which recounted the daringly amorous activities of the dashing Duc de Chartres. In pre-publicity interviews, though, denied his own choice of picture, he put aside his sulks and dutifully promised, as Natacha had coached him, to be once again the Great Lover, providing romance and excitement for all.

Disappointed, but still hoping to salvage a box-office hit and ensure delivery of the right mixture of passion and beefcake, Lasky called for the original script to be pepped up, and was staggered, but delighted, when Natacha agreed. She did not approve, however, of the first script of Booth Tarkington's novel and when Lasky suggested that production of the film be postponed until the New Year, when the rewrite would be finished, Natacha again concurred. She and Rudolph would spend Christmas, and see in 1924, with her mother and stepfather in the south of France. Overjoyed to find co-operation coming from such an unexpected quarter Lasky volunteered for the studio to pay all their travel expenses.

The Valentinos re-embarked for Europe on the *Aquitania* and, having anticipated a full-scale American-style celebration, Rudolph had bought sufficient decorations to fill two large tea chests stored in the liner's hold.

On their arrival, he insisted on the Hudnuts installing a huge Christmas tree in the hall. They spent most of their first night dressing the tree with dozens of coloured balls, tinsel, cotton wool snowballs, glittering ornaments, crackers and gifts. About 100 candles in clip-on holders completed the decorations.

Mrs Hudnut was against lighting the candles, but on Christmas Eve Rudy insisted and his mother- in-law reluctantly gave in. Anything to keep her son-in-law happy.

Valentino and Natacha, standing on stools, used long tapers to light the candles, and had almost finished when he spotted one towards the back which they had missed. As he reached through the branches, the flame accidentally brushed a snowball and, in moments, the whole tree was ablaze.

As the others panicked and Valentino dashed out to fetch a hose, Mrs Werner, unflappable as ever, collected the presents piled near the foot of the tree and moved them to safety. While Mrs Hudnut screamed for everyone to save her valuable tapestries and furniture, pails of water and Rudy's garden hose finally quenched the blaze. But the festive spirit was badly dampened and Mrs Hudnut no longer had the same fondness in her eyes when she looked at her son-in-law. Even Natacha was not immune to the tension and, at the first decent opportunity, on the morning after New Year's Day, they began their return journey to New York.

The newspaper reports that Valentino was about to begin shooting his comeback film prompted an unprecedented display of adulation from his fans.

Absence from the screen in new films had not done any damage to his reputation among his female admirers, and news that he was to film on Long Island had caused a rush on rented properties there. When shooting started, there wasn't a single room to be had within 20 miles of the studio.

Women pleading for just a few moments alone with the star, and the chance to gaze directly into those smouldering eyes, camped outside the studio gates and refused to move. The studio switchboard was flooded with calls, many of them of an extremely intimate nature, and hundreds of letters were delivered daily. Some of the writers enclosed snippets of their undergarments and beseeched Valentino to touch them, preferably with his lips, and return them to the sender. Others enclosed extremely candid nude photographs of themselves and detailed descriptions of what they would do to the lover of their dreams. To be ravished as the sheikh had ravished Diana, without scruple, was their greatest heart's desire, they wrote.

A flattered, but slightly perplexed Valentino professed amusement in public, and demanded that a round-the-clock bodyguard be provided by Paramount to keep his worshipping fans at arm's length. He had not forgotten the frenzied attack outside the Hollywood boutique two years earlier.

Newspapers and magazines revealed to their readers that Valentino did not confine his amorous activities to the screen. Not all his fans were turned away disappointed, it was hinted. Valentino tried to laugh off these reports, saying it was just good publicity for the film. But Natacha shouted him down in front of the whole cast and crew and snarled that he was a spineless fool to put up with such mortifying treatment from the Paramount chiefs. They were using him as they had always used him. Furiously, she demanded that all reporters be banned from the studio. Paramount executives promised this would be done, then secretly ordered the publicity department to leak further 'intimate disclosures' to the gossip writers.

From the day shooting started, Natacha had been in an evil temper, constantly berating her husband both in public and private. She criticised his acting, his posture and his make-up and, because he failed to stand up to her, Valentino earned added criticism from his fellow actors and the film crew. Believing that only Natacha could lift him to the great heights his talent deserved, he was content to let her have her way and supported her whenever there was opposition to her meddlesome activities around the studio. After each day's filming, she would gather the cast and director, Sydney Olcott, about her and review their performances, delighting in exercising the authority which the studio had awarded her as part of their settlement with Valentino.

Olcott's protests increased and his phonecalls of complaint to Lasky became significant daily events. Natacha constantly interfered with his direction and questioned even his smallest decisions. She was making him virtually redundant, he wailed.

To Lasky, it was all a question of *déjà vu*, for once again he was required to use all his persuasive talents to prevent a director from walking out on the Valentinos, but the daily rushes far exceeded anything they might have anticipated, and his pleas to Olcott and virtually everyone else associated with the production were to keep calm and stay the course. Miraculously, in view of the open hostilities which surrounded each day's shooting, Lasky succeeded, and the film was completed only a few days over schedule.

For the spectacular production, with triple the budget of his last two pictures, and on Natacha's orders, Paramount had used two assistant directors and more than a score of specialists never before employed in the making of a movie. These included a director of etiquette, a fencing master, a dancing master and Valentino's private fiddler and poetry reader. And to assist her with her designs – many of which were made up in Paris by top couturier, Poiret – she had 15 specialist assistants to cope with scenery painting, set design, costumes and lighting, and a couple of French academics to advise on eighteenth-century behaviour and etiquette.

For Natacha, style, design and romance were the main issues in the making of *Monsieur Beaucaire.* Valentino was draped in powdered wigs, silk stockings and incredibly tight pants and love patches were stuck to his face. As an aristocratic French lothario, he was called upon to seduce a string of beautiful women, which would probably go down well with his female fans, but there was little in the film to attract the men. Those few action sequences contained in the script were reduced still further on Natacha's orders and the best of these were cut out during the editing.

What George Ullman noticed was that the extravagant 'extras', provided by the studio to ensure the smooth production of Valentino's comeback picture, did nothing to contain the actor's grandiose ideas and, despite frequent stern warnings from his manager, he had begun another period of lavish spending.

Most of his purchases were expensive antiques to complete the furnishing of his Whitley Heights house in California, and his expenditure was outpacing his income by several thousand dollars a week. By the last day of filming on *Monsieur Beaucaire*, a disillusioned but wiser Ullman had to inform his irrepressible charge that he was again in debt to Paramount. Valentino was unrepentant.

In August, the film opened in New York to favourable notices from the critics and long queues outside the theatres. Valentino's performance received ecstatic reviews and *Variety* predicted that women would go for this one in their thousands. Initially, at least, it seemed that he was still the greatest box-office attraction in America, even after a two-year lay-off.

The *New York Times* called it the finest production of its type, one that should not be missed, even by people who didn't usually go to the movies.

Certainly, Douglas Fairbanks was unable to compete when his latest film, *The Thief of Bagdad*, opened in New York soon afterwards. Forty-Sixth Street was mobbed with people who wanted to see Fairbanks and Mary Pickford arrive for the première.

The two major stars planned to have everyone seated before making their entrance and thought they were the last to arrive. But, half a block from the theatre, Fairbanks heard the excited screams of hundreds of women.

Lowering his car's window, he heard cries of 'We love you, Rudy!' and 'Rudy, you're wonderful!' from the ecstatic fans, as Rudolph Valentino made his entrance into the theatre.

No one could follow that, Fairbanks decided. After the reception the great lover had just been given, his own and Mary's arrival would be an anti-climax. Grabbing his equally daunted co-star, he hurled himself on the floor of their limousine and shouted to the chauffeur to make another turn round the block.

Meanwhile, inside the theatre, Rudy swept through the lobby and, to deafening cheers, strode to the first box. All around, women in the first-night audience were in confusion. Men were staring in open envy at the handsome Italian who, with professional modesty, bowed slightly and sat down, eyes fixed on the screen, waiting quietly for the lights to go down and the picture to begin.

Only after the orchestra had struck up the theme music and the first images were flickering on the screen did Mary Pickford and Douglas Fairbanks creep into the darkened theatre through the stage door. Valentino had completely stolen their glory.

Valentino's popularity with the people at Paramount remained in direct proportion to the amount of time he was accompanied by Natacha. Valentino alone, they loved. Valentino with his wife had become an unacceptable package. No amount of success with *Monsieur Beaucaire* could persuade the Natacha-worn Sydney Olcott to direct another Valentino picture if the 'she-devil', as he had dubbed her, retained any kind of authority.

Joseph Henaberry was brought in to replace him for Valentino's last film with Paramount, a South American adventure story adapted from Rex Beach's novel *Rope's End*, to be retitled *A Sainted Devil*. To demonstrate her authority to the end, Natacha personally chose the two leading ladies – Nita Naldi and Jetta Goudal.

Jetta, a beautiful and talented French actress, was captivated by Valentino's striking looks and Continental charm and made no secret of her off-screen interest in him. He considered it harmless to indulge in light flirtation, but reckoned without his wife's jealousy and, worse, her incredible pride. That Rudy should publicly show even the slightest interest in any woman other than herself was considered a direct insult by his fiery spouse.

The young Frenchwoman's days on the picture were numbered, and the incident which clinched her premature departure came during an inspection of the costumes, which Natacha had designed. Jetts stared incredulously at the clothes and burst out laughing. They must be intended for effeminate men and deformed women, she shrieked. Jetta Goudal would never allow herself to be photographed in these ridiculous garments.

Natacha stormed from the set, her mouth twisted in a snarl, and next morning it was announced that Miss Goudal had been dismissed from the cast for indiscipline. Her place would be taken by Valentino's good and platonic friend, Dagmar Godowsky.

As filming of *A Sainted Devil* proceeded, a new torrent of complaints about Natacha again began pouring in to Jesse Lasky's office, and he estimated that, if anything, the ferocity and number exceeded even her previous power-play antics.

Paramount's Vice-President praised God that this was the last occasion he would be called upon to adjudicate between the Valentinos and his other employees and, with skill accumulated from long practice, smoothed the ruffled feathers of his director and assistants and advised that the sooner they finished the picture, the sooner they could all be rid of Natacha. On set, the unceasingly hen-pecked star silently suffered his wife's tantrums and criticism and was always ready to agree when she scolded one of the other actors or clashed with the director and technicians.

It seemed to outsiders as though Natacha desperately wanted to prove she was more important to the picture than her husband, and that he was quite prepared for this to be so. Whatever the reasons, he endured her harangues with smiles and fortitude. Surprisingly, the film was completed without another major incident.

'Miraculously' was how Jesse Lasky put it, as he beamed across at Paramount President Adolph Zukor, and toasted the departure of their 'Number One Headache'. Natacha had now become the problem of JD Williams and his unfortunate colleagues at the virgin Ritz-Carlton studios.

Williams's first inkling of what lay ahead came during their first meeting to discuss Valentino's début picture.

He was informed by Natacha that she, and she alone, knew how to exploit her husband's talents. To that end, she had written a thrilling screen story of love and war in medieval Spain under the pseudonym Justice Layne.

The dumbfounded studio boss was then told that Natacha intended to direct the picture, to be retitled *The Hooded Falcon* from her original story, *The Scarlet Power*, and she would also design all sets and all costumes.

When Lasky was told of the ultimatum by his spies in the Ritz-Carlton company, he again gave thanks for his timely deliverance from Natacha's hands and told his co-directors, 'Her narcissism has completely taken her over. That woman is now certifiable and should be locked up.'

Valentino would not have been in accord. Natacha, he assured a deeply concerned George Ullman, was his true mentor and guide. Only she could be trusted with his precious talent.

At Ritz-Carlton, he nodded his agreement as Natacha went on to explain how they intended making a tour of Spain to purchase authentic costumes and props and do further research. The cornered Williams, faced with the combined personalities of the formidable pair, could only mumble his consent, though he did add an earnest plea that they keep their expenses down to a maximum of $50,000.

Natacha's scornful answering look following this request should have warned him. The plundering expedition to Spain was to be carried out in truly lavish Valentino style.

23

'THE SACKING of Spain', as JD Williams came to call the Valentinos' jaunt across the Iberian peninsula, set the studio back a little over $100,000.

As the spendthrift couple swooped on town after town, leaving stunned but substantially richer antique merchants in their wake, they were pursued by a series of telegrams, each more frantic and belligerent than the last, demanding they curb their spending and confine themselves to buying only necessities for the forthcoming production.

But these missives from New York served only to spur the 'researchers' on to new heights of extravagance. Fresh crates of antique armour, weapons and furnishings, carpets, tapestries and costumes, matador outfits and *mantillas*, books, paintings and ornaments were dispatched daily to America. Finally, in a state of near exhaustion from their efforts, the Valentinos, and Natacha's mother, arrived in Seville, where they accepted an invitation to the Sunday bullfight.

Recalling his own endeavours in the ring during the filming of *Blood and Sand*, Valentino temporarily slipped back into his role of Juan Gallardo and made an entrance, every bit as impressive and arrogant, as the three matadors who were to face the afternoon's quota of bulls. Sitting below the President's box, the two women were treated to a running commentary on the action by a highly excited Valentino, who at one stage had to be physically restrained from leaping into the ring and assisting in dispatching one of the magnificent animals.

'This is real man's work!' he yelled. 'Making films is only for sissies.'

Only the prompt intervention of two stern-faced policemen prevented his breaking free from his wife and mother-in-law to join the matadors, but afterwards he insisted on being taken to their disrobing room to congratulate the heroes on their performances. During their return train ride to the Hudnuts' French château, he spoke enthusiastically of giving up his film career and devoting himself to the Corrida de Toros, and on arrival at the Hudnuts' home Rudolph could scarcely contain himself until a projector had been set up and he was able to watch a private copy of *Blood and Sand*.

Among themselves, the Hudnuts and their other guests agreed privately that they preferred *Monsieur Beaucaire*, but in front of Valentino they praised his skill in portraying the courage of Gallardo so convincingly and managed to stifle their yawns as the film was screened six times during that weekend.

Ignoring several new appeals from JD Williams to speed their return to America, the couple opted instead to tour the château region of France, to enable Natacha to make further studies of fourteenth-century European costume. Essential, she cabled Williams, to the film's integrity.

Valentino, under his wife's prompting, used this period to grow a small but distinguished-looking beard which, with make-up to darken his olive skin even further, she assured her hesitant spouse, would make him a very convincing Moorish lord.

Eventually, the cables from New York became so ominously emphatic that even Natacha felt they could no longer disregard them and they set sail for America in the *Leviathan*. On arrival, they were met with disappointing news from an extremely disgruntled JD Williams.

June Mathis was having difficulties with the script of *The Hooded Falcon*, and it had also been decided, because of technical difficulties and lack of studio space in New York, that the film would have to be made on the West Coast, with a budget limit of $500,000.

The whole studio, therefore, was being moved to Hollywood. Valentino and Natacha found it difficult to argue. If they wanted the picture to be made on the lavish scale she had envisaged, they must have the necessary space. Williams also warned that the picture would not be able to absorb the cost of all the articles they had bought in Spain, and some of them might have to be considered their private acquisitions.

While they they were still digesting this piece of news, Williams revealed that, because preparation of *The Hooded Falcon* might well run into many more weeks, he had bought the film adaptation of *Cobra*, a successful Broadway stage play, which was ready to go into immediate production.

His backers at Ritz-Carlton were becoming restless at the delay in seeing a return on their investment, he warned, and urged them both to accept the new arrangement.

'But do we have your promise that *The Hooded Falcon* will be next?' Natacha asked.

'Certainly,' replied Williams. 'You have my word on it.'

'In that case, Rudy will do *Cobra*,' consented Natacha, and to Williams's intense surprise and relief, for he had heard disturbing reports about her shrewish interference in production, she added, 'I will have no part in the filming of it. This is the kind of modern story that bores me to tears. I will concentrate on the designs for *Falcon*.'

Unfortunately, she could not resist demonstrating her power to the studio in some way. As a simple reminder to them of who was really in control, she insisted on a re-write of the script, incorporating some of her own storylines.

'It could have been much worse,' Williams told his backers. But that was before they saw the finished picture!

Meanwhile, Valentino's arrival in New York with a beard had caused a storm of protest among his admirers and Lasky, at Paramount, seeing the controversy as a fresh source of publicity to help launch *A Sainted Devil,* had his publicity chief contact the American Master Barbers' Association.

If Valentino kept his beard, wives all over the country would urge their husbands to follow suit, they warned.

The great lover's goatee became a subject for hot debate among the country's barbers and the Association passed a resolution declaring that its members were pledged, along with their families and friends, not to attend showings of Rudolph Valentino's pictures so long as he remained bewhiskered.

The male population, they said, was likely to be guided by the actor to the extent of making beards fashionable again, and such a fashion would not only injure their trade, but would utterly deface America and make its citizens difficult to distinguish from Russians.

Bowing to the demands of his fans, and the barbers, and because he secretly agreed with them, Rudy submitted to having his beard shaved. It had, he admitted later, caused him a good deal of discomfort anyway.

It was almost two years since the couple had bought their house on Whitley Heights and now they were to have their first opportunity to live in it.

Several tons of furniture had been dispatched there in the intervening period and most of it was now found to be totally unsuitable. Only the best items were kept, including a toilet seat trimmed with real gold, and the rest was sent off to be auctioned, at a fraction of its original cost, or placed in storage.

That was, in itself, a serious financial blow, but Natacha, far from being satisfied with her new home, complained that it was much too small, and demanded that Valentino find something grander and more appropriate to their needs and status.

Ullman, with dire warnings of an imminent financial crisis, managed to calm her with promises that he would discreetly begin a search for something more suitable. Apart from this one complaint, she seemed to be making a genuine effort to please her husband during the first months after their return to Hollywood.

Her present to him that Christmas was to become one of the most talked-about gifts, from any woman to any man, since the days of Mark Antony and Cleopatra.

She designed the present herself and sent their ex-cop bodyguard-cum-handyman, Luther Mahoney, to Tiffany's with the drawings. Meanwhile, Valentino was planning his own surprise. Recalling how much she had admired a diamond-studded locket watch at the time of their engagement, he asked George Ullman to visit the jewellers and, if it were still for sale, buy it.

At 6.00am on Christmas morning, Natacha phoned Ullman and invited him to drive immediately round to the house with his wife and their six-year-old son, Danny. When they arrived, Natacha was waiting outside and kept them talking until a shout came from inside that all was ready. Valentino met them in the hall and led them through to the living room where, covering the entire black marble floor, was a network of railroad tracks, tunnels, houses, electric switches, rail and passenger cars, platforms and level crossings. It was laid out like the main rail terminal of a large city and had cost Valentino a small fortune. It was, he said, a present for Daniel in appreciation of the work Ullman had done for Natacha and himself.

Natacha revealed that he had spent the entire night assembling the set, and caught a cold sitting on the bare marble floor. But Daniel's happiness in operating the giant layout more than compensated for all his efforts, and Rudy, she chided, had enjoyed himself putting the terminal together almost as much as in presenting it.

Fortunately, there had been something for him to do, she confided to Ullman, because they had quarrelled furiously on Christmas Eve and had barely spoken to each other until his family arrived.

Any lingering resentments from the quarrel were quickly dispelled when Natacha produced her special gift for her husband – a platinum slave bracelet, which she solemnly placed on Rudy's wrist. Recognising the symbolism of it, he took Natacha in his arms and kissed her passionately, oblivious to the embarrassed stares of the Ullmans. Declaring his slavery to her beauty and devotion, Valentino swore that he would never remove the bracelet.

Though it later aroused heated controversy among his fans, and a sneering attack in the press, he never went back on this promise.

Then it was Valentino's turn to present his gift to her. When Natacha opened the white velvet case and saw the jewel he had bought her, she hurled herself back into his arms.

For the remainder of their married life, she rarely removed it from her wrist.

The weeks that followed were among the happiest Valentino could remember. He was in peak condition, and rarely arrived on the set of *Cobra* later than 6.00am. The prizefight scenes in the picture enabled him to show off his physique, and he was overwhelmed when Williams arranged for the world heavyweight boxing champion Jack Dempsey to act as technical adviser and give him boxing lessons. After one of their regular sparring sessions, Dempsey joked that if Valentino ever decided to quit acting and turn to boxing, professional fighters would be in for a tough time.

'He was a hard fella,' said Dempsey. 'He could hand them out all right, and take them if he had to. I heard rumours that he was a homosexual – but that wasn't true. He was one of the most macho masculine men I ever met, in or out of the ring.'

Playing the part of an Italian count, and with Natacha absent from the set, Valentino could be himself for the first time on film. After his early-morning bouts at the studio with sparring partner Gene Delment, who was appearing frequently at the American Legion Stadium in Hollywood, he would drive himself home in his high-powered Voisin, and reappear an hour later after breakfasting.

Cheering news then came from George Ullman, who had discovered a Mediterranean-style house in Bella Drive, overlooking Beverly Hills, which met with Natacha's approval and, with a little juggling, fell within a price bracket they could cope with.

The gardens – eight and three-tenths acres of scenic hilltop – were beautifully landscaped with nearly fifty trees, mostly Italian Cypress, and many rare European and Oriental shrubs. The house, an Italian-cum-Spanish stucco type, with a terracotta-tiled roof, was constructed on two levels. The 16 rooms included three master bedrooms, three bathrooms, servants' room, wardrobe room, film laboratory and laundry room on the lower level, and on the upper level a library, small office, large living room, dining room, kitchen, cook's and butler's pantries, a servants' ante room and a large reception room with adjoining cloakroom and washroom. There was a garage for four cars, with six rooms above it as servants' quarters, stables large enough to accommodate four horses and kennels for 12 dogs next to the groom's quarters. The house, built the previous year, was going for $175,000, including undeveloped land adjoining the property.

Joseph Schenck agreed to stand behind the purchase and Ullman obtained the deeds. In honour of Natacha's film, declared Rudolph, they would rename the house Falcon's Lair. But Natacha was not impressed. After an idyllic few weeks, she had reverted to form and the couple's quarrels became increasingly vicious. Friends who had taken to calling at the Whitley Heights house stopped coming. They could no longer face the embarrassment of witnessing Valentino enduring his wife's violent, destructive tirades. She questioned his prowess as an actor, an artist and as a lover. He was, she accused, too spineless to fight for decent roles in decent pictures. He was a fool with his talent, with his money and with his choice of friends, who, she rightly claimed, loathed her.

People at the studio noticed a dramatic change in the star. He no longer arrived each day relaxed and friendly and eager for work. Now he seemed morose and disinterested and spent most of his time, when off the set, locked in his dressing-room, alone. His moodiness quickly began to affect the other members of the cast, and even the technicians found the new ambience dispiriting.

Valentino took to meeting his friends away from the house. 'It was a nightmare,' he confided. Natacha was one shrew who was not going to be tamed by him or anyone else. Making love to her was no longer an antidote to her persistent goading and criticism as she rejected any form of physical contact. They were no longer living as man and wife, he admitted dejectedly.

Many details of their quarrels were inevitably repeated, and just as inevitably ended up in the gossip columns. Did the slave bracelet force him to accept all Madame Valentino's outbursts without retaliation, asked one columnist. But this only made him more defensive of his wife in public, while making her more bitter towards him and his friends, whom she now barred from the house, not appearing to notice that they had voluntarily stopped visiting.

Adding to Valentino's misery were reports from the cutting-room that they had a visual disaster on their hands. The chief cameraman had quit early in the production and the second cameraman had failed to adapt to the same style. Joe Henaberry, who had managed to salvage a reasonably finished product from A Sainted Devil, had failed to come through with Cobra. Nita Naldi and Valentino played their roles as though half asleep, and the only time the great lover came to life was in the boxing sequences. Natacha's insistence on changes in the story had also removed what little plot existed. It was, in Hollywood parlance, a turkey.

Depressed by this news, and yearning for a less stormy matrimonial state of affairs, Valentino insisted that Natacha accompany him to Palm Springs for a short holiday away from the studios, their friends and the snipers on the gossip columns. He had often talked of the time babies would be in his home, and now he believed the one certain road to her heart, the condition that would soften her temper, turn her frowns to smiles and make him welcome again in her bed, was motherhood.

Natacha was dismayed. 'How can we have children when you are living the kind of life you do?' she snapped. 'I will start having babies when you stop being an actor. Not until. It's nonsense to think of starting a family when we are in this abnormal profession.'

Valentino was saved from having to answer by a telephone call from George Ullman in Hollywood. JD Williams had disowned them. With hefty criticism of his star, whom he claimed showed a distinct lack of manliness in facing up to his wife, he had announced the liquidation of Ritz-Carlton. Pre-production costs of *The Hooded Falcon* had been written off as a total loss and Williams was going out of picture making. What could have been a prosperous and lasting partnership between Valentino and the studio had been ruined by their irresponsible behaviour.

Chastened, Valentino rushed back to Hollywood for a meeting with his business manager. Natacha went, too, and immediately began to denounce the Ritz-Carlton syndicate, but Ullman cut her off brusquely. Perhaps, he reminded her, a little less of her voice and interference in the past might have placed her husband in a much stronger position to deal with the studios.

But all was not lost. United Artists were prepared to sign a contract with Rudy that would bring him more than a million dollars a year. This, on condition that they agreed to one special clause – Natacha would not be permitted to have a voice in the selection of material, cast, design, staging or the employment of director and other technical assistants.

In fact, she would be allowed no official connection with any part of his pictures, and Joseph Schenck personally had said he would prefer it if Natacha did not even enter the studio gates.

A relative once described Natacha to her biographer Michael Morris, author of *Madam Valentino*, thus: 'Natacha had the mind of a man in the body of a woman. She saw herself as a man's equal, treated him as such, and had little sympathy for those women whose identity was overshadowed by their husbands' fame.'

It was a description which aptly described her at this crucial moment.

Natacha's face contorted. 'Rudy will never sign a contract like that,' she declared. 'He knows he is totally unable to perform unless I am there to advise him. No one understands him as I do. Who can choose the right material to further his career if I can have no hand in it? He's incapable of doing it himself.'

Valentino leapt to his feet and, taking his wife by the shoulders, pushed her down into her chair. 'You have cost me my friends and humiliated me in public,' he shouted. 'You have mocked my work and abused my talent. But this time I will take George's advice and do things my way. Your job is to have babies. My job is to make films. And that is what I am going to do.'

He turned to an astonished George Ullman and told him, 'Tell Mr Schenck I am prepared to sign a contract on those terms immediately.'

A hired assassin could not more effectively have killed their marriage.

NATACHA RAMBOVA, if nothing else, possessed a well-developed sense of timing and a well-honed ability to judge her husband's emotional moods and manipulate him accordingly. Valentino's taunt about her role in life being confined to breeding his heirs had, not surprisingly, in view of her reluctance to start a family, failed to strike an answering chord in her far-from-maternal breast.

But, with characteristic cunning, she waited until his own stepping-stone to future greatness – a signed contract with Schenck – had materialised before revealing her own formula for virtuosity in the motion picture industry. The crowning recognition of Valentino's talent as an actor barred her from any participation in his glorification, but did not instil in her any degree of enthusiasm. To Natacha, the ultimate narcissist, only one person's achievements mattered – her own.

Elated after his latest meeting with Schenck, Valentino returned to Whitley Heights bubbling with news of his first project for United Artists. The studio chief had revealed he was to star in *The Eagle*, a film adaptation of Alexander Pushkin's *Dubrovsky*. This costume role as a daring and amorous Russian Robin Hood, in the same mould as *The Sheik*, delighted Valentino. United Artists had also secured Vilma Banky, the blonde Hungarian beauty discovered by Sam Goldwyn in Budapest, to be his leading lady.

His inwardly-fuming wife, who had recently been living up to her old Hollywood nickname 'The Icicle', embraced him warmly and led him to a double settee, where a fresh drink – a glass of chilled white wine – was waiting for him on a side table. Her revealing gown and jewelled turban were further evidence of a well-rehearsed scenario, but the overjoyed

Rudolph was in too euphoric a mood to notice. Since Ullman's bombshell she had been frostily polite in public and ominously silent in private. This new mood, he thought, augured well for the future.

In his hand, he clutched a sheaf of cablegrams from the founding stars of United Artists – Charlie Chaplin, Mary Pickford, Douglas Fairbanks and Norma Talmadge – welcoming him to 'the team'. On top of everything else, he told her, instead of a dressing-room, he was being provided with a luxuriously-fitted bungalow, a personal chef and a dresser.

'At last, I've found someone who knows how to treat me as a star,' he told Natacha. 'This will be the greatest film I have ever made. It will make me a millionaire.' For, in addition to a salary of more than half a million dollars a year, United Artists had granted him 42 per cent of profits on his films.

'And I am to have no part of it?' asked Natacha.

Valentino stared at her, his guilt clearly written across his handsome features. 'But with this I can provide you with anything you want,' he said.

It was what she had been waiting for. Quickly, before his guilt evaporated, she outlined her own project. If she could not work with him, she would become an independent producer and make her own pictures. She would write the stories herself and direct stars like Nita Naldi and Nazimova, who would willingly support her project. Frantically, Valentino back-pedalled, suddenly aware of the silken and potentially bankrupting noose he had helped place around his own neck. But Natacha pressed home her advantage, using all the feminine wiles and persistent argument for which she was notorious. Her first film, she revealed, would be a satirical tale of the agonies suffered by women in the beauty parlour, to be called *What Price Beauty?*

Eventually, as she knew he must, Valentine yielded and instructed George Ullman to make $50,000 available to Natacha, who immediately signed Nita Naldi to star in her picture and doubled the cost of production. At least, Rudy told his manager, it kept her happy while he got on with the business of making *The Eagle.*

But separate careers, one still in the ascendancy and the other predestined for failure, did not provide the magical solution to their domestic problems that Valentino was seeking. From the time Natacha began making her own films, she became even more possessed by her passion to be a power in the motion picture world.

George Ullman commented later, 'When her dictatorship was taken from her, it was not long before her loyalty to Valentino, not only to his business interests, but to him as a wife, began to fail her. When she ceased to collaborate, she also failed to co-operate – in more ways than one.' It was a relationship that could only deteriorate.

By early August, Falcon's Lair was ready for occupation, but Natacha refused to make the move. She refused even to visit the house and deliberately made a point of being out with friends when Valentino came home to Whitley Heights. Her bad temper was partly due to her being unable to find a distributor for *What Price Beauty?* and, declaring that only on the east coast could she arrange for release of her picture, she informed Valentino that she was moving to New York.

Failing to dissuade her, he insisted that she take George Ullman to act as a business adviser, and on 13 August, a prophetically unlucky day to begin their separation, Valentino drove his wife to the station in their new Isotta-Fraschini. Crowds turned out to see the departure and press photographers pushed each other aside to snatch pictures of the couple's farewell kiss. No one knew it at the time, but it was to be their last. Natacha Rambova would never set eyes on Valentino again.

Looking sad and depressed, Valentino followed her on to the platform and, as the train pulled away, began walking, then running, alongside her compartment. Then he stood alone, waving, until the train disappeared around a curve in the track, and turned and walked slowly, head bowed, to his car.

Opposite Natacha, in the drawing room of their private suite, Ullman asked, 'Do you love Rudy?'

She shook her head. 'I don't know,' she whispered.

'Do you want to go back to him?' asked the concerned manager.

'I don't know,' she said again.

'Do you want a divorce and lose Rudy out of your life for ever?' he persisted.

'I don't know,' choked Natacha for a third time, and burst into tears.

Hardly had the couple separated than the press began hinting at a serious rift in their stormy marriage. Her statement to one newspaper that 'this marital vacation will be a good thing for us both' shocked Valentino. Desperately, he tried to reach her on the telephone, but there was no answer from her apartment. A frantic exchange of telegrams with George Ullman did nothing to ease his anxiety.

Natacha, Ullman reported, had asked him to find her a part in a picture, and he had secured a role in a film called, fittingly, *When Love Grows Cold*. Valentino countered newspaper speculation with a statement that Natacha had no intention of suing for divorce. Their separation, he said, was due to a difference in temperament.

'We have been happy together and may be again,' he announced. 'I am sorry that this had to happen, but we cannot always order our lives the way we would like to have them.'

It was during the filming of *The Eagle* that Valentino began doing his own stunts. One scene called for him to control a team of runaway horses, but they bolted and dragged him across rough ground for 100ft. He was scratched and badly bruised, but insisted on continuing with the shoot. His friends believed this devil-may-care attitude was the result of the split with Natacha. It was almost, said Kerry, as though having lost her he didn't give a damn any more.

To combat the sadness of the separation, Valentino sought solace and a cure for his enforced celibacy in the company of Vilma Banky, his co-star, and they began appearing regularly together in public at parties, film openings and society gatherings.

Rumours of a passionate love affair between the two stars of *The Eagle* were steadfastly denied by both Valentino and Miss Banky, but the newspapers gave the supposed romance considerable coverage, which did not find favour with Natacha, who by this time was in France, visiting her mother and buying clothes for her forthcoming film.

Newspapers also carried the story that Imre Lukatz, the Hungarian nobleman to whom Vilma Banky had been engaged before leaving her homeland for America, had threatened to kill the great lover if they ever came face to face. 'Better deny it, darling,' Vilma advised Valentino, 'because he's quite capable of killing us both!'

Another sneering statement from Natacha brought a comment from her husband that she could not appear in pictures and be his wife at the same time. She must choose which she preferred. He did not know if they would be reconciled or divorced, but she could not return as his wife if she wished to pursue a career. 'If she wants her freedom or wants to be a star in pictures – all right. She understood that before she left here.'

In November, Valentino travelled to New York for the opening of *The Eagle* and was mobbed at every stop. In New York, he had to be provided with a five-strong bodyguard to walk the few yards from his hotel to a waiting limousine. Everywhere he appeared, vast crowds gathered to scream and cheer. His companion that night was Beulah Livingstone, a girl from the studio's New York publicity office.

Valentino had planned a quiet night out. A visit to the cinema to see Marilyn Miller's new picture, then dinner in a small restaurant and perhaps a nightclub.

But when he was spotted inside the cinema all their plans had to be scrapped. He was mobbed by autograph-hunters but, after ten minutes, the situation started to get out of hand as hundreds of women fought to reach him. The manager called for the police and he and several ushers managed to get the couple to the exit, but the crowd was now so dense that police couldn't reach them. As they struggled towards their limousine, dozens of women began tearing at his clothes and hair. By the time police reinforcements beat a way through to them and opened a path to the limousine, Valentino had lost his tie, cufflinks, scarf and handkerchief. One sleeve of his dinner jacket had been ripped away, together with a lapel, two pockets and all his buttons. His shirt was torn and there were several shades of lipstick on his cheeks and hands where women had kissed him. Beulah's dress was ripped and her wrap was shredded.

'Is it always like this?' she asked him tearfully. 'I was really scared.'

'I was, too,' he admitted. 'We have to take care these days,' he told her. 'I think they're trying to show me how much they love me. They don't realise how close they come to killing me.'

The next day, police leave was cancelled in that precinct and reserves were marshalled and detailed to travel with the star for the rest of his stay in the city. A police spokesman said they had never experienced anything like it before. 'Nobody else in the world produces this kind of hysteria in women,' he said.

On the day *The Eagle* opened at the Mark Strand Theatre, thousands of fans queued all day in the hope of getting seats but when the box office closed, several thousand were still waiting outside. On his arrival, Valentino was given a tumultuous reception which even that city had rarely witnessed and, when the film had been shown, the audience stamped and cheered until he appeared on stage.

The standing ovation he received after thanking his admirers for their kindness lasted several minutes and, eyes blinded by tears, he had to be helped from the stage. The critics were no less enthusiastic in their report of his performance, and *The Eagle* played everywhere to packed houses.

Joseph Schenck had proved that, with the right picture and the right director, and without the menacing and interfering presence of Natacha Rambova, Valentino was still the undisputed box-office champion.

On 10 November 1925, Valentino applied for American citizenship. On the same day, Natacha returned from Europe, but the two did not meet. She refused to comment on divorce rumours but, when asked if she considered a sheikh an ideal husband, she retorted, 'I can't say. I have never been married to a sheikh.'

Two days later, Valentino was told that his wife had applied, in Paris, for a divorce. He issued a statement saying he would not contest her action. He intended to defer to his wife's wishes in the matter. 'It is no longer a question of love, but of pride,' he said. 'She wanted to isolate me as much as possible. That was her nature.'

On 14 November as Valentino departed for Britain and the European première of *The Eagle* in London, Natacha told reporters that it was still her intention to have a career. If her husband wanted a housewife, she said, he would have to look again. Observers thought she had seriously misjudged her husband's reaction to the threat of divorce, but if she was disappointed at his not rushing to her side and begging for another chance, she was too experienced a hand in the game of marital fencing to let it show.

A S HE BOARDED the *Leviathan* to sail, once more, from America to England, a grim and unsmiling Valentino remembered the honeymoon voyage he had made with Natacha, just two years before, when it seemed that nothing could mar their idyllic existence. 'Now that is all over,' he told journalists who saw him off and reported how sad he appeared.

When he arrived in Britain, on a dull and depressing November day that matched his mood, he switched on his professional brave face. 'Your dull London weather is a welcome change from California's perpetual sunshine,' he said. 'Pleasing as the sun is, you can get a bit weary of him, and London does you good as a change.'

Valentino was very concerned that the British public should never believe the image of him, presented by certain magazines, as a smooth lounge lizard, lying around smoking scented cigarettes and oozing the irresistible attraction of a carefully-nurtured hot-house plant. 'I know,' he told pressmen, 'that I am thought to be largely an indoor man. But, actually, I don't suppose anybody lives more out of doors than I do.'

It was a substantial claim, which Rudy was only too willing to back up. 'I have just bought a new home further out of Hollywood – which is becoming slightly overbuilt – and there are five or six acres around it, in which I have arranged a fine big ring. I go for a gallop in it about five o'clock every morning. I keep five horses, one of which is specially trained and pampered for film work. Then I do a good deal of fencing and boxing.

'Recently, I have been learning from Jack Dempsey some of his most effective punches. The learning was slightly dangerous at times, but I survived.'

What he chose not to reveal to them was that he was suffering from regular and debilitating stomach pains, but refused to see a doctor. His preferred treatment was bicarbonate of soda which he swallowed almost by the handful.

Action Man needed all his skills for survival a few days later when he turned up for the opening of *The Eagle* at the Marble Arch Pavilion. For hours before the première, thousands of women and girls had besieged the cinema, struggling with police and haggling with touts, who were asking more than £5 for tickets and blocking the entrance to those lucky enough to have been invited.

It was just as bad as New York! When Valentino arrived, the severely-tested police could cope no longer. Screaming women broke through the cordon and surrounded the star, grabbing at his coat, his arms, his hair. Those who could not get near shrieked his name again and again in a chilling, monotonous litany. Others, clambering to get a better view, pulled down advertisement boards, the glass of which shattered and broke.

With police shoving and pulling hysterical girls away from him, Valentino shouldered his way into the cinema, where attendants struggled to close the doors against a surging mass battling to keep them open.

Inside, and safely installed in a box usually reserved for royalty, a shaken Valentino was asked to address the audience. 'See if they like the film first,' he said, and they did, cheering and applauding every time he appeared on the screen.

Afterwards, to get to the stage without being mobbed by the crowds who still surged round every doorway, he reverted to his action man role, following a lamp-carrying attendant up a flight of stairs, across the cinema roof, down an iron ladder, back into the building, down more stairs, through a concrete cellar under the stage ... and eventually into the limelight. The audience went wild as he appeared on stage, immaculate in evening dress, even after the mobbing outside and all his exertions.

As he held up his hands for silence, the spotlights flashed on that slave bracelet they'd all read about, and the screams went a few decibels higher.

'My last picture,' he tried to say above the noise, 'was not such a very good one ...'

'No, no, Rudy,' they yelled. Middle-aged ladies and smartly-dressed gay young things joined over-excited schoolgirls in the chorus of protest. 'No, no, Rudy!'

'But now,' he added, with ludicrous understatement, 'I think I have won back a place in your hearts.'

It was too much. 'Yes, yes!' they screamed, 'Oh yes, Rudy, yes!'

And then he was gone, slipping out of a side door to avoid the mob, many of whom would wait until long after midnight, believing that he wouldn't go without saying goodbye to them, somehow, personally.

As he left, one intrepid reporter stuck close to him to ask a last, though often-posed question: 'What is your secret? How do you do this to women?'

'I don't know,' he said. 'This is a matter-of-fact age and everyone is starving for romance. I suppose they like me because I bring that romance into their lives for a few moments.'

For a man from whose life the romance had so recently gone, it was a curiously apposite remark.

Shortly afterwards, he was in Paris, and the French capital noted that one thing had not been changed by his separation from Natacha – his spending. He entertained in both London and Paris on a lavish scale, and the bills forwarded to Ullman in America were enormous, prompting him to speed urgent cables to Valentino advising him that he was again running seriously into debt.

The incident which caused Ullman and the United Artists hierarchy most concern, and which sent shivers of dread speeding up their spines, also occurred in Paris. It ended in fiasco, but might easily have robbed his manager and studio of their biggest earner.

Valentino was leaving his hotel one evening when he was confronted by a well-dressed stranger, who introduced himself as the Baron Imre Lukatz, the Hungarian millionaire who had fallen in love with Vilma Banky, and who had threatened to kill the great lover on sight. Faced with the man he had publicly declared to be his arch enemy, the Baron began to scream abuse, and launched a two-fisted attack on the actor. Valentino responded with an uppercut which would have earned fulsome praise from his friend Jack Dempsey and deposited the Hungarian on his back. By this time thoroughly roused, Valentino challenged the Baron to a duel, which was accepted.

The Baron specified swords and, after appointing seconds, the two men agreed to meet at dawn the following morning in the Bois de Boulogne.

Accompanied by his seconds, Valentino was the first to arrive. The Baron turned up 20 minutes late, minus his sword, and immediately offered his apologies. He had heard, he said, that Valentino's relationship with Miss Banky had been confined to the screen. He recognised him as a man of honour and begged his forgiveness.

Greatly relieved, for he also had been having second thoughts, Valentino shook the Baron warmly by the hand, declared that honour had been satisfied and walked arm in arm with him to their waiting limousines.

A month later, before the Tribunal of the Seine, with neither party present, the French judges heard Natacha's plea for divorce. In evidence, it was stated that for two years, Monsieur Guglielmi had failed to provide support for his wife. The three judges deliberated briefly and ordered the decree granted.

The same day, Valentino boarded his favourite transatlantic liner, the *Leviathan*, at Cherbourg and set sail for New York, once again a single man.

WITH HIS HAIR slightly thinning at the temples and two disastrous marriages behind him, Rudolph Valentino once again became the most eligible man in America. His reputation as the great lover might have been based on celluloid evidence, but there were millions of women throughout the world who would have willingly sacrificed everything for just one hour in his arms.

Of all those women, only a handful had the opportunity to meet him and press their suit in person, and one of these was Pola Negri. Tempestuous, passionate, volcanic, hot-blooded and hot-tempered, she wanted Rudy in a very basic and physical way, and made no secret about her earthy ambitions. 'Once Rudy has experienced my love,' declared the tigerish Polish actress – who, like Natacha Rambova, had started out as a ballerina – 'he will forget about all other women. I am ready when he is.'

Valentino read of her boast with amusement, but was certainly not averse to using this means of exorcising the ghost of Natacha. He had ordered George Ullman to get rid of everything in Falcon's Lair that could remind him of his second wife. What better than a much-publicised and light-hearted romance to smooth over any lingering doubts in people's minds that he regretted the departure of Natacha? The fans were demanding a romance. They didn't like to see the great lover they worshiped without a suitable Venus in his arms.

He had briefly become involved in a hot-blooded affair with Nita Naldi, who invariably registered the supreme moment in their lovemaking with extremely loud and dramatic vocal accompaniment.

One of the few places he could take her, without worrying about the reaction her joyful screams were having on sharp-eared neighbours, was the cabin of his motor cruiser, moored out at sea. Her vocal fireworks at first flattered and amused him, but he quickly tired of having to head out to sea whenever he felt the urge to make love.

Later, he came to regret deeply the affair with Nita when the one-time friend of Natacha's began spreading vicious rumours among the Hollywood set that his second wife had arranged three abortions during their marriage, rather than have a child forcing her to abandon her career. Valentino never believed her stories, which were given much credence in other quarters, and denounced Nita as a vindictive and treacherous liar.

It was after the Naldi affair that Valentino turned his attention to Pola Negri, the $10,000-a-week star who had been described by one Hungarian playwright, Ernest Vajda, as 'the greatest actress of our time'.

Pola, who was often seen walking her pet panther on a leash in Hollywood, was herself sensuously feline and stalked Valentino with the guile and dedication of a trained seductress. The woman who claimed to have captured the heart of Chaplin, and worn his engagement ring, was this time looking for a more permanent union. Marriage was what she had in mind and she openly announced her intention of leading Valentino up the aisle.

The woman chosen as go-between to arrange the first meeting of the Hollywood couple was Marion Davis. On several occasions, she invited the pair of them to her home, but each time Pola would telephone and make an excuse for not being there. Fully aware that these tactics were designed to arouse his curiosity, Valentino played the game, the humour and tolerance of his younger days now fully restored.

Attempting to bring them face to face became an amusement which half the Hollywood community indulged in, but it was, as predicted, Marion Davis who finally brought them together. Valentino did not take his eyes off Pola as he bent to kiss her hand. She bowed her head in confusion. No director could have wrung a finer performance from either star.

Later, Pola said she found him handsome, artless and desperately sincere, though completely lacking the intense sexuality that dominated his screen personality.

There was a look of unhappiness in his dark eyes, she said, that appealed more to the maternal than the amorous. His true character, she believed, had come across in *Blood and Sand* when, in the magnificent matador costume, he was rather like a vulnerable child all decked out in fancy dress.

Marion Davis winked at Pola as the couple parted and said teasingly to Valentino, 'You've got your wish. Maybe now you'll stop hounding me.' As they walked away, laughing, she signalled to the orchestra who struck up a popular tango, 'La Comparasita', and the newly introduced couple began to dance.

'Call it fatalism,' Pola said afterwards, 'but from our very first meeting, I knew this man either had to destroy my life or so irrevocably alter its course that it would never again be the same. I knew it, and waved it away. I had met someone acknowledged to be the world's most desirable man, and I desired him. That was all. The rest was no more than romantic gibberish, probably inspired by the indefinite conclusions of that first encounter.'

The next time the couple met was at the Biltmore Restaurant. Pola was throwing a dinner party for Michael

Arlen and Valentino was hosting a party at a nearby table. The fiery, volatile actress tried hard to concentrate on her guests but found it impossible to keep her eyes from straying across to the handsome profile just a dozen feet away. The Italian appeared not to have noticed her, but suddenly Pola felt a hand on her shoulder and, turning, looked up into Rudy's smiling face.

I'd like you to dance with me,' he said.

For Pola, there was no resisting, she confessed afterwards. Almost as though in a trance, she glided into his arms and was whirled across the room. Just the sensation of his voice breathing in her ear caused tremors of sensuality to surge through her whole body, she said.

'I must see you alone,' said Valentino. 'Get rid of your guests and I'll take you home.'

Pola simply nodded. There was no question of wanting to avoid the inevitable outcome of this move. That night, Pola became – several times over, she later boasted – qualified to discount any rumours that Valentino's two bizarre marriages had reduced him to near impotency.

Sated with love, the naked couple lay on the bed in the master suite at Pola's beautiful Beverly Drive mansion, talking properly to each other for the first time. Their urgent need for each other's bodies, Pola told friends gleefully, meant that the things that are normally said before lovemaking had to be said afterwards.

From that moment, Pola became Valentino's almost constant companion. He was her escort at all the main parties, balls and premières, and Pola was a regular overnight guest at Falcon's Lair. Alberto, Valentino's brother, who was making his first visit to America and Hollywood with his family at the star's expense, was also a guest at the house on Bella Drive, and did not approve of this immoral relationship being conducted so openly. But Rudy laughingly explained that he was a single man again, and this was how a single man behaved among the Golden People of Hollywood. The great lover, he said, was simply trying to live up to his reputation.

That reputation was due to be even further enhanced by his next project for United Artists. For Joseph Schenck, underlining his skill as a business man and his ability to judge the right film vehicle for the superstar, had purchased the screen rights to Edith Hull's new novel, *The Sons of the Sheik*. One of the twin sons would be written out and Valentino would portray the other.

The film, Ullman predicted jubilantly, would earn for Valentino more than $1 million. Inspired by this prospect, Rudy startled United Artists chiefs by suggesting he play a double role. That of the son and also of the original sheikh, Ahmed Ben Hassan, the part that had first launched him as the most romantic figure in cinema history.

Adding to his excitement was the news that George Fitzmaurice was at last to direct him in a picture, and 'his good chum' Vilma Banky was to be his co-star. Schenck had even secured Agnes Ayres to recreate her portrayal of Diana, the old sheikh's wife.

Valentino seemed to thrive on the hardship of filming in the Arizona and Californian deserts. He insisted on absolute realism in the filming of *The Son of the Sheik*, and although his fellow actors cursed the severity of sandstorms whipped up by the giant wind machines he insisted on using at full power, they thrilled with him at reports from the studio in Hollywood that the rushes were the best and most exciting ever processed.

This premature verdict was more than fully endorsed when the picture was premièred at Grauman's Million Dollar Theatre in Los Angeles. A huge gathering of stars, including the original big four with United Artists, and all Valentino's friends, were part of the packed audience which cheered, clapped and stamped their feet in approval and provided him with the greatest ovation ever received by a star on 'home territory'.

Unencumbered by the embarrassing presence of Natacha, Valentino was now a welcome visitor to the most exclusive homes on the West Coast, and if Pola Negri sometimes irritated with her inevitable talk of marriage, she was still an amusing, passionate and uncomplicated companion. His friends were now free to come and go in his home as they pleased. Soon, he would be a wealthy man.

Following completion of *The Son of the Sheik*, Valentino once more, inexplicably, became moody and unpredictable. Ullman put it down to the constant pestering he received from fans. Douglas Gerrard blamed it on the difficulty he was having sleeping, and Schenck claimed it was the natural, post-production depression from which most stars suffered. Only Paul Ivano and Luther Mahoney recognised that he was pining for Natacha. She may have come close to destroying his career, but he still loved her – and missed her desperately.

Whatever the reason, Valentino was not happy and this manifested itself in the way he drove his fast and expensive motor cars.

Soon, his driving, always reckless but now dangerously so, began to concern his friends, who refused to ride with him if he was behind the wheel. Douglas Gerrard agreed to accompany him to San Francisco in his Isotta-Fraschini limousine, only after Rudy hired a chauffeur to do the driving. But on the return trip, Valentino took over the wheel, after promising Gerrard he would keep to a reasonable speed. Inevitably, the speedometer inched higher, despite Gerrard's objections, and a few miles after San Luis Obispo the big limousine, going much too fast, skidded completely across the wet highway and careered over the parallel railroad tracks – causing the driver of an approaching Southern Pacific locomotive immediately to apply his brakes – and struck a telegraph pole. Valentino and Gerrard were uninjured though badly shaken, but both the chauffeur and valet were cut and bruised and required hospital treatment. All four men vere rushed to the nearest hospital in a police car and the star was treated for shock.

In need of treatment for shock, too, were Ullman and Joseph Schenck when they heard the details of the accident. If the hottest box-office property in Hollywood could not look after himself, argued Schenck, then he must be taken care of. He summoned the actor to his office and forbade him to make further driving trips outside the city and never to drive at more than fifty miles an hour.

Had the studio boss witnessed a scene at Pola Negri's Beverly Drive home a few nights later, he would have had far more cause for concern. Sitting with her in her living room, Rudy suddenly became very pale, got up and stumbled through the French windows leading to the garden. Alarmed, the actress hurried after him and found him doubled up in pain on a garden chair.

When she asked what was troubling him, he replied, 'It's nothing. It will soon pass. I didn't want you to see me like this. I feel so ashamed of myself.'

Gradually, his colour returned and he lit a cigarette, explaining to Pola that he was taking medication because he feared he was going bald, and that this seemed to be upsetting the rest of his body. With his natural fear of doctors he had not consulted an expert, but was convinced the attacks would cease if he gave up the patent baldness cure, which he had obtained from a local quack.

To cover his embarrassment, Valentino invited Pola to view his new motor yacht and join him on a trip to Catalina. This new toy, on which he had entertained the highly vocal Miss Naldi, was seen by his friends as great therapy for the actor. He did everything aboard for himself – cleaning, polishing, even cooking the meals. In common with most big eaters he was an excellent cook and Ullman once proposed he be awarded the diamond belt for cooking spaghetti.

Valentino also called up June Mathis. Their last meeting had been a harrowing one, for Natacha had accused June of sabotaging *The Hooded Falcon* by delaying production of a suitable script. Rudy met his old friend and the main architect of his career at a quiet restaurant in Hollywood and they spent hours together, chatting over his early days as a star and the making of *The Four Horsemen*. This eagerness to see June Mathis again and re-establish their former relationship before leaving for the East to publicise *The Son of the Sheik* suggested to some a pre-knowledge that it was the last opportunity he would have to heal the rift.

But, at the time, she was happy to find that Valentino seemed to have recovered all his old gaiety and irreverent humour, and even joked that, by dining with him so intimately, June seriously risked having her eyes scratched out by the notoriously jealous Pola, or featuring in the gutter press as his latest conquest.

A week later, early in July, Valentino left Hollywood by train for New York, intending to change trains in Chicago. As usual, a large crowd gathered at the station in Los Angeles to see him off. Among them was Pola Negri. As Valentino himself had done when saying farewell to Natacha at this same station, Pola violated the superstition of watching a loved one out of sight. She stood on the platform waving and shouting after Rudy, who hung from the back of the observation car, ignoring the efforts of the guard to close the door. He waved his hand until a curve in the track carried him from her sight.

It was the last time Pola Negri saw Rudolph Valentino alive.

27

FOR DAYS NOW, an oppressive, sweltering heat had hung heavily over the metropolis, leaving the citizenry lethargic, surly, short-tempered and highly susceptible to the offbeat or whimsical type of newspaper story which this annual period, known as the silly season, threw up.

It was just such a story, penned by an anonymous columnist, which was to create waves of laughter – predominantly male sniggers – and generally damaging innuendo throughout the country, and which would introduce a new word for effeminacy – 'poof' – into the English language. It would also haunt Rudolph Valentino for the rest of what was left of his life.

The reporter who was responsible stumbled across the story when he went to the toilet in one of Chicago's latest ballrooms. The management had installed a slot-machine in the men's room, which dispensed talcum powder, via pink powder puffs, for those customers wanting to perfume themselves for the night of love and lust which, hopefully, lay ahead.

It might, very easily, have been killed on a copy-editor's spike or, with judgement, have found its rightful place as an inconsequential paragraph. But Chicago in those days – as the late, great and eminently praiseworthy Ben Hecht (1894–1961) was later to recall with wit and stylish candour – was a frontier town with rich pickings for journalists. And this one was too good to lose.

The story was seized upon by a *Chicago Tribune* editorial writer, who proceeded to put his tongue very firmly in his cheek and humorously protest that Rudolph Valentino was solely responsible for the 'effeminisation of the All-American Male'.

He went at his task, and his typewriter, with unsuppressed glee, which expressed itself in the finished product:

A new public ballroom was opened on the north-side a few days ago, a truly handsome place and apparently well run. The pleasant impression lasts until one steps into the men's washroom and finds there, on the wall, a contraption of glass tubes and levers and a slot for the insertion of a coin. The glass tubes contain a fluffy pink solid, and beneath them one reads an amazing legend which runs something like this: 'Insert coin. Hold personal puff beneath the tube. Then pull the lever.'

A powder-vending machine! In a men's washroom!

The writer was by now boggling wide-eyed over the discovery.

Homo Americanus! Why didn't someone quietly drown Rudolph Guglielmi, alias Valentino, years ago?

And was the pink powder machine pulled from the wall or ignored? It was not. It was used. We personally saw two 'men' step up, insert a coin, hold a kerchief beneath the spout, pull the lever, then take the pretty pink stuff and put it on their cheeks in front of the mirror.

Another member of this department, one of the most benevolent men on earth, burst raging into this office the other day because he had seen a young 'man' combing his pomaded hair in the elevator. But we claim our pink powder story beats this all hollow.

What had all this to do with Valentino? The *Tribune* man was coming to that, finally, and somewhat tortuously:

Is this degeneration into effeminacy a cognate reaction with pacifism to the virilities and realities of the war? Are pink powder and parlour pinks in any way related? How does one reconcile masculine cosmetics, sheikhs, floppy pants and slave bracelets with a disregard for law and an aptitude for crime more in keeping with the frontier of half-a-century ago than a twentieth-century metropolis?

It is a strange social phenomenon, and one that is running its course not only here in America but in Europe as well. Chicago may have its powder puffs; London has its dancing men and Paris its gigolos. Down with Decatur; up with Elinor Glyn. Hollywood is the national school of masculinity; Rudy, the beautiful gardener's boy, is the prototype of the American male. Hell's bells. Oh, Sugar.

The piece brought from the *Tribune*'s readers what the writer intended – a giggle. From Valentino, it brought a fury which he allowed to overwhelm him, and which elevated a piece of journalistic jokery to that dangerous area where questions of honour and principle, of manliness and courage, are mouthed and, worse still, meant.

He read the editorial with mounting anger as he breakfasted at the Blackstone Hotel in Chicago, where he was waiting to change trains on the way from San Francisco to New York.

And the cool, controlled, unflappable lover of the screen exploded in a flow of curses, in English and Italian, that would have stunned his more mature and matronly admirers into shocked silence.

Ullman urged him, 'Forget it. That sort of rubbish is not worth worrying about.'

But Valentino would not be calmed. His pride was hurt. All the publicity work on his image with those manly, bare-torso beefcake photographs might as well count for nothing. Now he was being blamed for the feminisation of the American male. He cursed and stormed and threatened. 'Who wrote it?' he demanded of reporters in the hotel. 'I'll go right to his office and show him who's a man.'

Instead, when his rage subsided sufficiently, Valentino chose, to him, the obvious course of defending his honour – and made the massive mistake of issuing a direct challenge, in the form of an open letter 'to the Man (?) who wrote the editorial headed "Pink Powder Puffs" in Sunday's *Tribune*'.

In the challenge, which the *Tribune*'s rival *Chicago Herald-Examiner* was only too happy to publish, Valentino came straight to the point. 'The above-mentioned editorial is at least the second scurrilous attack you have made upon me, my race, and my father's name,' he complained. 'You slur my Italian ancestry; you cast ridicule upon my Italian name; you cast doubt upon my manhood. I call you, in return, a contemptible coward, and to prove which of us is a better man, I challenge you to a personal test.'

Although Al Capone and his associates were currently shooting themselves and Chicago into headlines and history, Rudolph planned to play this one strictly by the rules. 'This is not a challenge to a duel in the generally accepted sense,' he explained. 'That would be illegal. But in Illinois, boxing is legal. So is wrestling. I therefore defy you to meet me in the boxing or wrestling arena to prove, in typically American fashion (for I am an American citizen), which of us is more a man.'

Neither, he emphasised, was this to be a stunt. 'I prefer this test of honour to be private, so that I may give you the beating you deserve, and because I want to make it absolutely plain that this challenge is not for purposes of publicity. I am handing copies of this to the newspapers simply because I doubt that anyone so cowardly as to write about me as you have would respond unless forced by the press to do so.'

Who he was so stoutly challenging, he did not care. 'I do not know who you are, or how big you are,' he declared. 'But this challenge stands if you are as big as Jack Dempsey. I will meet you immediately or give you time in which to prepare, for I assume that your muscles must be flabby and weak, judging by your cowardly mentality, and that you will have to replace the vitriol in your veins for red blood – if there be a place in such a body as yours for red blood and manly muscle.'

Having laid the ground rules, he concluded, 'I resent with every muscle of my body attacks upon my manhood and ancestry!

'Hoping I will have an opportunity to demonstrate to you that the wrist under a slave bracelet may snap a real fist into your sagging jaw, and that I may teach you respect of a man even though he happens to prefer to keep his face clean. I remain, with utter contempt, Rudolph Valentino.

'P.S. I will return to Chicago within ten days. You may send your answer to me in New York, care of United Artists Corp, 729 7th Avenue.'

The challenge was thrown down and immediately picked up by the press – notably by the *Tribune*'s powerful rival *Chicago*

Herald-Examiner, a William Randolph Hearst production which knew a good story when it wrote one.

The silly season saga grew out of all proportion and Valentino v the Writer became a buzzing, if not a burning, topic of conversation.

Back in New York, Valentino faced several situations which gave him the chance to prove his courage. He accepted them all without question, severely testing the nerve of Ullman who, quite naturally, did not want to see his star charge's health jeopardised unnecessarily.

First, Frank O'Neil, the *New York Evening Journal*'s boxing writer, called Ullman wanting to know if Valentino was the athlete his publicity made him out to be. 'Would he,' O'Neil asked, 'agree to a friendly bout between the two of us?'

Ullman hesitated. O'Neil was a big man and something of an expert boxer. But Valentino insisted on accepting and, in a brief but well-publicised scrap on the roof of the Ambassador Hotel, had the great satisfaction of sending at least one uppity gentleman of the press crashing to his knees on the gravel-surfaced 'ring'.

O'Neil, who'd managed to get a few, well-intended slaps at the screen's most famed features, was nevertheless well enough to announce to colleagues after the fight, 'That boy has a punch like the kick of a mule. I'd sure hate to have him sore at me.'

Valentino was delighted at the success of his public demonstration of the manly art. 'This will show them all that I'm no powder puff,' he said. He liked and admired boxers, and some of them were his friends.

He would, incidentally, have been proud to know that, down in Louisville, Kentucky, he had a future fan in Odessa

Lee O'Grady who would give birth to one of the world's greatest boxers. When her first-born weighed in at 6lb 7oz on 17 January 1942, Odessa would name the pretty little boy after his father, who himself was named after a former American Ambassador to the Court of St James's, an unsuccessful Vice-Presidential candidate and leading Southern abolitionist – Cassius Marcellus Clay. Her second son, who would also become a boxer, she would name Rudolph Valentino Clay.

A few days later, after seeing brother Alberto off to Paris aboard the *France*, Valentino turned up for the New York première of *The Son of the Sheik* at the Mark Strand Theatre, and walked into more trouble. All day, crowds had been gathering, waiting in the stifling hot streets to catch a glimpse of the film's hero, and police chiefs, fearing trouble, ordered a mounted patrol to the theatre to control the crowds. They cleared a path for Valentino to get into the theatre, where he made a short speech to an audience of sighing, adoring fans.

Getting out afterwards was not going to be so easy. Thousands of women lay in wait outside, every one of them eager to get their hands on their hero. Ullman, fearing for Valentino's well-being for the second time in a few days, whispered to him, 'Follow me,' and Rudy knew the drill. Suddenly, Ullman, with Valentino's hands on his shoulders, head-charged the crowd, running in roughly the direction of their waiting car. As they ran, Valentino heard again the sound of buttons being ripped from his coat, felt hands reach out to grab his pocket handkerchief, others snatching the hat from his head, and even the cufflinks from his shirt. The car's motor was running as they reached it and slammed the door, only partly shutting out the hysterical, agonised screams of women who had been so close and yet so far from the man they idolised.

In comparative safety, Rudy turned to Ullman. 'We made it,' he grinned.

Ullman wiped his brow. 'Only just,' he said. 'Do you reckon you'll ever get used to this?'

'No,' said Valentino emphatically. 'And I'd rather avoid any further practice if I can.'

Then, as the limousine began to pull away with a police escort, to their horror they saw a woman jump from the crowd and hurl herself on to the running board. Equally as quickly, she was dragged back by the mob and fell to the pavement with a sickening thud that could clearly be heard above the screams.

'Stop, for God's sake, stop!' Valentino yelled at the chauffeur. It was too late; the woman had already disappeared into the crowd, how badly hurt they could not know. Back at his hotel, Valentino insisted on telephoning the local police stations immediately. Had there been any reports of a woman being hurt in an auto accident? he asked. 'Nope, nothing reported,' he was told.

Relieved, and needing to relax after a hectic day, Valentino contacted, of all people, Jean Acker, and suggested that they and a few friends hit the town. He never offered a reason for seeing her after so many years, but their outing was to be a gossip columnist's dream.

He knew exactly the place to hit – Texas Guinan's, a hot, crowded, lavishly-furnished speakeasy run by the personable former actress Mary Louise Cecilia 'Tex' Guinan, to which film and theatre stars, politicians and millionaires flocked for wild parties and striptease shows and the honour of paying absurd prices for 'champagne', which tasted strangely like souped-up soda water.

You could get a genuine bottle of whisky for not much over $100 and Texas, who was frequently raided by police and those damn sneaky prohibition agents, thought it good value. 'There's a lot of talk,' she explained, 'about how I take the customers for all they've got. It's not as bad as that – even if there aren't any charity wards in my club. The boys come here to spend, and I'm not going to disappoint them. When they drink ginger ale in my place, they are drinking liquid platinum, and they like it.'

It was the place for the gregarious and generous, free-spending Valentino to be seen, and before they could contribute funds towards Tex's future happiness, Valentino and Jean were bombarded by reporters with the inevitable question, 'Is there a possibility that you two might get round to remarrying?'

Jean smiled through closed lips. Valentino gave the inevitable reply, 'We are good friends, and always will be.' Beyond that, he refused to comment.

It was enough to make the gossip columns the next day.

Inside, Tex Guinan bounded up to Valentino's party. 'Great to see you. Can I introduce Rahmin Bey?' The Indian fakir, then amazing audiences with his feats of magic, bowed low and addressed Valentino.

'Would you care,' he asked, 'to help me with a little experiment?'

Rudy shrugged. 'Sure, what is it?'

'With your permission,' smiled the mystic, 'I will thrust a needle through your cheek – without pain, and without drawing blood.'

Valentino agreed – it might help spread the word that he was frightened of no man or physical test. But George Ullman, who in the past few days had seen his best asset only too willingly expose himself to danger, brawl in public and get mobbed by over-eager fans, put his foot down at this little exercise. 'Don't be crazy,' he told Valentino. 'There just could be an accident. You can't do it.'

By now, all eyes were on the star. The audience was expecting something sensational, and Valentino was not going to disappoint them. He agreed that the needle should be put through his arm, stood up, stripped off his coat and rolled up his shirtsleeves. Then, with the room hushed and expectant, and Ullman looking on with mounting anxiety, Valentino watched in fascination as the magician thrust the long needle through his forearm, and withdrew it, without drawing blood and without pain.

The audience gasped and broke into applause. Valentino smiled, rolled down his shirtsleeve and pulled on his coat. And Ullman, fussing like a mother-hen that the needle might not be clean and fearing an infection, called a waiter to bring alcohol to clean the affected area.

With prices like Tex's, it was highly expensive preventative medicine.

It had felt good being with Jean Acker, Valentino told Ullman. He had kissed her cheek when they said goodbye. It was the last time Jean saw Valentino alive.

It was, during his last days, the 'powder puff' affair which was his main preoccupation. He mentioned it increasingly to Ullman and to friends. He could not wait to get back to Chicago and, when he did, the reporters' questions were predictable. 'Have you received a reply to your challenge?'

'Who is your opponent?' 'When will the confrontation be?' He answered them all with a statement which brought the farce to an anti-climactic conclusion.

'It is evident you cannot make a coward fight, any more than you can draw blood from a turnip,' he said. And added, with heavy sarcasm, 'The heroic silence of the writer who chose to attack me without provocation in the *Chicago Tribune* leaves no doubt as to the total absence of manliness in his whole make-up. I feel I have been vindicated because I consider his silence is a tacit retraction and an admission I am forced to accept, even though it is not entirely to my liking.'

Still playing fair, he added a tribute. 'The newspaper men and women whom it has been my privilege to know briefly, or for a long time, have been absolutely fair, and so loyal to their profession and their publications that I need hardly say how conspicuous is this exception to the newspaper profession.'

And that, it seemed, was that. It should have been. But the whole ludicrous affair would not lie low. It preyed on his mind and continued to worry him. The insult did not lose its sting, and Valentino kept wondering if he'd played the whole scenario properly or if, by issuing his challenge, he had become the only possible loser by bringing himself into more ridicule. He should, perhaps, have gone for advice to one of those journalists. Maybe it was not too late.

The journalist he selected was Henry Louis Mencken – already a legend among newspapermen – who was puzzled when told Valentino wanted to see him. They had never met before. He had never written about him or even seen one of his films. But Valentino, reading a piece by Mencken, had judged him a shrewd observer, and wanted his advice on the problem that was bedevilling him. Mencken was pleased to oblige.

They met in a New York hotel as the heatwave continued, and Mencken's first impression of the star, when they both took off their jackets, was how absurd Valentino's extraordinarily wide braces looked on such a slim young man – especially on a hot summer night.

For an hour they suffered the heat, mopping their faces with their handkerchiefs, the napkins, the corners of the tablecloth, and towels brought by a waiter. It was only when a thunderstorm broke that they began to breathe properly, and Valentino poured out his troubles. Mencken listened patiently, but could offer no consolation. The damage, he said, had been done. Valentino should have shrugged off the Chicago journalist's jibe with a lofty snort – or perhaps, better still, a counter-jibe. He should have stayed away from the reporters.

But right now he felt insulted and ridiculed and there was nothing he could do about it, and so he should let the affair die a natural death.

'That's infamous,' Valentino protested.

'Nothing,' Mencken replied, 'is infamous that is not true. A man still has his inner integrity.'

They talked and sweated and seemed to get nowhere.

Then, Mencken recalled, in what was probably the shrewdest assessment ever made of Valentino's character, 'suddenly it dawned upon me – I was too dull or it was too hot for me to see it sooner – that what we were talking about was not really what we were talking about at all.

'I began to observe Valentino more closely. A curiously naïve and boyish young fellow, certainly not much beyond 30 and with a disarming air of inexperience.

'To my eye, at least, not handsome, but nevertheless, rather attractive.

'There was some obvious fineness in him; even his clothes were not precisely those of his horrible trade. He began by talking of his home, his people, his early youth.

'His words were simple and yet somehow very eloquent. I could still see the mime before me, but now and then, briefly and darkly, there was a flash of something else.

'That something else, I concluded, was what is commonly called, for want of a better name, a gentleman. In brief, Valentino's agony was the agony of a man of relatively civilised feelings thrown into a situation of intolerable vulgarity, destructive alike to his peace and to his dignity – nay, into a whole series of such situations.

'It was not just that trifling Chicago episode that was riding him; it was the whole grotesque futility of his life. Had he achieved, out of nothing, a vast and dizzy success? Then that success was hollow as well as vast – a colossal and preposterous nothing. Was he acclaimed by yelling multitudes? Then every time the multitudes yelled, he felt himself blushing inside.

'The old story of Diego Valdez once more, but with a new poignancy in it. Valdez, at all events, was High Admiral of Spain. But Valentino, with his touch of fineness in him – he had his commonness too, but there was that touch of fineness – Valentino was only the hero of the rabble.'

At first, Mencken judged, Valentino's situation must have only bewildered him. But now it was revolting him – and, worse, making him afraid. 'Here was a young man who was living daily the dream of millions of other young men. Here was one who was catnip to women. Here was one who had wealth and fame. And here was one who was very unhappy.'

28

IF HE WAS desperately unhappy, Rudolph Valentino was certainly not showing it. Back in New York, and thrilled with the success of the Chicago première of *The Son of the Sheik*, he hurled himself into a gruelling round of parties and enjoyment. 'I'm having the time of my life,' he told Ullman, as he turned night into day and played those days away.

Duty, in the form of promoting the new picture, occasionally called, and he travelled to Atlantic City to attend a showing of it at the Virginia Theatre. Afterwards, as a favour, he made another personal appearance at the Ritz-Carlton revue run by his old friend Gus Edwards, who presented him with a pair of boxing gloves. They might, Edwards suggested, be needed to thrash that *Chicago Tribune* writer.

Smiling, Valentino accepted the gift, but declined an invitation to dance with a girl from the revue. Edwards insisted, and eventually he agreed. But as the music began, and Valentino swept the girl across the stage, neither he, nor she, nor the audience, could know that this was his last tango.

After another *Son of the Sheik* opening in Brooklyn, he was free until 16 August, when he was due to make a personal appearance in Philadelphia, and he filled the days with fun and the nights with friends. He called Adolph Zukor and, over a friendly lunch, told him, 'I'm sorry about the studio trouble I made.'

Zukor shrugged, 'Forget it. In this business, if we can't disagree and then forget about it, we'll never get anywhere.' And then he added the words he would never be able to forget. 'You're young. Many good years are ahead of you.'

There was no reason to think otherwise. Shortly before, a doctor had passed Valentino as perfectly healthy, and only hermits or enclosed orders of nuns had avoided seeing at least one photograph of him at his keep-fit exercises. 'How beautiful! How strong!' oozed the caption-writer of Hearst's *New York Daily Mirror* – a close copy of its British namesake – under one picture of the semi-naked star, flexing his muscles all over page one.

For some time, though, he had suffered stomach pains, often acute, and friends had urged him at least to mention them to a doctor. 'Indigestion,' he said, and kept on taking only bicarbonate of soda to ease the pain while he continued eating his beloved Italian dishes, chain-smoking and living life to the full. Constantly, Ullman begged him to ease up, to relax more, sleep more. Valentino, as though bent on wringing the last minutes of pleasure from his free time, ignored him. His parties went on, and the pace began to tell.

George Ullman would always remember Saturday night of 14 August 1926. As Valentino prepared himself for yet another party, Ullman noticed that the colour in his face had changed. 'Come home early,' he suggested, 'and get some rest.' Another session of personal appearances, he reminded him, were starting the following week.

Valentino looked up, eyes ablaze. 'Rest?' he laughed. 'Why, I feel wonderful. I don't need rest.' And he left for the party.

It was being held in his honour at the apartment of one Barclay Warburton Jnr, and attended by 16 people. It began around 10.00pm and lasted until the early hours and was the last party Rudolph Valentino would ever attend. In the early hours of the morning he became ill, and turned down an invitation to go to a party in the apartment of actress Lenore Ulric. Still in pain, he was driven back to his hotel by the chauffeur, but no one thought to call a doctor.

The following day, shortly before noon, he collapsed in his bedroom at the Ambassador Hotel, where Ullman found him clutching his stomach, writhing and moaning in obvious agony.

He called doctors, who said that Valentino must be transferred immediately to New York's Polyclinic Hospital. There, at 6.00pm the same evening, he was operated on for acute appendicitis and a gastric ulcer. By 7.00pm the operation was over, and shortly after 10.00pm, when the effects of the anaesthetic had worn off, the patient opened his eyes and asked a doctor, 'Well, did I behave like a pink powder puff or like a man?'

The operation appeared, at first, to have been a complete success, and doctors said the ulcerous condition was more of a menace to his health than the appendicitis. During the next few days, the VIP patient, appearing to be on the mend, slept most of the time and was allowed visits only from Ullman.

Sitting up in bed, wearing white silk pyjamas, he told his manager, 'No, don't send for my brother. Just cable him and say I'm a little indisposed and will soon be all right. And wire Pola the same.' When Ullman said he wished it was he who was in the hospital bed, Valentino protested, 'Don't be silly. You have little children and family responsibilities, whereas I ...' His voice trailed off and he turned his face away.

Later he asked for a mirror and Ullman, not wanting him to see the tired, white face of an ill man, asked why. 'I just want to see what I look like when I'm sick,' said Valentino, 'so that if I ever have to play the part in pictures, I'll know how to put on the right make-up.'

He was thinking again of his films and his fans, and they were constantly thinking of him. From the time the news of his illness broke, crowds of women had besieged the hospital, hoping to see or just hear of their idol. An armed guard was put at his door, in case the more hysterical of them tried to rush to his bedside. There was little hope of that; even close friends were not allowed near and Jean Acker, distressed that she was refused permission to see him, had to send in instead a coverlet and pillows, with his name embroidered on them.

Cables and telegrams poured in from all over America and the world, and a special secretary was hired to look after them. Bouquet after bouquet of flowers arrived, along with other gifts, health cures, Bibles, words of advice and prayers and lots and lots of love and deep concern.

The patient, meanwhile, appeared to be making excellent progress. By the Thursday, he was reported to be 'in good spirits' and doctors, noting his courage and 'remarkable constitution', were confident that his recovery would be a complete one. Ullman cabled this news to both Pola Negri in Hollywood and Natacha Rambova in the south of France.

His fans outside were not so certain. When a rumour that he had died swept like wildfire through the country, thousands telephoned the hospital and extra staff were drafted in to man the switchboard.

'Is it true,' the callers hardly dared ask, 'about Rudy ...?'

'Mr Valentino,' intoned the operators, 'is alive and his condition is the same.'

'Thank God, thank you ...'

By Saturday, he was thinking about leaving hospital. When he woke up at 7.00am that morning, he told Ullman, 'I feel fine now. The pain is all gone and I can feel the place where they made the incision. By Monday I can have friends in, and by Wednesday I can go back to the hotel – taking the nurses, of course.'

His own bulletin on his condition more than worried the doctors who had held out high hopes for him. They made yet another thorough examination and consulted together for almost an hour. Their verdict: the cessation of pain Valentino had talked about was an exceedingly bad sign. Pleurisy had brought about a relapse, and had been followed by septoendocarditis, a poisoning of the wall of the heart.

The doctors considered every possibility open to them, including a blood transfusion. Edward Day, a hospital engineer, volunteered to give a pint of his blood, but it was decided that Valentino was too weak to be able to withstand the extra strain on his heart.

By early on Sunday morning, his fever had increased and his pulse was more rapid. Ullman, hating himself for fearing the worst but realising that Valentino might want a confessor, called Father Leonard, a priest who had come often to the hospital to ask about Valentino, and left him alone in the patient's room. Joseph Schenck and his wife Norma Talmadge, also contacted by Ullman, arrived at the bedside in the early evening, and later Frank Mennillo, a long-time Italian friend, talked to Valentino. 'Don't worry, Frank,' the actor whispered to him. 'I'm going to be well soon.'

After a quiet night, Valentino woke in great pain at 4.00am on Monday morning and was given a morphine injection to ease his suffering. Even then, he was convinced he would soon be fully recovered. Cheerfully, he asked Dr Howard D Meeker, 'Do you know the greatest thing I am looking forward to?'

The doctor asked, 'What is it?'

Valentino told him, 'The fishing review next month. I hope you have plenty of rods.'

He became irrational, talking mainly in Italian, but around 6.00am he recognised Ullman by his bedside and called him by his name, in a voice so much stronger than before that, for a moment, there was fresh hope. Then Valentino began talking again, in a rambling, irrational way, and all hope faded. 'Wasn't it an awful thing that we were lost in the woods last night?' he asked.

Ullman, unable to speak, smiled and stroked his hair.

'On the one hand,' Valentino continued, 'you don't appreciate the humour of that.'

'Sure I do, Rudy, sure I do,' murmured Ullman.

'On the other hand,' said Valentino, 'you don't seem to appreciate the seriousness of it, either ...'

The sun was rising. Ullman walked to the window to pull down the blind, but Valentino waved a hand and protested, 'Don't pull down the blinds. I want the sunlight to greet me.'

By 8.00am he had lapsed into a coma, opening his eyes occasionally when his name was called. By 10.00am Father Joseph Congedo, a priest who claimed to be from Valentino's home town of Castellaneta, had administered the Last Rites of the Holy Roman Catholic Church, although his alleged credentials were never confirmed.

By 11.00am, news of the star's critical condition had spread and the whole country, the *Los Angeles Record* reported, was 'waiting each word from his sick-room almost as it waits for a word from the sick-room of a President'. Crowds of men, women and children, including many Italians, gathered outside the hospital, waiting quietly, praying for a miracle they knew now would never come. Police, watching the crowd growing, were forced politely but firmly to move them on.

One last, desperate hope disappeared when a racing plane, flying from Detroit with a special antiseptic preparation for Valentino, had to make a forced landing because of fog before it reached New York. Time was running out and calls to the hospital switchboard were pouring in by the thousand. All morning, the question was the same. All morning, the reply was a terse 'Critical ... condition unchanged.'

Then, shortly before noon, with Valentino's temperature at 105°F, his pulse hammering 140 strokes per minute and his respiration at 30 per minute, an official bulletin declared him 'rapidly failing'. Soon afterwards, at 12.10pm, on Monday, 23 August 1926, 'with Father Leonardo's crucifix pressed to his lips', Rudolph Valentino died 'without pain'.

At 12.15pm, Joseph Schenck walked slowly down the hospital stairs and read out a brief bulletin signed by three doctors. Rudolph Valentino was dead, at the age of 31, of septic pneumonia and septic endocarditis.

Immediately, the constant flow of calls to the hospital switchboard increased in volume. Now, instead of the clipped, terse, official statement of the patient's condition, the callers heard the news they dreaded, delivered by girls who had joined them in their anguish.

'Oh, he's dead ... Rudy's dead.'

29

D ISBELIEF AND utter incomprehension that he could be dead at such an age, after all those keep-fit pictures and an apparently successful operation, was a general reaction – and a reaction which, almost inevitably, was to bring rumours that he had died from something far more serious than a stomach complaint.

The first people to hear the news, those who had kept vigil outside the Polyclinic Hospital, took in the awful fact more readily than others would do and, because of their immediacy, reacted much more violently. Within minutes of the announcement, women outside the hospital wept bitterly and screamed hysterically and tore their hair in grief. Some, overcome with emotion, slumped unconscious to the pavement. Others, fainting in the crowd still pressed around the hospital, were stretched out where they lay. Ambulance staff were fetched to carry them away and police waded in to break up the mounting, mourning mob.

As the news was flashed around the world, and pre-written obituaries were hurriedly updated to make massively morbid headlines, the life of Rudolph Valentino was already beginning to become legend. In cities throughout America, women fought their way to news-stands, snatched copies of the early editions and, after a few seconds' reading, broke down and wept openly.

Their despair was soon shared by millions as the news reached the capitals, cities and towns of the world, and for many of those millions the death of Valentino brought a real and personal grief. For years, they would remember vividly exactly where they were, who they were with and what time it was when they heard that he was dead.

When Natacha Rambova heard the news she was in the Hudnut château in France, and read it in a cable from George

Ullman. She became prostrate with grief and locked herself in her room, sobbing and refusing to eat for three days.

When Jean Acker heard the news she was in New York and wept, 'He is gone. What good is it to talk now?'

When Alberto heard the news he was in Italy and made immediate plans to sail to America for his brother's funeral.

When Edith Maud Winstanley heard the news she was in Derbyshire, and was saddened that the man who had brought her work to a wider audience than she could ever reach was dead.

When Charles Chaplin heard the news, he said, 'The death of Rudolph Valentino is one of the greatest tragedies that has occurred in the history of the motion picture industry. As an actor he attained fame and distinction; as a friend, he commanded love and admiration. We of the film industry, through his death, lose a very dear friend, a man of great charm and kindliness.'

When Cecil B DeMille heard the news, he said, 'In Mr Valentino's death, we have lost a great artist. But, fortunately, we can look on death as progress and not as the finish.'

When Rita and Ada Maldarizzi heard the news they were at home in Castellaneta and wept, remembering the visit their childhood friend had paid them, when they had known, somehow, it was the last time they would see him. They prayed for the repose of his immortal soul.

When Pola Negri heard the news she was in the Ambassador Hotel bungalow in Hollywood, where she had been working night and day to finish the film *Hotel Imperial* so that she could rush to Valentino's bedside. Studio officials had sent messengers to her bungalow to break the news as gently as possible.

They were too late. Newsmen had already reached the star and informed her of Valentino's death. She immediately fainted. Her maid, frantically crying for help, summoned a hotel doctor, who brought Miss Negri back to consciousness. Then, totally distraught, she began to weep and wail bitterly. A few moments later, her grief became hysteria and, in a dialect of mixed Polish and English, she began to scream his name again and again: 'Rudy ... Rudy ... oh, Rudy!'

The doctor, now joined by her personal physician, managed to quieten her with a sedative, and a woman friend stayed to comfort her. 'The star's hysterical condition,' newsmen reported, 'prevented her from issuing any statement,' but all work on her film was abandoned, and it was assumed that she would leave, as soon as she was well enough, for New York. Assumed? You could put your last dollar on it, said Jean Acker.

When the rest of Hollywood heard the news, it came to a standstill. Flags were lowered to half-mast, directors shouted 'Cut!' and called off work for the day, and actors hurried to executive offices to ask if they knew anything more than that first bare announcement.

Women stars wept dramatically and the men tried just as dramatically to put on brave, unflinching faces.

When Valentino's bodyguard-cum-houseman, Luther Mahoney, heard the news, he removed jewellery and cash from the star's secret hiding place in Falcon's Lair, to prevent some future owner of the property discovering an unexpected windfall, and all of Pola Negri's nighties and underwear from his bedroom to prevent journalists posthumously exposing his boss's sex life.

Only at United Artists, the gossip had it, was work even more feverish than usual, as laboratory staff put in overtime producing extra prints of *The Son of the Sheik*.

Even though its star was dead, he could still appear and make money in the cinemas. And now he would be more in demand than ever.

MOURNING FOR Rudolph Valentino did not merely occur quietly, respectfully, decently and privately. It broke out like some wild, contagious disease and, fanned by interested parties stage-managing positively his last public appearance, brought about one of the most bizarre public farewells in history and mob scenes that New York police described as the worst in the city's records.

Had he known what havoc he was to wreak, Valentino would never have asked his manager to agree to any public request for his body to lie in state. But he did and, complying with that wish, Ullman arranged for Valentino to be moved to Frank E Campbell's Broadway funeral chapel later on the afternoon of his death. There, morticians worked through the night, embalming the body, making up the face until it resembled a wax dummy, which some suspicious mourners later swore it was, dressing it in full evening clothes and laying it to rest in a bronze and silver coffin, with the face and shoulders exposed to public view.

Even as they worked, crowds began to gather outside and, by the early afternoon of the next day, as a Valentino secretary issued a statement thanking the 10,000 people who had sent messages of sympathy, thousands of personal mourners were creating havoc outside the funeral parlour. More than 12,000 of them – celebrities, shop girls, clerks, high-society women, youths aping the Valentino look with their slicked-back hair – blocked every street around the chapel, waiting and watching as florists delivered massive bouquets from the star's friends, and little bunches of field-flowers arrived from his fans.

And then it began to rain. A gentle rain – 'from Heaven', more than one observed – became a sudden downpour, and police lost all control as the vast crowd began to struggle to reach whatever shelter they could find.

Tough, experienced and pathetically few New York cops swore and cursed, bullied and threatened as the mob surged towards the place where their idol lay. As they did so, the pressure on the chapel's large plate-glass window proved too much and it shattered into thousands of pieces, raining down on screaming, panicking women and girls.

From then on, chaos reigned. Mounted police were forced to make repeated charges into the crowd to try to restore some sort of order. In a mad scramble, one woman was trampled under the hoofs of a police horse and pulled, moaning, from the fray. Scores more were bruised and injured or cut by the flying glass. Others fainted and were carried along by the crowd. Children were torn away from their parents. Police battled to get those hurt to a room in the mortuary which had been turned into an emergency hospital.

When the funeral parlour doors opened, it could only, and did, get much worse. The mob, knowing now that their patience was about to be rewarded, surged towards the door, sweeping aside police and anyone and anything else that stood between them and the laid-out superstar. They swarmed, shouting, screaming and swearing, into the Gold Room where Valentino's body lay, amid an aroma of incense and scented candles, wreaths, bouquets and golden drapes. 'As unreasonably as marching ants,' one reporter said in his dispatch from the improbable battle-front, 'the crowds pressed forward in a manner which, hurriedly summoned, extra police were entirely unable to block.'

But they were not to stay long. It soon became clear that if drastic action were not taken, and quickly, the room would be completely wrecked by those wishing to 'pay their respects'.

The doors were closed, and the coffin was moved to a smaller room on the first floor, with emergency exits through which people could be hurried back into the streets. Those streets were now littered with torn clothing, broken straw hats, shoes wrenched from feet in the melée and, here and there, bars of soap which the more malicious among them had rubbed on the pavements to bring down the police horses.

When the doors were reopened, it looked for a while as though some sort of order reigned. People were rushed upstairs, rushed past the body – skilfully lit and behind protective glass – and rushed back downstairs and out again. 'Come on, step lively!' ordered police and attendants as men, women and children, some weeping, some merely staring curiously, others giggling, were hurried through.

Those who tried to snatch souvenirs in the room, or step forward to kiss the glass casing, were hustled away with little delicacy. A two-second glance was allowed. Those who appeared to collapse in tears or fall into a faint were just as quickly carted off in the direction of doctors, who said that few were genuine cases of uncontrollable grief. One girl wearing a tragic, tear-stained expression was found to have an onion tucked conveniently into her handkerchief. But then even doctors were not above suspicion. A 'Dr' Sterling C Wyman, who had been appointed chief physician to help the injured, was later unmasked as an ex-con man cashing in on the proceedings.

Outside, another store window had been demolished, and the crowd, now swelled to an estimated 20,000 or more by people who had finished work for the day, were becoming impatient. More women had fainted, more people had been hurt, more police had been called, bringing their numbers to around 150 – including Police Commissioner 'Mac'

McLaughlin, who had decided it was about time he got along to see for himself what the hell was going on down there.

He soon found out, and ordered the doors of the chapel to be closed once more until order prevailed. It was not easy, but by some major miracle of planning and persuasion, police eventually organised a queue and, from 7.30pm until midnight, when the doors were closed for the night, up to 40,000 had glimpsed Valentino for the last time.

Among the last to arrive were a group of men who brought the biggest surprise of the surprise-packed day. As police dispersed the lingering thousands from the area and workmen erected wooden barricades to protect the chapel's remaining windows, the black-shirted men told officials they were from the Fascisti League of America and brought a wreath from no less than Benito Mussolini, who wanted them to mount a guard of honour around their fallen compatriot. The impressed executives of Mr Frank B Campbell's emporium professed themselves only too glad to welcome them. When a man like Mussolini dictated his wishes, they agreed, it was best to comply.

It rained again the next day. The heavens, they said again, were weeping for Rudy. But from early morning, thousands more turned up to view the body, and this time the police were ready for them. They ordered the soaked mourners into a controllable, organised queue and, from 9.00am, allowed them in to see the coffin, which had been moved again to a ground-floor room to speed up the passage of people through the building. Among them, reporters noticed Mrs Richard Whittemore, alias 'Tiger Lil', whose husband, a bandit-gang leader known as The Candy Kid, had been hanged only recently in Baltimore. Lil, not averse to posing for press photographs, explained that she had met Valentino at a party some years earlier and was there to pay her respects.

The photographers were busy again in the early afternoon when Jean Acker, with members of her family, arrived. Other people were cleared from the room while she said a private farewell to her former husband. Later, between sobs, she was able to say, 'I have always loved Rudy. We always retained our love for each other. Of late my affection has been that of a mother or sister. We had not thought of remarrying.' Near to collapse, she was escorted away.

More drama came later in the day when militant anti-Fascists confronted the black-shirted guard of honour, accusing them of shaming the name of Valentino, who was, they said, an all-American anti-Fascist himself. The Italian Government, they claimed, knew nothing about a wreath from Mussolini, and had not ordered the guard to be posted. On investigation, the embarrassing truth was discovered; a funeral parlour press agent had hired the Fascisti to lend 'dignity' to the proceedings. George Ullman, horrified at the disclosure, and by the sordid goings-on, turned up late in the evening and announced that he would tolerate no more of it. Reversing a decision to allow the body to remain on view until Saturday evening, he said it would be removed at midnight to a vault where it would be seen by only genuine, private mourners.

The behaviour at the bier appalled him. 'It is sordid, disgusting, irreverent and morbid,' he said, as the last of the day's estimated 50,000 visitors waited to gain admittance.

As New Yorkers caught their last glimpse of Rudy's corpse, British people were catching their first; readers of the one-penny *Daily Sketch* were treated to a picture of Valentino's body lying beneath a page one headline which boasted VALENTINO LYING IN STATE. Below it, a caption explained, 'This exclusive picture of Rudolph Valentino lying in state was transmitted by wireless from New York to London in less than an hour. It is reproduced,' it added, half-apologising for the poor quality just as it was received. 'By arrangement with the Radio Corporation of America and the Marconi Telegraph Company in London, special operators were retained in New York and London to expedite the transmission of the photograph.'

Meanwhile, the subject of this super-scoop was moved once again to the Gold Room where, despite crowds still besieging the building, he was to lie in comparative peace until his funeral the following Monday.

But if wagging tongues could reach and wake the dead, Rudolph Valentino would by now be sitting bolt upright, listening in fascination and horror. From the very moment he died, rumours about his sudden demise had been spawned, spread and embroidered and widely believed by those who could not accept the fact that a gastric ulcer and its complications could snatch away one so young and apparently healthy.

They said he had been shot or stabbed by a jealous rival, poisoned by a spurned woman, coldly done to death by arsenic. Only foul play, the theory went, could be responsible for such a sudden departure.

The shooting rumours began with the mention, on the death certificate, of perforations. Bullet holes obviously, the suspicious nodded knowingly. But they were up against the poison rumour-mongers, who claimed that only arsenic could be responsible for the violent pains which caused Valentino to be rushed to hospital in the first place. Their case was backed by a Brooklyn lung specialist who said that, if Valentino's face had changed after death, as had been suggested, poisoning could be the cause. 'Septic poisoning alone could not do that,' he declared, and passed on his opinions to Assistant District Attorney Ferdinand Pecora, with a request for an autopsy.

The rumours gained momentum when mystery developed over where Valentino had spent his last night. Ziegfeld Follies beauty Marion Kay Benda claimed that she and Rudolph, who were deeply in love, had spent the early part of that Saturday evening at two clubs, including Tex Guinan's, where he had become violently ill. Another version had it that he had spent the entire evening at the party, from which he had been rushed directly to the hospital by ambulance at 8.30am.

All that was dismissed by the junior Mr Warburton, who said there had been no party at his home, and was then himself rushed into hospital for a mysterious operation. Had the poisoner struck again? To try to end the rumours, Dr Meeker and his assistant doctors issued a statement repeating their original diagnosis of the cause of death. Valentino, said Meeker, 'simply had not taken good care of himself. He must have had a chronic stomach disorder – there were holes in the lining of his stomach as big as your finger.'

Holes? Those bullet holes again, obviously. Or probably stab wounds. The rumours went on and on. He had been found in a gutter. Jack de Saulles's friends had taken their revenge. He had been discovered in the arms of a lover and gunned down by her enraged husband. Everyone, it seemed, had a pet theory that they would not give up. Even a year later, Italy's *Secolo* carried a report saying that two rivals, with motives of jealousy and the love of a woman whom Valentino had captivated, had laced his food with small quantities of poison, leaving, of course, no trace after it had been absorbed. Police in America, it was revealed, were carrying out secret investigations.

So secret, in fact, that no one ever heard of them again.

HAVING SENT ahead the biggest floral tribute of all, a hugely expensive concoction of red roses, with her name picked out in white, Pola Negri descended on New York to say a personal farewell to her beloved Rudy. It was a sensational performance.

When her train drew into Grand Central Station on the day before the funeral, she emerged in mourning weeds of stunning severity which, a handy press agent revealed, had cost $3,000. Weeping, and supported by a maid and Mrs George Ullman, she walked slowly to the barrier where she screamed and promptly fell into a faint. Half-carried to a waiting car, she was driven to the Ambassador Hotel, where Rudy had been so cruelly stricken down, and promptly fell into another faint.

Having recovered, she left for the funeral parlour and wound her way through the still waiting crowds into the Gold Room, where her love lay at rest. At the sight of him, she had to be physically supported by attendants and, after kneeling in prayer, she moaned and wept and collapsed. But she was soon well enough to tell reporters, 'My love for Valentino was the greatest love of my life. I shall never forget him. I loved him not as one artist loves another, but as a woman loves a man.'

Then, in wretched condition, she was led away.

'*In nomine patris, et filii et spiritus sancti ...*'

The priest's words broke the silence in the actors' church of St Malachy. 'In the Name of the Father, and of the Son, and of the Holy Ghost ...' In front of him lay the rose-covered coffin of the man who had caused so much chaos and comment during the last few days and who now, like any other mere mortal, was to receive the last blessing and farewell of his holy mother church in the solemn sacrifice of the Mass.

'Kyrie eleison Christie eleison ...'

'Lord have mercy, Christ have mercy ...' Except that even this seemed to some like a star-studded showbusiness occasion mounted for a curious, morbid public. Thirty minutes earlier, crowds had watched as the silver and bronze coffin was carried from the funeral chapel and placed in the hearse. Then, with an escort of 12 motorcycle police escorts, it set off slowly through streets lined with people pushing, clambering, manoeuvring to get a better vantage point for the last farewell.

In the car behind the hearse, they spotted Pola Negri, a tragic figure in black, her face hidden in her handkerchief, being comforted by the Ullmans. Behind her car came others with Jean Acker, Mary Pickford, Norma and Constance Talmadge and Nora Van Horn, representing Natacha Rambova.

All along the two-mile route, police struggled to keep back spectators who gathered to watch the passing show, and the area around the church on West Forty-Ninth Street had been closed to all other traffic. That was where you spotted the most celebrities as they arrived to take their ticket-only pews: Douglas Fairbanks, George Jessel, Gloria Swanson, Bonnie Glass, Marilyn Miller, Viola Dana, Gertrude Astor ... some 500 of them, and many of them faces the crowd knew like their own.

'Requiem aeternam dona eis, Domine, et lux perpetua luceat eis ...'

'Eternal rest grant unto them, oh Lord, and let perpetual light shine upon them.'

In between the priest's solemn incanations, one could hear the sobs and sniffles, the scratching pens as reporters noted down the details of dresses and outfits and behaviour in grief; Pola Negri, who had to be helped up the aisle to her place, looked at times as though she might collapse. Jean Acker did faint, and had to be assisted to the door. A white-coated doctor and nurse stood by in case of emergency caused by emotion.

'*Ite missa est ...*'

'Go, the Mass is ended!'

The injunction came as a relief and the congregation muttered their reply.

'*Deo gratias.*'

The coffin was once more taken back to the funeral parlour to await its last journey, and Pola Negri retired to her hotel to hide her sorrow in silence. But not for long.

Soon, between sobs, she was reading to reporters a letter written by Dr Meeker which had lately come into her possession:

Dear Miss Negri;

I am asking Mary Pickford, an old friend and patient of mine, to deliver this message to you ...

About four o'clock Monday morning, I was sitting by Rudolph alone in the room. He opened his eyes, put out his hand and said, 'I'm afraid we won't go fishing together. Perhaps we will meet again – who knows?' This was the first and only time he realised he would not get well. He was perfectly clear in his mind. He gave me a message for the Chief, Mr Schenck, and then said, 'Pola – if she doesn't come in time, tell her I think of her.' Then he spoke in Italian and went into his long sleep. I feel an obligation to get this message to you.

Yours sincerely,

Harold D Meeker

She said no more. She merely read the letter and withdrew. But the meaning she intended to convey was quite clear to those who heard it – she was Rudy's last love.

And who else should be waiting on the dock on 1 September to greet Valentino's brother Alberto as he arrived to see him buried? Pola Negri, dressed in black, kissed and embraced him with tears in her eyes, before going with him to the funeral parlour to see the body.

Afterwards, with the heartfelt thanks of those who feared that he would be taken away from them and buried in some far-flung Italian town with a strange name, Alberto announced, 'My brother belonged to America and his resting place will be in California, which he loved. My sister feels this way, too.'

And so, next day, Rudolph Valentino set off on his last journey by train to his final resting place, accompanied by Alberto, Pola and the Ullmans. All along the route, people looked out for the train, hoping to see something of the coffin, and when it arrived in Chicago, thousands turned up at the station to pay their respects.

In the Church of the Good Shepherd in Beverly Hills, on the morning of 7 September, an opera star sang 'Ave Maria' at the Mass before burial. Again, tens of thousands lined the route from the church to the Hollywood Cemetery, where June Mathis had said Valentino could be buried in her family crypt until a permanent resting place could be decided upon.

Two of the pallbearers were Charles Chaplin and Samuel Goldwyn.

A plane buzzed overhead dropping blossom to the ground as Alberto said a silent prayer and Pola wept. The cameras whirled. Celebrities sobbed. A priest spoke the final words. The coffin was moved into the crypt and the marble slab lifted into place. 'You can rest here, Rudy, until I die,' June Mathis whispered. The world had seen, but not heard, the last of Rudolph Valentino.

RUDOLPH VALENTINO might have been dead but, according to one allegedly reliable source, he was certainly not taking it lying down. In fact, declared American psychic Dr George Benjamin Wehner, he was having the time of his life, or death, in the Great Blue Yonder and making frequent excursions to mingle with lesser, living mortals on Earth.

Dr Wehner's spirit messages from the late star featured prominently in *Rudy, the Intimate Memoirs of Natacha*, first published in London, and later in America soon after his death.

And although there were cynics who said that Natacha, in death as in life, was putting words into Valentino's mouth, a curious public was intrigued enough to pay out ten shillings and sixpence to read how he was 'living' beyond the grave.

Meanwhile, back down on Earth, all was not peace and light. They were going through Valentino's affairs and finding them a debt-ridden mess. To his credit were two houses and land valued at $240,000, but mortgaged to the hilt; four large cars ($40,000) and four small ones (unvalued); eight horses ($4,000); 12 dogs ($10,000); a yacht ($6,000); jewellery ($40,000); costumes and furniture ($12,000); an insurance policy ($40,000); and an estimated $1,400,000 from films. Unvalued were his collection of firearms and birds from two aviaries, 1,000 pairs of socks, 300 ties and cravats, 40 suits, 50 pairs of shoes, 20 hats, 3 fur coats, 7 watches and several hundred shirts.

It was George Ullman's task to turn the debt into a profit. In well publicised auctions, he sold off Valentino 'junk' worth around $28,000 for around $76,000. An adoring public, who had now elevated their idol from the Great Lover to the

God of Love, with shrines to his memory in their homes, clamoured to have a relic of the true Rudy ... a sock, a handkerchief, a tie, a garter. His paperback books, with a newly-printed 'Rudolph Valentino' bookplate, freshly inserted on Ullman's orders, went for $5, $10 and even more. 'When Valentino died,' Ullman's lawyer reported, 'he owed the Art Cinema $132,000. His estate was covered with liens, mortgages and everything else. The only thing he really did own was all but two shares in his production company.'

Ullman was Secretary and Treasurer, and the only assets of the corporation were his 40 per cent stake in two of his pictures. Out of these, Ullman made about $400,000 for the estate, by showing them everywhere – even in China, where they did not know, until many years afterwards, that Rudolph Valentino was dead!

George Ullman, who would go through years of mounting work and legal fights in clearing up the estate of the man he helped to success, died in September 1975. In his memoirs, *Valentino As I Knew Him*, he described Rudy as 'a sacrificial victim of Natacha's narcissism'.

Alberto and Maria had a third share each in the will, along with Aunt Teresa Werner, whom Valentino wished to thank for her kindness after Natacha left to get her divorce. Maria married an Italian architect and Alberto, changing his name to Albert Valentino, and his nose, by plastic surgery, in operations similar to the one previously performed on Jack Dempsey, went into movies.

He did it, he said, on the advice of June Mathis. But his one film was far from good and soon forgotten. The first 'talkie' would be filmed that year, starring Al Jolson, and there would be many career fatalities among the silent movie stars who could not make the transition. An amateur actor like Alberto, tied to aping his famous brother in silent movies, and doing it badly, had very little chance.

Jean Acker was not mentioned in the will. 'I didn't expect to be,' she told reporters, who so recently had believed that she might again become Valentino's wife.

Natacha Rambova fared little better. She received the sum of $1 – 'this sum and no more' is what Valentino decreed in his will – and showed neither anger nor surprise. 'Rudy,' she said, 'has explained everything. I understand.'

His true and everlasting feelings for her, she said, were contained in the words of one of his poems, 'Poverty', written to express his love for her.

Possessing the jewels of the earth. Holding within my grasp the sceptre of the universe.

All these would but make me a pauper – Were I beggard of your love.

But she had a lot more to say, in her book, about accusations that she had sacrificed Valentino's career for her own selfish ambitions, to become a power in the film world.

Her fault, she claimed, was not ambition but conceit. 'I was conceited enough to imagine that I could force the producers into giving Rudy the kind of production which our artistic ambitions called for. I could not understand why, with his ability, romance, magnetism and proved drawing power, Rudy should not have the best, why he should continually be thrust into small, trifling, cheap, commercial pictures, while other artists of much less ability and popularity were given big stories and big productions. The injustice of it made me furious, and I stubbornly made up my mind that he shouldn't be used so.'

In 1932, Natacha married a Spanish nobleman, Don Alvaro de Urzaiz. They were later divorced and she went back to America to live with her widowed mother. Selling up the villa in France, she said she could no longer bear its associations with Valentino and the constant stream of fashionably-dressed women who arrived there from all over the world, bringing flowers and begging to be allowed to inspect the house, to touch his clothes, to sit on his favourite chairs.

After her divorce, she had been, in turn, actress, fashion designer, spiritualist, photographer in the Spanish Civil War and latterly had become a keen archaeologist and Egyptologist.

Natacha died in hospital in Pasadena, California, at the age of 69, in June 1966. She rated a 16-line obituary in the *Times*. But they managed to spell her name wrongly.

June Mathis was at a theatre in New York, in July 1927, when she collapsed and died. The tragedy caused a problem over Valentino's resting place, for she had said he could lie in her crypt 'until I die'. It was solved when his body was moved to an adjoining crypt reserved for her husband, Sylvano Balboni, but which was eventually bought by the Guglielmi family. Even then there was little peace. Women made their way to the grave from all parts of America and the world. One wife living in mid-America sued for divorce on the grounds that her husband would not let her live near the mausoleum. Vandals chipped pieces from the vault, a marble pedestal was broken and its fragments sold as Valentino souvenirs, and five men discovered trying to break into the crypt were suspected to be 'ghouls, planning to steal the body for commercial purposes'.

A memorial to Valentino – a symbolic bronze nude standing on a globe with its head gazing towards the sky – also became the target for vandals after its unveiling in Hollywood's De Longpre Park in May 1930.

After being toppled twice from its plinth, it was removed by park staff for safe-keeping.

The Lady in Black, who was to mystify pressmen for years, first appeared when she knelt in prayer before the statue on an early anniversary of Valentino's death. One of several mourners clad entirely in black, and carrying red roses, she paid her tribute at the crypt every year

But it was not until November 1945 that she was revealed as the same Marion Wilson – the former Ziegfeld Follies beauty Marion Brenda – who claimed to have been with Valentino at the Warburton party before he was taken ill, and was his last mistress. No one has ever come forward to confirm her claims.

Carmel Myers, already a star when Valentino was struggling for recognition, remained a much sought-after actress for films and television for a further 50 years after his death.

In the 1970s, while researching a biographical project on Valentino for the fiftieth anniversary of his death, I spent several weeks in America talking to many of the former silent movie stars, directors and technicians who had known him well.

One of these was Carmel Myers, who was then living alone in a beautifully furnished apartment between Hollywood and the Pacific coast.

We talked at great length about the Valentino years. 'It's hard to believe so many years have passed since Rudy was alive. I thought he was wonderful,' she said. 'He had such personality and style. And that voice of his sent shivers running right through me. My only regret is that I was too young to be allowed to socialise with him alone. It was a tragedy that he died so young, just when he was reaching his peak as an actor. But Rudy was one of those people who will always be remembered by those who knew him. You couldn't exaggerate either his talent or his personality. He was one of the truly great ones.'

Viola Dana retired early and left the Beverly Hills house she shared with her sister during Valentino's lifetime. In her stylishly furnished home in Santa Monica, ten miles from the Hollywood studios where she was a star in the Twenties, she remembered, 'They called Rudy "the Great Lover". I would call him "the Great Dancer". He was supreme on the dance floor. He was such a splendid person, and all man. But no one could understand his first marriage. Perhaps he didn't understand too well himself. It was sad to see him unhappy, because he wasn't the kind of person anyone likes to see suffer. He was one of the lovely, vibrant people who kept us all amused. I knew him well, before he was famous and his life started to get distorted. So much was made up about him. But I think when he talked to me about his life in Italy and New York, it all happened the way he said it did. It wasn't always a very pretty story. But very few people ever knew very much about Valentino. He was too much of a loner. Anyone who says different is lying. He didn't have a lot of friends. Not real friends.'

Gertrude Astor, long retired from film making when I met her, lived for decades as a semi-recluse in Hollywood, preferring people to remember her as a star – young and beautiful. She lived alone, spending much of her time re-running her old movies and remembering the way it was.

'As far as I was concerned,' she said, 'Rudy was quite all right. He was very conceited inside, but didn't show it. He knew what his future was and he took good care of himself, except for his marriages. His first marriage was difficult to figure out. Jean loved girls, not men. Everybody but Valentino knew that.

'The second was even less comprehensible. That was ridiculous. He was making the same mistake all over again. It was all very hard to understand, because he really knew what to do with a woman. His reputation wasn't just founded on play-acting, believe me! I know.

'But Natacha was using him. He just couldn't see it. She used sex as a weapon and, when he didn't toe the line, she cut off his supply. In the end, the poor man had no physical contact with her at all. But he never stopped loving her, and wore that silly slave bracelet into his coffin.'

After her retirement in 1964, Pola Negri lived with her memories in San Antonio, Texas, rarely granting interviews, seldom talking of Valentino. But she remembered him as 'a wonderful human being – a man, but one who often acted like a little boy, simple, shy and insecure and uncertain of his relationships with others. Off-screen he was quiet, even reserved. But he was charming.

'He had tremendous sex appeal and an uncanny fascination for audiences. There was no one who could touch him afterwards as a screen hero or lover. There is no one like Valentino now. There never will be.'

Pola Negri died in January 1981.

Harold Grieve, who was a technician on several of Valentino's pictures, was able to shed some light on two of the frequently posed questions about Valentino's relationship with Natacha Rambova. Was theirs a genuine affair, physically, and what was her real bond with Nazimova? He told me his most vivid, and most lasting, memory of the star was of catching him making love to Natacha Rambova in his dressing-room.

'We all thought she was a lesbian,' he said. 'One of Nazimova's lovers. It shows what she was prepared to do to get Valentino in her clutches.

'Marrying one lesbian was a foolish accident. Marrying a second was really dumb,' he concluded emphatically.

Rita Maldarizzi, aged 70 when we talked at her home on the Via Ospedale in Castellaneta, said she and her sister were the only people then living in the town who had such close contact with Valentino in his early days.

'He was in our home more often than he was in his own,' she said. 'He was always hanging around. My father said he never had the slightest intention of doing any work of any kind. He didn't go out and look for it, certainly, just sat around all day with other boys at the cafés. But he did have this obsession to go to America. He had heard so many tales of success, fortunes being made, and dollars.

'Everything was dollars to him, and if he'd lived today he would have been off to Hollywood all the faster.

'I think he got all his wild ideas from his mother, Donna Beatrice. When she was carrying him, right up to almost the last month of her pregnancy she would be dancing, my mother told me. She was a wild, happy, beautiful woman, always cheerful, laughing, dancing. That's what gave Rodolpho this funny head of his, always wanting to do mad things, running off and making dollars. Everyone said in those days, "It's because his mother was dancing."

'I'll never forget the day he brought a woman back to town. He must have been in his teens then – 16 or 17. He brought this girl here. She was a pretty young thing, one of those roving folk singers, and he escorted her round the streets all day. What a sensation he was. It was sheer impudence. She was all over him. But we knew he'd never marry a local girl and settle down. His main fascination was always the tales of emigrants, the good life overseas, making fortunes, earning stacks and stacks of dollars. He simply made that dream come true.

'That day he came back, after he'd become famous, we girls were thrilled by his lofty talk, dizzy listening to his stories of Hollywood. There was no cinema here in those days and we had never seen a film. What he spoke of seemed to be a fairytale world to us. But he had changed. He was wholly different. Everything about him seemed so strange, so theatrical.

'Some people here were nasty to him. They jeered and shouted abuse at him because he wouldn't give them money. He was looking for old friends – not hate. We cried when he had gone. A short time later, our father died, and we had a long message of condolence from Rodolpho, but we never heard from him again. We knew, somehow, that we never would.

'But we still have the coffee service that Mama brought out when he came, and the divan on which he lay back, telling those stories. Of course, we've since seen an old film or two of his as a curiosity. We could see that it was him on the screen, naturally. But it wasn't our real Rodolpho. He'd changed so much from the time he was a boy in Castellaneta.

'There's a street named after him now, the Via Rodolpho Valentino, and a cinema. And there's a plaque on the house where he was born and a statue in the park. But nobody ever comes to look at it now. After he died, somebody in England used to send a huge bouquet of flowers to the family grave here on the anniversary of his death. It happened every year until 1972 and then suddenly stopped. The Mayor tried to find out who had been sending them, but he couldn't trace the person.

'Everyone assumed it was a woman – and that she had died.'

Jack Dempsey had retired from his famous New York restaurant and was an old man when I spoke with him, but said he retained a clear memory of Valentino. 'The most virile and masculine of men,' he said. 'The women were like flies around a honeypot. He could never shake them off, anywhere he went. What a lovely, lucky guy.'

My thanks to these and to many others who confided their memories of the infant silent movie industry, and the making of Valentino into its first megastar; to the men and women journalists who recorded the events in magazines and newspapers as they happened – or, at least, mostly happened; to the Librarians of the Academy of Motion Picture Arts and Sciences who painstakingly assisted in my research; and to their colleagues at the British Museum Library who were similarly helpful.

Valentino's Leading Ladies

VIOLA DANA

VIOLA DANA befriended Valentino at one of the unhappiest times in his life. His first wife had rejected him on their wedding night, his attempt to break into movies had stalled and he was reduced to working again in cabarets. She was 22, two years younger than him, but already a star when she invited him to spend Christmas 1919 in her home. Her parties were the envy of Hollywood and he became one of her favourite guests. She introduced him to leading directors and studio chiefs and helped him get back into pictures.

Born in Brooklyn, New York, in 1897, she was the middle sister of three actresses, and changed her name from Virginia Flugraph to Viola Dana for her Hollywood screen début in *Molly the Drummer Boy* aged 17. Between then and 1929, she starred in over a score of pictures, receiving top billing until her retirement at the age of 32. She had married at 18 but her first husband, John Collins, was killed three years later. Her second marriage to Maurice Flynn came in 1925, but ended in divorce.

Of Valentino, she said, 'We had great fun together. We were just kids trying to make movies. The least we could do was give each other a little help and affection. He was such a splendid person. All man.'

Her last public appearance was on television in *A Hard Act To Follow*, a documentary on Buster Keaton, in 1987. She died that same year aged 90.

ALLA NAZIMOVA

VALENTINO ADMIRED Nazimova's artistic accomplishments but disliked her as a woman. She publicly insulted and humiliated him when she was a famous star and he a penniless beginner, and he never forgave her, although he went on to become her leading man in *Camille*.

Nazimova's scandalous exploits as a bisexual were well known in Hollywood, as was her lesbian relationship with Valentino's first wife, Jean Acker, and her questionable affiliation with his second wife, Natacha Rambova.

Born of wealthy Jewish parents in Yalta, Russia, in 1879 as Adelaide Leventon, she was an acclaimed student of the violin in Switzerland before turning to the stage. By 1903, she had become the toast of St Petersburg, and changed her name to Nazimova. After a two-year tour of Europe, she moved to America where she found fame on New York's Broadway.

Nazimova – she rarely used her first name – was 37 when she made her début in pictures in *War Brides*, in which she appeared with her protégée, Richard Barthelmess. She briefly became a Metro star but most of her films were produced and scripted by herself. Some were spectacularly stylish, but did badly at the box office.

She made 17 silent movies before returning to the Broadway stage in 1925. Financial hardship took her back to Hollywood in 1940 where she appeared in 'talkies' for the first time. After making five films, she suffered a fatal heart-attack in 1945. She was 66.

CARMEL MYERS

VALENTINO'S FIRST role as leading man was opposite Carmel Myers in *A Society Sensation* in 1918. He was captivated by her darkly exotic looks, but any thoughts of romance were squashed by her chaperone mother. The devout Jewish girl had started in pictures at the tender age of 15 as a protégée of DW Griffith, who hired her father, a rabbi, as religious adviser on her first movie. Carmel was well liked in Hollywood and counted Mary Pickford among her closest friends. She was bowled over by Valentino's charm and staggering good looks and intervened with Universal chief, Carl Laemmle, to have him hired for a follow-up picture as her leading man in *All Night*.

'That voice of his sent shivers right through me,' she remembered years later. 'My only regret is that I was too young to be allowed to socialise with him alone. He was one of the truly great ones.'

She did, however, become one of his first true friends in Hollywood, and they remained close until his death in 1926.

Carmel successfully adapted to talkies and went on to star with some of Hollywood's top names, including John Barrymore and Lon Chaney. She continued in films until 1946, when she discovered a new career in television, which continued to call on her acting services almost up to her death in 1980.

GLORIA SWANSON

GLORIA SWANSON was the biggest female star at Paramount when Valentino achieved superstar status in 1922, and it seemed only natural to studio bosses to cast them together. In *Beyond the Rocks* they failed to hit it off, and the resulting film did little for either of their reputations. Swanson was 22 years of age and enormously popular, and was already earning over $500,000 a year. She felt insulted when Valentino rejected her famous 'come on', quoting his love for Natacha Rambova. After this, understandably, there was just no sparkle in their scenes together, and Gloria told Paramount she would never appear with him in another picture.

Born in Chicago as Gloria May Josephine Svensson in 1899, she was a 16-year-old sales clerk when a film director pulled her out of a crowd and gave her a small part in his movie. She went on to appear in Charlie Chaplin's first comedy before moving to Hollywood and stardom in 1917.

She waltzed through the sound revolution and received her first Oscar nomination for Best Actress in *Sadie Thompson* in 1928. She was to receive two further Best Actress nominations before her final retirement from pictures in 1975. The last was for her role as Norma Desmond in *Sunset*

Boulevard in 1950, which was voted twelfth in the 100 greatest movies of all time, by the American Film Institute in 1998.

Seven times married, Gloria earned and spent a multi-million-dollar fortune in her lifetime. She died in 1983 aged 84.

MAE MURRAY

ONE OF THE brightest and most strikingly beautiful of the Ziegfeld Follies girls who found a new career in films, Mae Murray was quickly dubbed 'The Girl with the Bee-Stung Lips'. She conquered Hollywood as she had conquered Broadway and became 'Queen of the Lot' at MGM. As an ex-dancer, she was first attracted to Valentino in Maxim's cabaret in New York. When she spotted him, in Los Angeles in 1919, she asked him to take her in his arms again, but this time for purposes other than whisking her around a dance floor. Her desire won him his first big role, as her lover, in *The Big Little Person*, in which, it was noted, she put a great deal more into her love scenes than was usually required.

Mae wanted more of his passionate kisses and insisted on a follow-up picture, *The Delicious Little Devil*. The love scenes between them were even more hot-blooded than before, and the director, her husband Bob Leonard, vetoed a third picture.

In 1925, after her film *The Merry Widow* with John Gilbert broke box-office records, she foolishly divorced Leonard, the top MGM director, and quit the studio at the urging of her fourth husband, Prince Mdvani who wanted to control his glamorous meal ticket. From $10,000 a week, she quickly faded into obscurity. Mdvani divorced her when the money ran out in 1933, leaving her bankrupt and in poverty. She died in a Motion Picture charity home in 1965, aged 81.

NITA NALDI

NAUGHTY NITA NALDI, the most gorgeously evil vamp in silent movies, was another of the Ziegfeld beauties who answered Hollywood's call and became a star of the silent screen. She was 21 when she made her cinema début with John Barrymore in 1920. Two years later, she was hot enough to be paired with Valentino in his greatest picture *Blood and Sand*. Through this she became Natacha Rambova's closest friend and, despite her fearsome reputation as a ladykiller, made two further pictures with Valentino – *A Sainted Devil* and *Cobra* – without becoming romantically linked.

This changed dramatically after Natacha divorced him. Against all the odds, for Pola Negri had already staked her claim to the great lover, it was Nita who first occupied the spot in his bed vacated by his ex-wife. It was a hot-blooded affair, but her ear-splitting vocal fireworks when she was sexually aroused, though at first both flattering and amusing, soon became tedious, and he opted for an equally passionate, but less deafening, affair with Pola.

Nita – formerly Donna Dodey from Virginia – quit Hollywood in 1929. In later years, she made rare appearances

337

on stage and in television, and laughingly debunked her former screen image by dubbing herself 'Dracula in drag'. Her last 25 years were lived out in New York's Wentworth Hotel, subsidised by the Actors' Fund. She died there in 1961 of a heart-attack, aged 62.

VILMA BANKY

GOSSIP COLUMNISTS claimed, during his separation from Natacha that Valentino was having a passionate affair with his *Eagle* co-star Vilma Banky, nicknamed 'The Hungarian Rhapsody'. They appeared regularly together at parties and other social gatherings but denied a romantic link. Months later in Paris, her lover, Baron Imre Lukatz, attacked Valentino for seducing his mistress and the actor challenged him to a duel. By daybreak, both had had second thoughts and their sword fight was called off.

Vilma, who was also the leading lady in Valentino's last film, *Son of the Sheik*, was born Vilma Longit, in Budapest, and was the daughter of a renowned Hungarian actor. She was spotted by Sam Goldwyn who took her to Hollywood and silent movie stardom. But tragically, like the great Mary Pickford, she was unable to transfer her stardom into talkies.

Her strong Hungarian accent, coupled with poor English, was panned by fans and critics alike, and after *The Rebel* in 1933, she received no further offers of work.

Married to Rod La Rocque, the Twenties matinée idol, she lived in Los Angeles until her death in 1991, at the age of 93.

POLA NEGRI

POLA NEGRI was Rudoph Valentino's last big affair. She claimed they were engaged to be married but he never confirmed this. The tempestuous Polish beauty, as hot-blooded as she was hot-tempered, had sworn to enslave him after his divorce from Natacha. She had once been engaged to Charlie Chaplin and was a brilliant self-publicist, often walking her pet panther on a leash down Sunset Boulevard. Fans said it was hard to tell which of them was the more sensuously feline, the big cat or Pola. Her relationship with Valentino was hardly a balanced one. He saw it in purely sexual and physical terms. She wanted marriage and a family.

It was generally agreed that, at his funeral, her performance as the grieving 'not quite widow' outdid anything she had achieved on screen. She wept and wailed and fainted and looked distraught and declared to anyone and everyone that he was the only man she had ever really loved.

But a few months later, she married Prince Serge Mdvani, the brother of the scoundrel Mae Murray was to marry two years later. The two men were of similar, rotten character, and the Prince abandoned her after less than four years of marriage.

Following this disappointment, she appeared in only a handful of films and retired to become a recluse in San Antonio, Texas, in 1970. She died there in 1987 aged 92.

GERTRUDE ASTOR

A FUN-LOVING party girl, Gertrude Astor befriended Valentino shortly before his meeting with Natacha Rambova, and made him a regular invitee to every event in her bachelor-girl mansion in Hollywood. She was already a popular star, although she didn't appear with Valentino until 1922 in *Beyond the Rocks*. It was only her presence on the picture, he said, which made the weeks of frosty hostilities with Gloria Swanson bearable.

AGNES AYRES

RUDY'S LEADING lady in *The Sheik,* the movie that changed him from mere superstar into the first male sex symbol, caused Agnes Ayres to become the most envied woman in the world. When, as the sheikh, he ordered the captive Agnes to 'Lie still, you little fool,' women sighed and whimpered to the point of ecstasy and tried to imagine what it actually felt like to be ravished by this passionate Adonis. Many believed the only one who could offer a first-hand account was Agnes Ayres, whose post bag suddenly swelled from a dozen or so to over 500 letters a week. Some were so basically phrased that studio chiefs ordered them to be kept from their innocent young star.

Reprising the same role, Agnes appeared in Valentino's last picture, *Son of the Sheik,* which produced a similar postal deluge.

CLARA KIMBALL YOUNG

IT WAS VALENTINO'S role in *Eyes of Youth*, in which Clara Kimball Young starred, which really launched his career. He did not even appear until the third part of the film and was on screen for only a few minutes, but it was enough for scriptwriter June Mathis to offer him the starring role in *The Four Horsemen of the Apocalypse*, the first million-dollar production in cinema history.

A L I C E   T E R R Y

ALICE TAAFFE had been a fellow extra on Valentino's first movie, *Alimony*, in 1918, and he was delighted when hugely talented director, Rex Ingram, picked her to play Marguerite, the leading female role in *Four Horsemen of the Apocalypse*. By this time, she had changed her name to Alice Terry and had become Ingram's fiancée. His faith in her was justified. The role made her a star.

Rudolph Valentino's Films

VALENTINO – THE FIRST SUPERSTAR

Alimony (1st National 1918). Directed by Emmett J Flynn. With Josephine Whittel, Lois Wilson, George Fisher, Ida Lewis. Valentino's first screen appearance was as an extra; he was merely atmospheric ballroom background.

The Married Virgin (Fidelity 1918). Directed by Joseph Maxwell. With Vera Sisson, Edward Jobson, Frank Newburg, Kathleen Kirkham, Lillian Leighton. Release was held up by litigation. Issued 1920. Reissued in 1922 as *Frivolous Wives*.

Virtuous Sinners (Pioneer 1919). Directed by Emmett J Flynn. With Norman Kerry, Wanda Hawley, Harry Holden, Bert Woodruff. Valentino is only to be glimpsed as background, although Flynn kept him on the payroll throughout shooting.

A Society Sensation (Universal 1918). Directed by Paul Powell. With Carmel Myers, Alfred Allen, Fred Kelsey, Harold Goodwin, Zazu Pitts. Valentino was billed as M Rudolphe di Valentina.

All Night (Universal 1918). Directed by Paul Powell. With Carmel Myers, Charles Dorian, Mary Warren, William Dyer, Wadsworth Harris, Jack Hall.

The Delicious Little Devil (Universal 1919). Directed by Robert Z Leonard. With Mae Murray, Harry Rattenbury, Richard Cummings, Ivor McFadden, Bertram Gassby. Mae Murray gave him the part.

The Big Little Person (Universal 1919). Directed by Robert Z Leonard. With Mae Murray. Leonard was Mae Murray's husband and became jealous of Valentino during filming.

A Rogue's Romance (Vitagraph 1919). Directed by James Young. With Earle Williams, Brinsley Shaw, Herbert Standing, Katherine Adams, Maude George. From an HH Van Loan story.

The Homebreaker (Ince-Paramount 1919). Directed by Victor Schertzinger. With Dorothy Dalton, Douglas Maclean, Edwin Stevens. Most of Valentino's role ended up on the cutting-room floor.

Out of Luck (Griffith-Artcraft 1919). Directed by Elmer Clifton. With Dorothy Gish, Ralph Graves, Raymond Canon, George Fawcett, Emily Chichester, Porter Strong, Kate V Toncray.

Eyes of Youth (Equity November 1919). Directed by Albert Parker. With Clara Kimball Young, Milton Sills, Edmund Lowe, Gareth Hughes, Pauline Starke, Sam Southern, Ralph Lewis. It was Valentino's role in this picture, seen by June Mathis, which won him the part in *The Four Horsemen of the Apocalypse*.

An Adventuress (Rep. Dist Co. 1920). Directed by Fred J Balshofer. With Julian Eltinge, Virginia Rappe, Leo White. Reissued in 1922 as *The Isle of Love*.

The Cheater (MGM 1920). Directed by Henry Otto. With May Allison, King Baggott, Frank Currier, Harry Van Meter. An adaptation of Henry Arthur Jones's play *Judah*.

Passion's Playground (1st National 1920). Directed by JA Barry. With Katherine MacDonald, Norman Kerry, Nell Craig, Edwin Stevens, Alice Wilson, Virginia Ainsworth, Howard Gaye. Adapted from a CN and MA Williamson novel.

Once to Every Woman (Universal 1920). Directed by Allan J Holubar. With Dorothy Phillips, W Ellingford, Margaret Mann, Emily Chichester, Elinor Field, Robert Anderson.

Stolen Moments (Pioneer 1920). Directed by James Vincent. With Marguerite Namara.

The Wonderful Chance (Selznick 1920). Directed by George Archainbaud. With Eugene O'Brien, Martha Mansfield, Tom Blake, Joe Flanagan, Warren Cook. Adapted from an HH Van Loan story.

The Four Horsemen of the Apocalypse (MGM 1920). Directed by Rex Ingram. With Alice Terry, Joseph Swickhard, John Sainpolis, Alan Hale, Wallace Beery, Stuart Holmes, Jean Hersholt, Mabel Van Buren, Nigel de Brulier. Valentino's first starring role, that of Julio Desnoyers. A June Mathis adaptation of the Ibañez novel.

Uncharted Seas (MGM 1921). Directed by Wesley Ruggles. With Alice Lake, Carl Gerard, Fred Turner, Charles Mailes, Rhea Haines.

Camille (MGM 1921). Directed by Ray C Smallwood. With Nazimova, Arthur Hoyt, Zeffie Tillbury, Rex Cherryman, Edward Connelly, (Patsy) Ruth Miller, William Orland, Consuelo Flowerton, Mrs Oliver. Valentino played Armand in this June Mathis modern version of the Dumas novel and play, with settings designed by Natacha Rambova.

The Conquering Power (MGM 1921). Directed by Rex Ingram. With Alice Terry, Ralph Lewis, Eric Mayne, Edna Demaury. A June Mathis adaptation of Balzac's *Eugenie Grandet*.

The Sheik (Paramount 1921). Directed by George Melford. With Agnes Ayres, Adolph Menjou, Walter Long, Lucien Littlefield, George Wagner, (Patsy) Ruth Miller, RR Butler. Adapted from EM Hull's popular novel.

Moran of the LadyLetty (Paramount 1922). Directed by George Melford. With Dorothy Dalton, Walter Long, Charles Brindley, Maude Wayne. An adaptation of the Frank Norris novel.

Beyond the Rocks (Paramount 1922). Directed by Sam Wood. With Gloria Swanson, Alec B Francis, Edythe Chapman, Gertrude Astor, Mabel Van Buren, Helen Dunbar, June Elvidge. Written by Elinor Glyn.

Blood and Sand (Paramount 1922). Directed by Fred Niblo. With Lila Lee, Nita Naldi, Walter Long, Charles Belcher, George Feld, Rose Rosanova, Leo White. A June Mathis adaptation of the Ibañez novel.

The Young Rajah (Paramount 1922). Directed by Philip Rosen. With Wanda Hawley, Pat Moore, Charles Ogle, Fanny Midgely, Robert Ober, Joseph Swickard, Bertram Grassby, J Farrell MacDonald, George Periolat, George Field, Maude Wayne, William Boyd, Spottiswoode Aitken.

Monsieur Beaucaire (Paramount 1924). Directed by Sidney Olcott. With Bebe Daniels, Doris Kenyon, Lois Wilson, Lowell Sherman, Paulette du Val, Flora Finch. Adapted from Booth Tarkington's novelette.

A Sainted Devil (Paramount 1924). Directed by Joseph Henaberry. With Nita Naldi, Helena d'Algy, Dagmar Godowsky, Jean del Val, George Seigmann, Louise Lagraige. Adapted from Rex Beach's *Rope's End*.

Cobra (Paramount-Ritz-Carlton 1925). Directed by Joseph Henaberry. With Nita Naldi, Casson Ferguson, Gertrude Olmstead, Hector V Sarno, Claire de Lorez, Eileen Percy, Lillian Langdon, Henry Barrows, Rose Rosanova.

The Eagle (U-A 1925). Directed by Clarence Brown. With Vilma Banky, Louise Dresser, Albert Conti, James Marcus, George Nichols, Carrie Clark Ward. Adapted from Pushkin's *Dubrovsky* by Hans Kraly.

Son of the Sheik (U-A 1926). Directed by George Fitzmaurice. With Vilma Banky, Agnes Ayres, George Fawcett, Montagu Love, Karl Dane, Bull Montana. Adapted by Frances Marion from EM Hull's sequel to her successful earlier novel.

BIBLIOGRAPHY

The Sheik by E. M. Hull
Rudy, Intimate Memories of Natacha by Natacha Rambova
Madam Valentino by Michael Morris
Valentino by Irving Schulman